Living on the Ragged Edge *Workbook*

PUBLICATIONS BY CHARLES R. SWINDOLL

Books for Adults

Active Spirituality
Bedside Blessings
Behold . . . The Man!
The Bride
Come Before Winter
Compassion: Showing We Care in a Careless World
The Darkness and the Dawn
Day by Day
Dear Graduate
Dropping Your Guard
Elijah: A Man of Heroism and Humility
Encourage Me
Esther: A Woman of Strength and Dignity
The Finishing Touch
Flying Closer to the Flame
For Those Who Hurt
Getting Through the Tough Stuff
Getting Through the Tough Stuff Workbook
God's Provision
The Grace Awakening
Growing Deep in the Christian Life
Growing Strong in the Seasons of Life
Growing Wise in Family Life
Hand Me Another Brick
Home: Where Life Makes Up Its Mind
Hope Again
Improving Your Serve
Intimacy with the Almighty
Job: A Man of Heroic Endurance
Job: Interactive Study Guide
Joseph: A Man of Integrity and Forgiveness

Killing Giants, Pulling Thorns
Laugh Again
Leadership: Influence That Inspires
Living Above the Level of Mediocrity
Living Beyond the Daily Grind, Books I and II
The Living Insights Study Bible—General Editor
Living on the Ragged Edge
Make Up Your Mind
Man to Man
Moses: A Man of Selfless Dedication
The Mystery of God's Will
Paul: A Man of Grit and Grace
The Quest for Character
Recovery: When Healing Takes Time
The Road to Armageddon
Sanctity of Life
Simple Trust
So, You Want to Be Like Christ?
Starting Over
Start Where You Are
Strengthening Your Grip
Stress Fractures
Strike the Original Match
The Strong Family
Suddenly One Morning
The Tale of the Tardy Oxcart
Three Steps Forward, Two Steps Back
Victory: A Winning Game Plan for Life
Why, God?
You and Your Child

Minibooks

Abraham: A Model of Pioneer Faith
David: A Model of Pioneer Courage
Esther: A Model of Pioneer Independence

Moses: A Model of Pioneer Vision
Nehemiah: A Model of Pioneer Determination

Booklets

Anger
Attitudes
Commitment
Dealing with Defiance
Demonism
Destiny
Divorce
Eternal Security
Forgiving and Forgetting
Fun Is Contagious!
God's Will
Hope
Impossibilities
Integrity
Intimacy with the Almighty
Leisure
The Lonely Whine of the Top Dog

Make Your Dream Come True
Making the Weak Family Strong
Moral Purity
Our Mediator
Peace . . . in Spite of Panic
Portrait of a Faithful Father
The Power of a Promise
Prayer
Reflections from the Heart—A Prayer Journal
Seeking the Shepherd's Heart—A Prayer Journal
Sensuality
Stress
This is No Time for Wimps
Tongues
When Your Comfort Zone Gets the Squeeze
Woman

Books for Children

Paw Paw Chuck's Big Ideas in the Bible

Living on the Ragged Edge Workbook

~

Coming to Terms with Reality

BASED ON THE BOOK BY

CHARLES R. SWINDOLL

Produced in association with CREATIVE MINISTRIES
Insight for Living

NELSON REFERENCE & ELECTRONIC
A Division of Thomas Nelson Publishers
Since 1798

Published by Nelson Reference & Electronic, A Division of Thomas Nelson, Inc., Post Office Box 141000, Nashville, Tennessee, 37214.

Nelson Reference and Electronic books may be purchased in bulk for educational, business, fundraising, or sales promotional use. For information, please email SpecialMarkets@ThomasNelson.com.

All Scripture quotations, unless otherwise indicated, are taken from New American Standard Bible (NASB). Copyright © 1960, 1962, 1963, 1968, 1971, 1973, 1975, 1977, 1995 by The Lockman Foundation, La Habra, California. Used by permission.

Other Scripture references are from the following sources:

J. B. Phillips: The New Testament in Modern English, Revised Edition (PHILLIPS). Copyright © J.B. Phillips, 1958, 1960, 1972. Used by permission of Macmillan Publishing Co., Inc.

An effort has been made to locate sources and obtain permission where necessary for the quotations used in this book. In the event of any unintentional omission, a modification will gladly be incorporated in future printings.

Editorial Staff: Shady Oaks Studio, 1507 Shirley Way, Bedford, TX 76022
ISBN 1-4185-0346-0

Printed in the United States of America
05 06 07 08 VG 9 8 7 6 5 4 3 2 1

Charles R. Swindoll has devoted his life to the clear, practical teaching and application of God's Word and His grace. A pastor at heart, Chuck has served as senior pastor to congregations in Texas, Massachusetts, and California. He currently pastors Stonebriar Community Church in Frisco, Texas, but Chuck's listening audience extends far beyond a local church body. As a leading program in Christian broadcasting, Insight for Living airs in major Christian radio markets around the world, reaching churched and unchurched people groups in language they can understand. Chuck's extensive writing ministry has also served the body of Christ worldwide and his leadership as president and now chancellor of Dallas Theological Seminary has helped prepare and equip a new generation for ministry. Chuck and Cynthia, his partner in life and ministry, have four grown children and ten grandchildren.

Based on the original outlines, charts, and transcripts of Charles R. Swindoll's sermons, the workbook text was developed and written by Michael J. Svigel, Th.M., Dallas Theological Seminary. Contextual support material was provided by the Creative Ministries Department of Insight for Living.

Insight for Living

Editor in Chief: Cynthia Swindoll
Director: Mark Gaither
Research Intern: Michael Kibbe
Editors: Marla Alupoaicei, Kathryn Moore, Greg Smith, Amy Snedaker

Contents

Contents

Contents

A Letter from Chuck

King Solomon was the Donald Trump of the ancient world—a person of power, immense wealth, and remarkable creativity and charisma. As author, songwriter, poet, architect, king, diplomat, and philosopher, he was a Renaissance man centuries before the Renaissance. So impressive was this man and his kingdom that other dignitaries stood in awe of him. His empire became a synonym for unparalleled greatness, a standard of quality no one else could reach.

Yet Solomon the Great took a maddening journey in his adult life when over-the-top things of the world lost their luster, when the roots of his life were exposed to the damaging rays of under-the-sun reality. Solomon applied the wisdom God gave him to the quest of finding what shreds of happiness, meaning, and fulfillment he could from a life apart from God . . . and his conclusion still echoes through the corridors of time. The empty cry sounds like it could have been shouted today: "Vanity of vanities! Everything is vanity!"

Solomon kept a journal of his dark and desperate journey as he came to terms with reality and searched for meaning. That journal, preserved for us, is the book of Ecclesiastes. Its words are as relevant to today's hedonistic, workaholic, and entertainment-frenzied culture as they were during the time the ancient monarch was on his long and lonely drift. Here is the harsh reality of under-the-sun living—the pleasure-seeking lifestyle in the raw. Here is emptiness personified. Here is life on the ragged edge.

May the Lord use these studies to convince all of us that life apart from God is one miserable, futile mess. Without Christ as the center and source of our lives, we drift through a desert of despair in a world of darkness. I pray that each lesson will touch all who are spinning their wheels along their own journeys to find meaning and purpose in a fallen world. May all of us heed the warnings and wisdom of Solomon's desperate journey toward peace and fulfillment.

How to Use the Living on the Ragged Edge Workbook

~

Ecclesiastes 12:12 says, "The writing of many books is endless, and excessive devotion to books is wearying to the body." With these words, Solomon warned the reader to beware of the endless reasoning of worldly philosophers and of worldviews that contradict the wisdom of God's Word (Ecclesiastes 12:10–11). With this workbook from our Insights and Application line of biblical resources, we hope to point you to the Word of God as the primary text in your study. As with all of our materials, the goal is to help you dig deeply into the truths of Scripture and apply them to your life. Therefore, this workbook can be used as a guide for personal devotions, a catalyst for small-group Bible studies, or as an aid to interactive classroom teaching.

Using the Workbook for Personal Devotions—When your one-on-one time with God needs direction, this workbook will guide you on the path toward greater knowledge, insight, and spiritual growth. The following approach is recommended:

- Begin each lesson with prayer, asking God to teach you through His Word and to open your heart to the self-discovery afforded by the questions and text of the workbook.

- Open your Bible to the passage of Ecclesiastes covered by the lesson. As you progress through each workbook chapter, you will be prompted to read certain passages from

As you read the biblical text, use this space for taking notes.

Ecclesiastes. As you read, use the space provided for taking notes, especially for jotting down any questions, insights, or difficult elements you encounter in the passage. This exercise will help you better interact with the biblical and workbook texts.

- As you encounter the workbook questions, approach them wisely and creatively. Not every question will be applicable to every person at every time. If you can't answer a question, continue on in the text. Let the Holy Spirit guide you in thinking through the text and its application, and use the questions as general guides rather than strict laws of application.

- Throughout the chapters, you'll find several special features designed to add insight or depth to your study, perhaps even answering some of the questions you noted during your reading of the biblical text. Use these features to enhance your study and deepen your knowledge of Scripture, history, and theology. An explanation of each feature can be found on pages xvi–xviii.

- As you complete a lesson, close in prayer, asking God to apply the wisdom and principles to your life. Then let go and watch God work! He may bring people and circumstances into your life that will challenge your attitudes and actions. You may discover things about the world and your faith you never realized before. You may apply the wisdom gleaned from this study of His Word to your life in ways you never expected. Trust that God will work out His will for you in His way and that His Word will bear fruit.

Using the Workbook for Small-Group Study—When your small group wants to lay biblical foundations for mutual growth, this workbook provides you with a blueprint for learning God's Word. The following options are recommended for a small-group study:

- Although this workbook is written with the needs of the individual student as its primary focus, we've made it easy to use for couples, mentors/mentees, or small groups by providing group-oriented discussion questions in each chapter. While these questions can also be answered individually, they are especially intended to promote discussion and dialogue among members of the study group.

- If your group time is relatively short (one hour or less), ask group members to work through each lesson before your group meets, using the suggestions for personal devotions above. During group time, after opening in prayer, a facilitator may read aloud the Bible passage covered by the chapter, then discuss several of the personal application questions with the group, focusing on some or all of the group discussion questions. Members may want to share their own answers to the questions, contribute their insights, or steer the discussion in a direction that fits the needs of the group. The facilitator should try to devote the final fifteen minutes to reading and discussing the closing application points of each workbook chapter.

- If your group has more time, or if it's unrealistic to expect members to study through the workbook on their own, a group facilitator or group members may simply read (aloud or silently) sections from the workbook during the group study time, following a format similar to the one for personal devotions. Be sure to read the Bible passage at the same time. Under this format, group members read and discuss questions only during the group meeting, rather than answering the questions on an individual basis beforehand.

In a group format, not all questions will be applicable, and some will be too personal to share. If a lesson isn't completed during a single session, simply continue where you left off in the next session. The goal is not merely to cover material, but to promote deep discussion of the biblical text with a view toward personal response and application.

Using the Workbook in Classroom Teaching—When your church body needs a resource that offers real answers to tough questions, this workbook offers biblical truth, straight answers, and life-application questions in a conversation-stimulating format. There are several ways to use this in the classroom.

- For experienced teachers who enjoy preparing their own lessons, this workbook can serve as a personal study for teacher preparation. The teacher can take notes, adapt illustrations, compile quotations, and use the teaching and application questions from the chapters in their own lesson preparation. Teachers are encouraged to modify the material to fit the needs of their particular classes.

- For teachers who desire a more structured curriculum, the workbook lessons can be adapted for a class presentation that allows for a high degree of class interaction. This approach would be similar to the small-group Bible study, except that the teacher will study through the workbook chapter prior to the group meeting and select workbook sections and questions to be taught to the class. The teacher should emphasize the application principles and questions at the end of the lesson and provide opportunities for classroom discussion. As supplemental curriculum, the workbook also serves as an excellent resource for students who want a more in-depth study of the material presented in class.

SPECIAL WORKBOOK FEATURES

The main text of each chapter is supplemented with a variety of charts, graphics, and special features to summarize and clarify teaching points or to provide opportunities for more advanced study. Some of these features appear in every chapter, while others occur intermittently through the workbook.

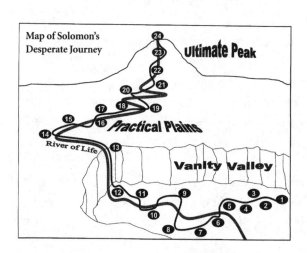

ROAD MAP FOR THE JOURNEY

As you follow Solomon's journey, it's easy to get tangled in the details and lost along the path. That's why each chapter provides a map that traces Solomon's trek through the Valley of Futility, across the Practical Plain, and finally to Ultimate Peak. Each chapter will provide a brief paragraph that connects the chapter to the map and to the overarching themes of Ecclesiastes described in the first chapter.

GETTING TO THE ROOT

While our English versions of the Scriptures are reliable, occasionally profound meanings and nuances can be brought to light by a study of the original languages. This feature explores the meaning of the underlying Hebrew or Greek words or phrases from a particular passage, sometimes providing parallel examples to illuminate the meaning of the biblical text we're studying.

DIGGING DEEPER

Various passages in Ecclesiastes touch on deeper theological questions or confront modern worldviews contrary to the Bible. This feature offers you the opportunity to gain deeper insight into specific theological, practical, and sometimes philosophical issues related to the biblical text.

WINDOWS TO THE ANCIENT WORLD

Sometimes the chronological gap separating us from the biblical readers clouds our understanding of a passage of Scripture. This feature will take you back in time to explore the surrounding history, culture, and customs of the biblical world.

GROUP DISCUSSION QUESTIONS

The group icon identifies questions that promote discussion and dialogue between members of a small group study. However, when the workbook is used for personal study, these questions provide opportunities for individual reflection as well.

Whether you use this workbook for individual, group, or classroom study, we trust it will prove to be an invaluable guide as you accompany Solomon on his journey to fulfillment and joy. May God's Word be for you a map of truth and compass of direction as you come to grips with *living on the ragged edge*.

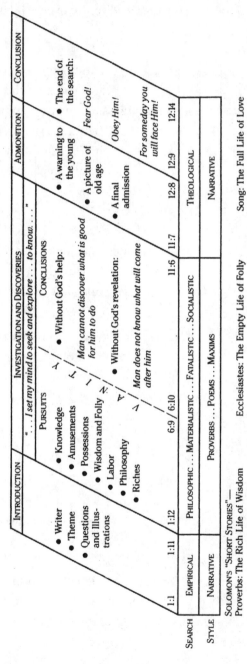

1 Journal of a Desperate Journey

[Ecclesiastes Survey]

Surf the internet, watch your television, meander through a bookstore, or scan the radio, and you'll be shocked at the pervasive message of meaninglessness targeting young and old alike. The problem is not only that people have been unable to find purpose in life but also that many have even given up looking. Today, people who are weary of wading through the muddy waters of broken promises and wallowing in the mire of pointless pursuits are coming to the same conclusion: life is meaningless. With this conclusion comes cynicism, sarcasm, relativism, and pessimism. The response to most questions—especially questions regarding truth—is "Who cares?"[1]

Of course, not everybody sees life this way. Not everyone has given up. Many are still in the midst of the rat race and are galloping faster and faster to reach the unreachable carrot always dangling just inches from their noses. Others are running on the treadmill of life, hoping that the feelings of going nowhere will pass and that the sacrifices they made to "the system" will start paying off. Some have even achieved the success they so desperately pursued, only to discover that the same void in their lives remains. At the top of the ladder of success they find that another rung awaits them, with a dozen more to climb. If they keep busy enough, though, they become numb to the painful reality that life in this world is meaningless. After dragging themselves through the desert of life toward the elusive paradise oasis just on the horizon, many find themselves chomping on the sand of a dismal mirage.

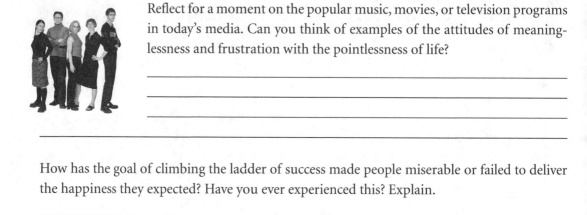

Reflect for a moment on the popular music, movies, or television programs in today's media. Can you think of examples of the attitudes of meaninglessness and frustration with the pointlessness of life?

_____

_____

_____

How has the goal of climbing the ladder of success made people miserable or failed to deliver the happiness they expected? Have you ever experienced this? Explain.

_____

_____

_____

_____

Life offers a smorgasbord of pursuits, an all-you-can-eat buffet of options promising to quench the insatiable appetite of the human soul. But very few people have the time and money to try it all. Many operate under the assumption—or even the hope—that the path to worldly happiness is there somewhere, if only they can stumble upon it. Others just accept things as they are and push to the furthest reaches of their minds nagging thoughts of something better. Most pass out of this world never having learned its cruel lesson—life is meaningless.

Few people in this world have had it all, seen it all, and done it all. And fewer still have not only realized the futility and emptiness of all they have done but also have turned from the world under the sun to the world above it. These rare individuals have discovered the emptiness of humanity and have exchanged it for the fullness of the divine. Finding such a person is like finding a diamond in a barrel of broken glass. The multifaceted insight he or she can bring to our lives is unparalleled.

Few people in history journeyed as far to investigate the happiness offered by the world as King Solomon did three thousand years ago. Having gone through a period in his life when all the treasures of this world had lost their luster, he investigated some of the most basic assumptions about existence. Thankfully, Solomon kept a journal of his desperate journey, a book in the Bible known today as Ecclesiastes.

A Man and His Perspective

One doesn't need to be a Hebrew scholar to realize quickly that Solomon's outlook on life seems pretty bleak. In fact his opening speech began, "Vanity of vanities! All is vanity" (Ecclesiastes 1:2). He said everything is futile, pointless, and empty. Why did Solomon characterize life this way?

DIGGING DEEPER

Ecclesiastes: The Five "Ws"

Who wrote it? Since the author didn't give his name but referred to himself only as "the teacher" or "preacher" (Hebrew: *Qōheleth,* Greek: *ekklesiastes*), we cannot be certain. However, most of the evidence suggests that King Solomon was the author. We can conclude this because the writer identified himself as a son of David and king over Israel in Jerusalem (Ecclesiastes 1:1, 12). The author of Ecclesiastes also said he was the wisest person to rule Jerusalem (1:16), he built extensive projects (2:4–6), and he had great wealth (2:7–8).

What is it? Ecclesiastes is probably best understood as a journal of Solomon's reflections on meaning and purpose from the world's limited perspective. It is his presentation of evidence based on experiences for those who have neither the time nor the resources to take the journey themselves.

Where was it written? Solomon said repeatedly that he was king over Jerusalem in Israel (1:1, 12), and this book was probably written there.

When was it written? Ecclesiastes was probably written about 925 BC, toward the end of Solomon's life. As an old man, Solomon wisely reflected on his life's journey, including his drift away from and back to God.

Why was it written? Solomon wrote Ecclesiastes to show that life apart from God is empty and meaningless. As he began his journal, Solomon said, "Thus I considered all my activities which my hands had done and the labor which I had exerted, and behold all was vanity and striving after wind and there was no profit under the sun" (2:11). Solomon ended by saying, "The conclusion, when all has been heard, is: fear God and keep His commandments" (12:13). While life apart from God is frustrating, life with God and enjoying His gifts with thanksgiving can be abundant, regardless of our daily circumstances.

Read Ecclesiastes 1:3–11. How would you describe the Preacher's tone and attitude?

_____

_____

_____

_____

GETTING TO THE ROOT

The Hebrew title of Ecclesiastes is *Qōheleth,* which is derived from the Hebrew root "to assemble," and probably means "teacher" or one who addresses an assembly.[2] In Greek the word for an assembly is *ekklēsia,* from which we get our word "ecclesiastical," relating to the church.[3] Thus, in the Greek translation of *Qōheleth,* the title is *ekklēsiastēs,* or, transliterated into English, "Ecclesiastes," meaning "preacher or teacher of the assembly."

When we view life from Solomon's perspective, we are forced to ask the same question: is life worth living? When hopelessness, despair, emptiness, and purposelessness abound, the search for meaning begins. When we fail to find meaning in the material world, despair increases and hope is lost. Daily activities become routine and ridiculous, and we wonder why we even wake up in the morning.

For the most part, life *is* routine. Dr. James Dobson calls the humdrum of life the "straight life." It's not glamorous, and it's not exciting. In fact, as Solomon indicated in Ecclesiastes 1:3–11, life can be downright boring. Dobson writes:

> The straight life for a homemaker is washing dishes three hours a day; it is cleaning sinks and scouring toilets and waxing floors; it is chasing toddlers and mediating fights between preschool siblings. . . . The straight life eventually means becoming the parent of an ungrateful teenager.[4]

For the working person the situation is just as wearisome:

> It is pulling your tired frame out of bed, five days a week, fifty weeks out of the year. It is earning a two-week vacation in August, and choosing a trip that will please the kids.

The straight life is spending your money wisely when you'd rather indulge in a new whatever.[5]

Think about your own "humdrum," day-to-day pattern of life. Does this cycle ever make you wonder if there's more to life? Have you ever lost sight of God's plan and purpose in the midst of the mundane? If so, briefly describe that experience.

_____

_____

_____

GENERAL SURVEY: THE FLOW OF THE JOURNAL

Introducing the Journey (Ecclesiastes 1:1–11)

In the opening verses of Solomon's journal, we read that all human tasks done "under the sun" are in vain: "What advantage does man have in all his work which he does under the sun?" (1:3). The general support for this assessment is the wearisome cycle of life as displayed both in the world around us and in our constant inability to find lasting satisfaction in our toil (1:4–11).

Pursuing and Exploring Life (Ecclesiastes 1:12–6:9)

After a rather shocking introduction to the meaninglessness of life, Solomon presented the report of his pursuits, leaving no stone unturned. At the buffet line of life he tried a little of everything to increase his worldly wisdom and knowledge, but he concluded that these bring only grief and pain (1:18). He found that the paths of pleasure and possession were futile (2:1–11). Worldly wisdom was pointless, for both the wise and the fool had the same end: death (2:12–17). One's life's work proved empty and meaningless (2:18–3:22). Finally, Solomon reported that the injustice of oppression and the accumulation of wealth brought frustration and dissatisfaction (4:1–16; 5:10–6:9). In the end, nothing the world had to offer could satiate Solomon's hunger for more.

Reflecting and Summarizing (Ecclesiastes 6:10–11:6)

By the time we reach this section of his journal, we find Solomon drawing a series of conclusions and lessons from his attempt to find meaning "under the sun." It's a rapid-fire record, an endless cycle of nothingness:

GETTING TO THE ROOT

The phrase "under the sun" is repeated twenty-nine times in Ecclesiastes and is found nowhere else in the Old Testament. "Under the sun" refers to our physical, earthly life, which is characterized by pointless and grievous labor (Ecclesiastes 1:3, 14; 2:11, 17–22; 8:17), endless cycles (1:9), injustice and wickedness (3:16; 4:1, 3, 7, 15; 5:12; 6:1; 8:9; 9:3), worldly pleasure and chance (9:6, 9), and a short lifespan (5:17; 6:12; 8:15). Life "under the sun" is the human experience considered apart from God.[6]

In today's world, the following philosophies are equivalents of the "under-the-sun" outlook on life described in Ecclesiastes:

- *Secular humanism*—man is supreme in the universe
- *Materialism*—the physical universe is all there is
- *Naturalism*—the natural flow of the universe is not disrupted by the supernatural
- *Agnosticism*—we don't know whether there is any God
- *Atheism*—there is no God to whom we're accountable

The phrase "under the sun" conveys a bleak, hopeless view of life in this world.

bleak, blank, and bland futility. No matter how varied the experiences of life, they fail to satisfy people's deepest desires. Without God's help, people cannot discover what's good for them, and without His revelation they cannot prepare for what's coming.

Being Young and Growing Old (Ecclesiastes 11:7–12:8)

Exhausted by chasing after the wind, Solomon dismissed his despair and presented a view of life under the sun that was as hopeful as one could reasonably muster: enjoy life because it's passing by faster than an express train at rush hour (11:7–10). Yet Solomon urged his readers to be guided by one thing: "God will bring you to judgment for all these things. So, remove grief and anger from your heart and put away pain from your body, because childhood and the prime of life are fleeting" (11:9–10). Because this is true, he reasoned, we must forsake our vain pursuit of meaning apart from God and remember our Creator in the days of our youth (12:1). A life of chasing after the wind, Solomon argued, will in the end find nothing and lose the one sure thing that was there all the while: *God.*

What things in today's world do people use to fill up their hunger for meaning and purpose? What are the results of these attempts?

_____

_____

_____

_____

Why do you think children and youth are statistically more likely to come to the Lord than older adults? How can maturing toward adulthood drive God further and further from our minds?

_____

_____

_____

_____

Drawing Some Final Conclusions (Ecclesiastes 12:9–14)

At the close of his journal, the wise preacher gave his bottom-line exhortation. He wrote, "The conclusion, when all has been heard is: fear God and keep His commandments, because this applies to every person. For God will bring every act to judgment, everything which is hidden, whether it is good or evil" (12:13–14).

How the Journal Relates to Our Journey

One author has written that the book of Ecclesiastes "gives the appearance of being written with our time in mind. . . . Consequently, many people have turned to this book for help when they have experienced disillusionment with their world and even with their God."[7] Perhaps few of us have viewed life with the stark realism of Solomon, but if we're honest with ourselves, we can't deny the accuracy of the book's portrayal of life apart from God. His "under-the-sun" philosophy is one that many share today, especially younger generations who have given up on standard answers to age-old questions. Solomon's words may be uncomfortable—even difficult—to hear, but they present the raw truth about life's emptiness that so many are facing. We can draw three initial principles for our lives from our flyover of Solomon's experiences and conclusions.

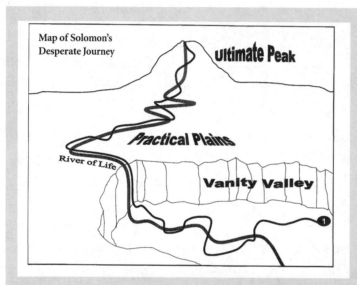

ROAD MAP FOR THE
JOURNEY
#1

Solomon's big idea throughout Ecclesiastes is rather simple: "God is God and we are not." In the course of his journey he will develop four other themes under this main idea.

God is God and we are not. Therefore,

1. God does as He pleases according to His perfect plan.
2. Our exploits apart from God are futile.
3. God gives all things to us as gifts to enjoy.
4. Our response should be to fear and obey God in wisdom.

Solomon begins his journey by examining the utter futility of life apart from God in the Valley of Futility, occasionally crossing the River of Life with rare insights of wisdom. He then climbs from the valley to discuss the practical applications of his discoveries in the Practical Plain. Finally, he ascends the Ultimate Peak for a glimpse of the ultimate purpose of life.

First, the sensual lure of something better tomorrow robs us of the joys offered today. The temptation is great to think the grass is greener on the other side. But we must resist the lure of this deception. We must choose to live to please God today rather than trying to build our empire to enjoy tomorrow. If we do, we'll find it easier to be content and less likely to catch ourselves chasing our tails in a vain pursuit of happiness.

Do you invest all of your time, talents, and treasures in an uncertain future when you believe you'll finally reap the rewards, or do you treat each day as a unique gift to be enjoyed and used to God's glory? Defend or explain your answer with specific examples.

_____

_____

_____

_____

Second, the personal temptation to escape is always stronger than the realization of its consequences. We seldom look beyond anticipated, immediate satisfactions to see detrimental, ultimate consequences. However, if we think about the effects of our actions, we'll take a firm step toward seeking the eternal priorities in life and forsake the meaningless pursuits of life under the sun.

Many of us want to escape the humdrum monotony of life's responsibilities. If you were to simply walk away from the "boring" duties in your life, what would be the consequences?

_____

_____

_____

_____

Third, the final destination will never satisfy if God is absent from the scene. Emptiness and a fleeting sense of contentment pervade a life lived without God's perspective and approval. The only cure for the disease of futility is a consistent walk of faith in and obedience to the living God.

Have you ever gone through a "dry spell" in your walk with the Lord? What did you do to fill the void? What was the result? Are you going through such a time right now?

_____

_____

_____

_____

Solomon was wealthy beyond comprehension and had the world at his fingertips. Yet that impressive king endured a period in his life when the world lost its luster, when the very roots of his life were dug up and exposed. He wrote a journal of that dark and desperate journey as he asked whether one could find meaning in the world apart from God. Solomon sampled the physical, intellectual, and emotional wares that the world under the sun had to offer—and they all came up short. Compared to a life with God, Solomon concluded, it was all empty, nothing, a chasing after the wind. It's a lesson about reality that many of us today need to learn and relearn daily.

2 Chasing the Wind
[ECCLESIASTES 1]

It can cause impaired thinking, irritability, restlessness, mood swings, and hallucinations. Its victims may hear unreal voices or music, feel invisible touches, or perceive things that aren't there. Under its influence, drivers have seen nonexistent hitchhikers, giant spiders, and animals in the road. What could cause such severe psychotic reactions? Is it some illicit drug? Abuse of alcohol? An overdose of narcotics? The answer might shock you: monotony.[1] These cases may be extreme, but the milder conditions of dissatisfaction, boredom, and apathy are much more common.

Dissatisfaction, boredom, apathy—the same-old drag of everyday life is an undeniable reality. Just look around. How many people do you know who awaken each morning motivated about their day? How many individuals can you name who genuinely enjoy their jobs and anticipate a new week with delight? With few exceptions, most people merely exist with a quiet yet pervasive sense of desperation. They see no future in their employment and little hope for their marriages, and they sincerely doubt that their lives will ever improve. For these, life is nothing more than monotonous futility and boredom.

Which things in your life do you find most monotonous? Which do you find most exciting? Does monotony or excitement best characterize your life overall?

_____

_____

_____

_____

Three thousand years ago, King Solomon described in the book of Ecclesiastes how the attempt to find meaning in this natural world was like "chasing after the wind," and how trying to overcome the humdrum of everyday life would result only in frustration and despair. The opening section of his journal exposed the hard realities of life and told the truth about existence apart from God. It's a truth that's too tough for some Christians to hear, but one that needs to be told if believers are to be honest about the difficulty of a life lived apart from Christ.

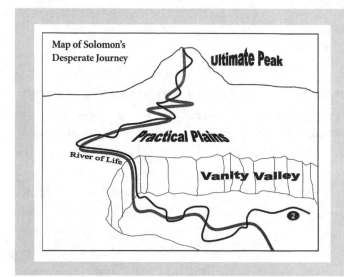

Map of Solomon's Desperate Journey

Ultimate Peak

Practical Plains

River of Life

Vanity Valley

2

ROAD MAP FOR THE JOURNEY #2

Solomon begins his journey in the Valley of Futility by arguing that since everything is set by God's sovereign and unknowable plan (1:9, 15), all merely human endeavors apart from Him are futile (1:2–3, 8, 13–14, 17).

EXPOSING FOUR LIES ABOUT LIFE

Several lies about life are often repeated as proverbial axioms—asserted as undeniable truths or heartwarming principles to help people smooth out life's ragged edges. However, while "chicken soup for the soul" can often warm us, following the wrong kind of advice will likely burn us. Let's look at four examples of worldly wisdom that can scald the unwary.

1. *"Laugh and the world laughs with you. Cry and you cry alone."* This proverb is often meant to force a smile. While it's a nice thought, it's simply not true. It does nothing but sugarcoat a harsh and tasteless world. As we'll see later, there's a time both for laughter *and* for tears (Ecclesiastes 3:4). Forcing a positive outlook can be self-deceptive.

Besides, sometimes we *do* laugh alone. Some people can't stand it when others are enjoying life more than they are. In fact, some people literally *hate* those around them who seem to have true inner joy. Have you ever had your "Good morning" met with a "What's good about it?" People who cry, complain, murmur, and grumble often draw a crowd—a phenomenon that many daytime talk shows count on!

Why do you think certain people resent those who find true joy in life?

_____

_____

_____

_____

2. *"Every day and in every way, our world is getting better and better."* If only this were true! Always looking at the world with hopeful optimism in human achievements may be a pleasant thought, but it's extremely naive. While we have made great strides in medicine, technology, and even government, we're still surrounded by death, destruction, pain, suffering, and the more intangible problems of depression and boredom. Humans may be advancing in knowledge, but overall we're neither progressing in morality nor growing in true, godly wisdom.

In which ways do you feel the world has improved during the last one hundred years? How has it gotten worse?

_____

_____

_____

_____

3. *"There's a light at the end of every tunnel."* This lie is meant to give people hope. But hope in hope alone is not true hope. Hope must be based on facts or reliable promises, not on vague, misty-eyed sentimentalism. While it's true that some tough times end in victory, the light at the end of the tunnel may very well be a freight train barreling down the track! If we hope in something other than God, our hope has no basis in truth.

Have you ever hoped in something other than God and been sorely disappointed? If so, briefly describe that experience.

_____

_____

_____

_____

4. *"Things never are as bad as they seem."* Unfortunately, things often *are* as bad as they seem. Sometimes they're even worse, and pretending won't help. Disengaging and running away from reality instead of facing the music will often worsen the situation instead of improve it.

Read Ecclesiastes 1:1–18.

What things, ideas, or activities do people use today to escape the reality of a bad situation or a depressing life?

_____

_____

_____

_____

TELLING THE TRUTH ABOUT EXISTENCE

Why do people believe and spread these and other lies about existence? Because they believe this world can provide purpose and happiness if they just hold on long enough. But the hope to which they cling ignores the fact that the world is corrupt, work is ultimately unfulfilling, and people are selfish. Life on planet Earth apart from God is not a bowl of cherries—it's the pits. Life's not a bed of roses—it's a vat of thorns. Let's take a look at the *truth* about life "under the sun," as eloquently expressed by King Solomon.

A Basic Premise (Ecclesiastes 1:1–3)

Solomon began his journal of Ecclesiastes by providing us with an arrow pointing to the final destination. He didn't wait until the end of the book to give us a glimpse of his conclusion. Instead, he told his readers up front what he had learned, and then he presented his evidence throughout the book.

From what perspective is Solomon's assessment about life under the sun in Ecclesiastes 1:1–3 true? From what perspective is it false?

_____

_____

_____

_____

Have you ever seen a small child try to catch a beam of sunlight in a dust-filled room, grasp a rainbow in a mist, or touch a reflection in a pool of water? These innocent actions seem reasonable at the time, but the child always ends up empty-handed. What appears real and tangible proves to be an elusive mirage. That's futility: a chasing after the wind.

GETTING TO THE ROOT

The word translated "vanity" in Ecclesiastes 1:2 is the Hebrew word *hebel*. It literally means a vapor or breath, and figuratively something worthless.[2] Repeating the word as Solomon does, "vanity of vanities" *(hebel hebalim)* expresses the superlative in Hebrew—with the sense that everything is complete and utter vanity.[3]

Examples of Futility (Ecclesiastes 1:4–11)

Having presented his basic premise, Solomon next painted a picture of tiresome cycles—a collage of futility that gives us a taste of the pointlessness of life without God. One example of futility under the sun is the endless passing of generations across life's empty stage (Ecclesiastes 1:4). People are born, and they die. The cycle goes on. Neither humanity nor creation escapes the futility of existence. Another example of futility is the cycles of nature (1:5–8). The sun continues to rise each morning and set each evening. The toil of today will repeat itself tomorrow.

According to Romans 8:19–23, when will the world be freed from its bondage to monotony? What will that look like for us?

_____

_____

_____

_____

These endless cycles frustrate people as they seek to discover the meaning of life, only to find more questions (1:8). Instead of changes that are new, fresh, and satisfying, the world brings repetition and sameness, for there is nothing new under the sun (1:9–11).

Think back in your life to things or events you once considered new and exciting. How do you feel about these things now? Have they kept their newness, or are they now just part of the routine?

_____

_____

_____

_____

GETTING TO THE ROOT

In Ecclesiastes 1:13, the Hebrew word translated "seek" is *darash,* which means to investigate the roots of a matter. The second word, translated "explore," is *tur,* meaning to investigate a subject on all sides.[4] Together, these two words imply an in-depth, broad, and thorough search that involves both theoretical and practical knowledge.

The Searcher and His Pursuit (Ecclesiastes 1:12–18)

As king, Solomon had the luxury of setting his mind and activities on discovering the meaning of life. He set out to thoroughly research every available approach to life and then to actively immerse himself in each. This might seem like an exciting and rewarding adventure to many people, but Solomon discovered just the opposite.

In Ecclesiastes 1:13–14, Solomon shared the results of his pursuit for the meaning of life: "It is a grievous task which God has given to the sons of men to be afflicted with. I have seen all the works which have been done under the sun, and behold, all is vanity and striving after the wind."

Review Ecclesiastes 1:12–18. In the chart that follows, write the methods Solomon used to pursue the meaning of life on the left, and write his conclusions on the right. An example is provided.

METHODS OF PURSUIT	RESULTS OF PURSUIT
(1:13) He set his mind to seek and explore	*(1:13) He realized it was grievous and an affliction*
(1:14)	(1:14)
(1:16)	(1:17–18)
(1:17)	

Solomon's description of his pursuit for meaning is pretty bleak, isn't it? When he looked for significance outside of God's purposes, he found only sorrow. This was reflected when he said in effect, "You can't make the crooked straight, so you might as well just leave everything 'as is'" (Ecclesiastes 1:15). When Solomon sought joy and contentment in knowledge, he found nothing but grief and pain (1:17–18). Life under the sun for Solomon was a drab, dull, and depressing mess.

THINKING THROUGH THE PRACTICAL RAMIFICATIONS

Solomon's journal entry is a despairing yet accurate portrayal of life lived with only an earthly perspective. If we walk around with our heads down, we'll see nothing but dirt. Thankfully, however, two thoughts emerge from Solomon's observations that point to something better for the child of God.

1. *If there is nothing but nothing under the sun, our only hope must be above it.* If an in-depth exploration of the monotony of life in the natural world leads to despair and frustration, then placing our trust in that unending carousel of life is utterly foolish. The object of our hope must be God, who dwells outside the cycles of this world.

DIGGING DEEPER

Nihilism

R. C. Sproul writes that the vanity spoken of by Solomon "captures the essence of a philosophical position called nihilism. To say 'all is vanity' is to say that *nothing* has meaning or significance ultimately. Nihilism means literally 'nothing-ism.' The *nihil* corresponds to what Nietzsche called *das nichtig* (the nothing)."[5]

Geisler and Watkins describe Friedrich Nietzsche's worldview as follows:

> Since God does not exist, the world is all there is. Matter is in motion, and life moves in cycles. The world is real, and God is an illusion. . . . Man's history, like his destiny, is cyclical. Neitzsche rejected any Christian goal-oriented end in favor of a more oriental view of cyclical recurrence. History is not going anywhere. There are no ultimate goals to achieve on earth, no paradise to regain.[6]

Francis Schaeffer was correct when he evaluated Nietzsche this way:

> Surrounded by some of the most beautiful scenery in the world, Nietzsche knew the tension and despair of modern man. With no personal God, all is dead. Yet man, being truly man (no matter what he says he is), cries out for a meaning that can only be found in the existence of the infinite-personal God, who has not been silent but has spoken, and in the existence of a personal life continuing into eternity.[7]

Nietzsche's view of nihilism would be correct if we perceived the monotony of this world as proof that God were dead or never existed. However, Nietzsche's view is dead wrong because God is alive, and He provides purpose and meaning to the most mundane experiences.

Imagine that a friend or relative shared Solomon's frustration over the meaninglessness of life found in Ecclesiastes 1:1–18. Now read Colossians 3:1–2. In what ways could you encourage your friend with these verses?

_____

_____

_____

_____

2. *If a man who had it all investigated everything visible and found nothing of lasting value, then the only thing needed must be invisible.* Like Solomon, we could spend all the money in the world on a pursuit to find meaning in people, places, and things of the visible world. And like Solomon, we'd end up with a world full of stuff and an empty soul. Visible things cannot fill an invisible void. But does this mean people can't experience lasting joy? Not at all! If our thirst for meaning cannot be quenched by things that are seen, we must turn our attention to the things that are unseen.

Read 2 Corinthians 4:17–18. What are some of the "invisible things" in your life that are often overshadowed by the visible things? How can you begin to place a greater emphasis on things that are not seen?

_____

_____

_____

_____

Consider the words of C. S. Lewis:

> Creatures are not born with desires unless satisfaction for those desires exists. A baby feels hunger: well, there is such a thing as food. A duckling wants to swim: well, there is such a thing as water. . . . If I find in myself a desire which no experience in this world can satisfy, the most probable explanation is that I was made for another world. If none of my earthly pleasures satisfy it, that does not prove that the universe is a fraud. Probably earthly pleasures were never meant to satisfy it, but only to arouse it, to suggest the real thing.[8]

Throughout history, the search for enduring happiness has led countless individuals to place their faith in the living God. In the person of Jesus Christ, the monotony grinds to a halt

(Revelation 22:13), the crooked is made straight (Luke 3:5), and wisdom and knowledge are fulfilled (Colossians 2:3). Where are you seeking the answers to Solomon's questions about life? Are you focused on the vain pursuits of the world around you, leaving you chasing after the wind? Or does your quest lead you to look above, where Christ is seated on the throne?

3 Eat, Drink... and Be *What?*
[ECCLESIASTES 2:1–11]

f it feels good, do it!" This is the golden rule for our postmodern generation, the mandate of our times. It comes in different forms, all of which point to the philosophy of hedonism as a means of finding fulfillment in life. *Hedonism* is defined as "the doctrine that pleasure or happiness is the sole or chief good in life."[1] The philosophy of hedonism draws on an ancient belief that the material world is all there is and that humans are merely physical beings. Therefore, hedonism asserts that only our pleasurable experiences can bring us joy and purpose as we absorb them with our five senses.

One revolting example of unrestrained hedonism comes from the life of Aleister Crowley. Born in 1875, this self-proclaimed "wickedest man in the world" sought to worship Satan by living according to one law: "Do what thou wilt." Throughout his life he gorged on sensuality through deviant sexual practices, witchcraft, pornography, drugs, and shocking exhibitionism. The end of his pursuit of carnal passions is described as follows:

> At the age of seventy-two, in a cheap boardinghouse in Hastings, England, Aleister Crowley, injecting eleven grams of heroin into his wasted body each day, begged for morphine to kill the pain. But the pain wasn't assuaged, and Crowley passed on to meet his Maker.[2]

Few people go to the extremes of Aleister Crowley, but almost all of us feel the sensual world's call to worship at the altar of indulgence.

Read 1 John 2:15–17. How would you describe someone who "loves the world" in today's terms? What would be some extreme and mild examples? Why do you think it's so easy to fall into an idolatrous love of the world?

_____

_____

_____

_____

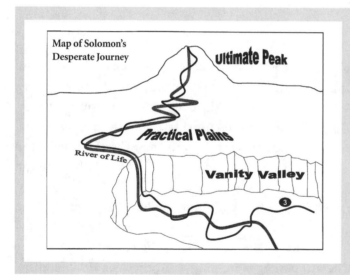

Map of Solomon's Desperate Journey

Ultimate Peak

Practical Plains

River of Life

Vanity Valley

3

ROAD MAP FOR THE JOURNEY #3

Continuing his trek through the Valley, Solomon demonstrates that apart from God's grace, our various forms of worldly entertainment and exploits are ultimately empty and futile (Ecclesiastes 2:1–11).

A QUICK REVIEW

Moment by moment, the world calls out to all of us, "Worship me! Love me!" It promises to provide true meaning in life, but it can't deliver. The world asks you to love it, but it can never love you in return. King Solomon arrived at this same conclusion nearly three thousand years ago.

As king over Israel, Solomon had the greatest political clout in the Near East and ready access to whatever he desired. He also reigned during a period of peace, which heightened his opportunity to enjoy life to the fullest. During what could be considered an ancient midlife crisis, the wise and wealthy king took advantage of his time, riches, and wisdom, applying them toward a vigorous pursuit of happiness in the world "under the sun." Yet, at the end of his search, Solomon determined that life apart from God as the source of purpose and meaning is "vanity and striving after wind" (Ecclesiastes 1:14).

Can the pleasures of the world satisfy our deepest needs? Can purpose and contentment be found in a playboy lifestyle? Can the golden rule of hedonism buy happiness, or does it only purchase cheap fool's gold? Let's join Solomon for a walk down the hallway of his life as we learn the answers to these questions and see their relevance to our lives.

The word *sensual* is often interpreted as *sexual,* but it really refers to activities that appeal to the various God-given senses. To make this topic more concrete, list an activity for each of the following senses that gives you enjoyment or pleasure. At this point, don't be concerned about whether the activity is positive, negative, or neutral. Just try to determine your most enjoyable pursuits.

1. Seeing _____

_____

_____

_____

2. Hearing _____

_____

_____

_____

3. Smelling _____

_____

_____

_____

4. Touching _____
_____
_____
_____

5. Tasting _____
_____
_____
_____

Read Ecclesiastes 2:1–11.

As you read through this chapter, keep these sensory pleasures in mind as you consider their proper place in the pursuit for meaning and God's life of blessing.

GETTING TO THE ROOT

The Hebrew word translated "pleasure" in Ecclesiastes 2:1, *simkhah,* refers to the enjoyment that comes from the physical senses.[3] In the Old Testament, the word can refer to pleasures that are positive or righteous (Proverbs 10:28) or negative and sinful (Proverbs 21:17). It's important to remember that the activities in which Solomon engaged were not *necessarily* wrong or immoral, although some of them were. Many were neutral activities done for the wrong reasons, either to find meaning and purpose or to smooth out the ragged edges of life.

An Open Invitation

Solomon's quest for meaning in life came as a result of the frustration, boredom, and endless cycles described in Ecclesiastes chapter 1.

Wild 'n' Crazy Fun 'n' Games (Ecclesiastes 2:1–3)

Solomon began his examination of worldly pleasure with a statement of his general conclusions: "I said to myself, 'Come now, I will test you with pleasure. So enjoy yourself.' And behold, it too was futility" (2:1).

Solomon warned his readers of the pitfalls of chasing worldly pleasures before he discussed his hedonistic pursuits (2:2–11). Many things in the world can benefit us and give us joy, but almost all things should come with the same warning: "Use only as intended; not for use in finding your ultimate purpose in life."

Think about some of the sensual pleasures you've tried in life. They may have been positive, negative, or neutral, but were ultimately unfulfilling. Write a "warning label" for younger generations who may be thinking about similar pursuits.

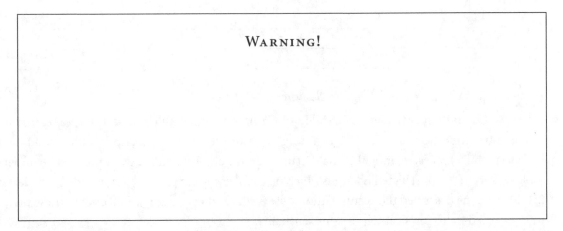

WARNING!

In Ecclesiastes 2:2, Solomon added amusement, humor, and laughter to his quest. Who doesn't like a good comedy or a clever joke? The gift of laughter is certainly something that makes us distinctly human. So Solomon vigorously pursued this avenue, hoping a life of frivolity would satisfy him.

Read again Solomon's conclusion in Ecclesiastes 2:2. How do you think humor can move from being a positive seasoning in life to being an unwise frivolity that distracts us from God and His purpose? Explain.

_____
_____
_____
_____

Another area of enjoyment Solomon explored to fill life's natural void was indulgence in alcoholic beverages (2:3). This doesn't mean that he drank himself into a stupor but that he engaged in a sophisticated pursuit of the world of fine wines. He sought to become a connoisseur of the "good things" in life, for throughout his quest Solomon's mind was guiding him wisely.[4]

Why do you think so many people believe alcohol (or other drugs) will lead to the joy and pleasure they seek in life? How has the media and other aspects of our culture encouraged this idea?

_____
_____
_____

Projects and Pools, Slaves, and Songs (Ecclesiastes 2:4–8)

Failing to find fulfillment in laughter and liquor, Solomon attempted to find it in great construction and beautification projects and acquiring fantastic wealth. In a description that could have been written by real estate mogul Donald Trump, Solomon outlined the great projects he undertook—a sort of "reconstructed Eden" in which he could enjoy the pleasures of beauty (Ecclesiastes 2:4–6). Then he described the accumulation of servants and livestock (vv. 7–8). All of these pleasures appealed to his physical senses—his sensuality.

Review Ecclesiastes 2:4–8. List the types of projects, personnel, and property that Solomon accumulated. To which of the five physical senses does each appeal?

_____

DIGGING DEEPER

Hedonism versus Asceticism

Is it wrong for us to experience any kind of pleasure in this world? Does God want us to go through life abstaining from the sights, sounds, scents, sensations, and sweetness of His physical creation? Absolutely not.

It's true that some Christian "ascetics" believe all pleasure in this world falls into one of three categories: it is sin, it will lead to sin, or it may appear to be sin. Their view of the ideal Christian is the puritanical prude, hiding himself away in a monastery or other compound, avoiding any contact with the "evil" physical world. These people view God as a cosmic kill-joy, prepared to put the instant kibosh on anybody having a good time. But nothing could be further from the truth.

One author writes, "Pleasure is good. God made a good world, and he made us capable of delighting in our sensations of it."[5] In fact, the apostle Paul told Timothy that extreme asceticism—denying people the enjoyment of things of this world—is a sign not of spiritual Christians but of heretics and false teachers: "For everything created by God is good, and nothing is to be rejected if it is received with gratitude" (1 Timothy 4:4). The enjoyment of God's gifts should be accompanied by an attitude of thankfulness and joy, returning glory to God for His graces. As Paul taught in the book of 1 Corinthians, "Whether, then, you eat or drink or whatever you do, do all to the glory of God" (10:31).

Worldly hedonism is an empty philosophy that ultimately leads to destruction. Religious asceticism, however, is a legalistic pursuit that replaces God's gracious gifts with our own self-righteousness and suggests that God never intended for people to live joyous, abundant lives in the physical universe He created. The balanced, biblical solution is to acknowledge the many blessings of God's physical creation, returning thanks to Him for His glorious gifts.

Look at the passage again. This time, note all the occurrences of the words *my, me, I,* or *myself.* Given his self-centered pursuits, why do you think Solomon ultimately found his projects unsatisfying? How could he have made many of these noble projects more meaningful?

_____

_____

_____

_____

The Good Life (Ecclesiastes 2:9–10)

After surveying the results of his projects and his accumulation of wealth, Solomon realized he was on top of the world (Ecclesiastes 2:9). He had achieved "the good life." His checkbook was fat, he had every new gadget imaginable, and he had plenty of beautiful women with whom to enjoy it all (2:10).

Yet in the midst of all this, Solomon was able to step back and evaluate the more valuable things in life with discernment, for he said, "My wisdom also stood by me" (2:9). One scholar notes that Solomon's "experiment with pleasure never fell to the level of mindless stupor. His rational capacity stood by him."[6] Solomon remained in a position to regard his accomplishments objectively in light of the ultimate realities of life. What was his conclusion? Had he achieved perfect satisfaction? Lasting accomplishment? A fabulous return to Eden? No!

It's Time to Face the Truth (Ecclesiastes 2:11)

At the end of his quest for meaning through gratification of the senses, Solomon concluded:

> Thus I considered all my activities which my hands had done and the labor which I had exerted, and behold all was vanity and striving after wind and there was no profit under the sun. (Ecclesiastes 2:11)

In other words, when Solomon sat down and tallied all of his accomplishments, weighing them to determine their eternal and ultimate value, he came to the following conclusion:

Net Worth = 0

WINDOWS TO THE ANCIENT WORLD

How Wealthy was Solomon?

You may recall a television advertisement in which a man drops a massive cell-phone bill on a table, and the edge of the table collapses under its weight. Nobody wants something like that dropped on their kitchen table—especially a cell-phone bill! But what about 150 pounds of *gold*—daily? Now that's a different story! The author of Ecclesiastes experienced that every day. First Kings 10:14 says that King Solomon's annual income of gold weighed fifty thousand pounds. That would be worth about 240 million dollars in today's currency. And that was just the gold!

First Kings 10:23 says, "Solomon became greater than all the kings of the earth in riches." He not only built the temple of the Lord—a magnificent structure in which nearly every part was either solid or overlaid gold—but he also built himself a house unmatched by any private dwelling you could find today. In fact, its dimensions (more than thirty thousand square feet of floor space) are comparable to those of the White House. Pure gold adorned the walls and pillars and overlaid the furniture. There was so much wealth and precious metal available to Solomon that he "made silver as common as stones" (1 Kings 10:27). Archaeological evidence of King Solomon's unrivaled building projects and vast wealth is still found today, nearly three thousand years after the height of his kingdom.[7]

Gold wasn't the only luxury item in Solomon's house. First Kings 4:22–23 says that the members of Solomon's household consumed five tons of flour, ten tons of meal, thirty oxen, and one hundred sheep—*daily*. Many of those people were probably stable hands hired to take care of Solomon's forty thousand horses. All things considered, calling Solomon the Donald Trump of the ancient world is an understatement!

This disappointing final analysis is never mentioned in the fine print of today's business and entertainment news. While marketing firms may lure us with trickery and our peers may pressure us with deception, God tells us the truth. In His Word, He tells us that earthly riches and pleasures simply cannot satisfy the deepest longings of our hearts.

Solomon discovered that the golden rule of hedonism—"If it feels good, do it"—is nothing but illusory fool's gold. At the same time, Solomon's hedonistic quest yielded at least three valuable gems of wisdom.

1. *Sensual pleasures make promises that lack staying power.* It doesn't matter if the alluring thrill is alcohol, drugs, sex, music, food, or anything else. Such pleasures never deliver the satisfaction they promise. They offer initial ecstasy (Ecclesiastes 2:10) but ultimate futility (2:11).

2. *Sensual pleasures offer to open our eyes, but in reality they blind us.* Propagators of hedonism tell us that if we follow our urges and lusts, a whole new world of incredible pleasures will unfold. But what actually happens is that a lifestyle of self-gratification leads us away from the truly important things of life: God, family, and friends.

3. *Sensual pleasures disillusion us, making us cover-up artists.* The pursuit of pleasure may satisfy for a time, but eventually it will leave us empty. That's a hard fact to face, and one many of us refuse to acknowledge. Rather than admitting the futility of our escapades, we con ourselves with hypocritical cover-ups, pretending we have found true satisfaction. We begin to manipulate our theology and ignore our common sense when we lead with our feelings and follow the lure of the world's plastic pearls instead of seeking the pearl of great price: the kingdom of God.

Are there any areas of your life in which you're being misled by pleasure's promises, blinded by its deceptiveness, or steeped in its hypocrisy? Copy the five activities you listed as "pleasurable pursuits" on pages 23–24 into the chart on the facing page and answer the questions *yes* or *no*.

Based on your answers, are there any activities you listed that might not fit with a growing, healthy walk with Christ? If so, what will you do about it?

_____

_____

_____

_____

List Activity:	1	2	3	4	5
1. Is this activity paying off the way I had hoped?	Yes	Yes	Yes	Yes	Yes
	No	No	No	No	No
2. Am I receiving these experiences with an attitude of thankfulness and glory to God?	Yes	Yes	Yes	Yes	Yes
	No	No	No	No	No
3. Are the results going to impact eternity?	Yes	Yes	Yes	Yes	Yes
	No	No	No	No	No

Living in the fast lane isn't limited to the twenty-first century. Solomon epitomized that lifestyle centuries ago. Pushing aside all restraints and ignoring every twinge of guilt, the king set out on a quest for meaning through sensual pleasures that makes the offerings of casinos, dance clubs, playboy resorts, and extravagant lifestyles pale in comparison. Solomon's world was an all-you-can-eat buffet of pleasure, and he put heaping portions on his plate. Hedonism was rarely pursued with greater commitment or determination to discern meaning and significance. When Solomon laughed, it was nothing short of an uproar. When he drank, it was from the finest selection of choice wines, and his meals were lavish feasts. No project was too grand—no dream unattainable. But what was the result of Solomon's great pursuit? Emptiness.

Into which voids of sensual experiences are you pouring your time and efforts? Take a few moments to pray about the empty pursuits in your life. Then turn to God for fulfillment and a proper perspective on the good material gifts He's given you to enjoy.

4 More Miles of Bad Road

[ECCLESIASTES 2:12–26]

Like an endless labyrinth, the paths of life can lead us down a twisting, turning course only to find a dead end. We seek release from sorrow, monotony, and pain. We seek an escape from futility and frustration. We think, *Perhaps the answer lies here, around this corner. Maybe it's there, down that corridor, or through that archway.* Then, as we approach what looks like an exit, we find nothing but a mirror and see our own empty selves staring back. Such is life under the sun. Often, the roads that seem so promising turn out to be either endless paths or dead-end pursuits.

This situation isn't just for unbelievers. Christians, too, can lose their eternal perspective and get tangled in the gears of the world system. In response to a sermon series on Ecclesiastes, one believer wrote, "*I'm empty.* I've come to the conclusion that living is a waste of time. All *is* vanity, striving after wind. There is not *one* thing on this earth to make it worth staying. I used to think that ministering to others was reason enough to live. It isn't. Neither is raising a family."

That's a pretty bleak outlook, isn't it? If we're honest with ourselves, we'll all admit that we've had similar thoughts—at least during moments of frustration. It's part of who we are as sinful humans. Even Christians experience the frustration of this material world as we await our resurrection to a new and perfect life with Christ for eternity.

On the following chart, where do you most often find yourself: *frustrated and hopeless,* as reflected in the quote; *fulfilled and hopeful,* so nothing in the world could affect you negatively; or somewhere *in-between?*

The Bible says that Christians living in the world function somewhere between frustration and fulfillment. In Romans 8:18–23, Paul described the "futility" to which creation has been subject since the Fall and in which Christians presently participate. However, many Christians feel obligated to say that they feel fulfilled in life when, in fact, they acutely feel the frustration brought about by sin.

GETTING TO THE ROOT

Paul used the Greek word *mataiotēs* for the word translated "futility" in Romans 8:20. This is the same word used in the Greek translation of Ecclesiastes for the word "vanity" or "futility." In Romans 8:18–23, several complementary terms are used with "futility" to describe this present world: "suffering," "anxious longing," "slavery to corruption," "eager anticipation," and "groaning."

It's best to be honest with ourselves and take Paul's words seriously—life is frustrating. If we find ourselves constantly fulfilled in this life, we're probably out of touch with God's reality. Our joy in Christ is an expression of hope, not a true satisfaction with the life we have in this world. Believers with a proper eternal perspective can balance the frustrations of life with the hope of a better life to come.

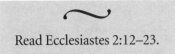

Read Ecclesiastes 2:12–23.

THE SEARCH CONTINUES

At this point in his desperate journey, Solomon has described his utter frustration after having traveled down paths that led to emptiness. All of these paths were "vanity and striving after wind" (Ecclesiastes 2:11). The king had tried intellectual pursuits, comic relief, building projects, and sensual pleasures (1:1–2:11). Although some of these pursuits produced good feelings for a time, they ultimately provided no lasting benefit. But running into a few dead ends didn't stop Solomon.

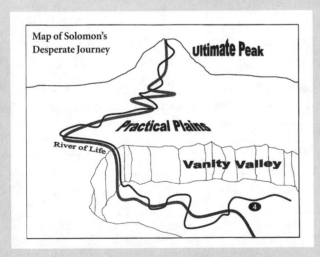

Map of Solomon's Desperate Journey

Ultimate Peak

Practical Plains

River of Life

Vanity Valley

ROAD MAP FOR THE JOURNEY
#4

As Solomon trudged along through the Valley of Futility, he realized another indication that God is God, and we are not. Since God Himself gives all things as He pleases—even wisdom, knowledge, and joy (2:24–26)—our own efforts at fulfilling our personal plans and achieving our goals in life appear futile apart from Him (2:19–23).

The next leg of Solomon's journey included distinct paths of mental exploration in the form of three comparisons: wisdom versus folly (2:12–17), the immediate versus the ultimate (2:18–21), and daily work versus evening relief (2:22–23).

Wisdom Compared to Foolishness (Ecclesiastes 2:12–17)

In Ecclesiastes 2:12–13, Solomon considered whether to embrace wisdom or folly as his guiding philosophy of life. On the surface, it seems like an easy choice. Solomon thought it was self-evident that wisdom was better than folly, but when he viewed life without an eternal perspective, the smooth path turned rocky as he followed his thought to its logical conclusion. Wisdom provides great benefits in the here and now, but it can appear foolish when we look at the natural outcome of life:

> And yet I know that one fate befalls them both. Then I said to myself, "As is the fate of the fool, it will also befall me. Why then have I been extremely wise?" So I said to myself, "This too is vanity." For there is no lasting remembrance of the wise man as with the fool, inasmuch as in the coming days all will be forgotten. And how the wise man and the fool alike die! (2:14–16)

Solomon chose to embrace wisdom but then questioned the value of accumulating knowledge because everyone dies anyway. Why are getting an education and pursuing knowledge important when viewed within the context of a godly, eternal perspective?

_____

_____

_____

_____

From a purely humanistic, secular worldview, Solomon was right: we all die in the end, so who cares? Why waste time, energy, and money on filling a brain that's just going to rot in the grave? Why try to build a legacy if we'll be forgotten shortly after we're gone? These thoughts plagued Solomon so much that he wrote, "So I hated life, for the work which had been done under the sun was grievous to me; because everything is futility and striving after wind" (2:17). One author aptly summed it up: "If . . . every card in our hand will be trumped, does it matter how we play? Why treat a king with more respect than a knave?"[1]

The Immediate Compared to the Ultimate (Ecclesiastes 2:18–21)

Solomon decided to make a U-turn and try another side street. He mused that if our earthly pursuits end in death and we're remembered no more, then perhaps the solution lies in shifting our emphasis from ourselves to others. He considered that if we can't enjoy wisdom and riches, at least we can pass them on to those who can! But we can't control whether others will use those resources wisely or foolishly. We have no choice but to entrust our legacy to God's management.

Many who believe only in a material world often try to find meaning in preservation and betterment of society—improving the world for the human race. Parents seek to leave an estate and life insurance to their children, world leaders seek to stamp out threats that could cause future human tragedies, and activists fight to improve health, safety, and the environment for coming generations. Solomon considered this route as well but quickly rejected it.

Review Solomon's conclusions in Ecclesiastes 2:18–21. Can you identify with Solomon's frustrations and feelings about the futility of work? Please explain. How does Colossians 3:23–24 affect your perspective?

_____

_____

_____

_____

Daily Work Compared to Evening Relief (Ecclesiastes 2:22–23)

After taking two side trails that led nowhere, Solomon was running out of options. First, he deduced that wisdom was no better than folly because we all die in the end. Second, he suggested that living wisely for our heirs is vanity because they may just waste it after all. What else was left?

Solomon turned his efforts toward life's daily grind for insight. He mused that if life as a whole is futile, and if future generations hold no promise, perhaps limiting our scope will do some good. Forget tomorrow—focus on today! Take your rewards in smaller increments. Enjoy your free time and rest while you can! Such was Solomon's mind-set as he compared daily work with evening relief.

Perhaps you, like Solomon, have trouble detaching yourself from your work for the sake of rest. The sad truth is that rest, leisure, and vacations are increasingly smothered by the stress of labor. If we work for the weekend, we'll be disappointed, because the weekend will present us with its own stress.

If we labor to earn a vacation, we could end up bringing work along with us, spending our time catching up on housework or yardwork, staying glued to our laptop or cell phone, or doubling our efforts to catch up once we return to the workplace. Solomon saw that without a divine perspective, we're stuck in a relentless cycle.

Read Genesis 2:2–3 and Exodus 20:10–11. The biblical principle of rest is found throughout Scripture. What can you do to give yourself time to recover from the daily grind? Why do you think true rest is especially necessary in our modern society?

_____

_____

_____

_____

Signposts of Insight (Ecclesiastes 2:24–26)

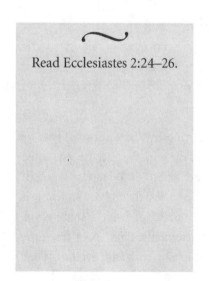

Read Ecclesiastes 2:24–26.

By the end of Ecclesiastes 2, Solomon had reached a dead end in yet another pursuit. Instead of a smooth journey toward fulfillment, he found more miles of bad road. Yet, along the way, he discovered three signposts of insight that guided him closer to the proper perspective on life.

1. *There's nothing inherent in humanity that allows us to extract fulfillment from the things we do.* Although there are a couple of ways of translating the Hebrew text of Ecclesiastes 2:24 into English, a literal rendering would be, "There is nothing good in man with which to eat and drink and view his own toil as something good."[2] This would mean that a person "does not possess anything within or outside himself to aid him in securing permanent happiness."[3]

God created humans with a need for fellowship with Him, including the need for significance and self-worth. Since the fall of Adam and Eve, humans have sought self-sufficiency, independence from God, and significance in the things and people of the world rather than in their Creator. But this is doomed to fail because God made us to find our significance in Him alone. If we lack the ability to find meaning in our fallen condition, what are we to do?

Read Psalm 14:1–3; Isaiah 59:7–8; and Romans 7:18. Why do you think people are incapable of finding significance and enjoyment in themselves, in others, and in the world apart from God?

_____
_____
_____
_____

2. *Enjoyment is God's personal gift.* Ecclesiastes 2:24–25 says, "This also I have seen that it is from the hand of God. For who can eat and who can have enjoyment without Him?" This is a common theme in Ecclesiastes: unless God gives us contentment and peace as a gift, all our pursuits will be empty. Any joy we experience in this life is by God's grace.

Read Psalms 42:1–2; 63:1; and 145:15–16. According to these passages, how are our deepest spiritual needs for significance met?

_____
_____
_____
_____

If God is not the source and center of a person's life, contentment will be a fleeting phantom. However, when Christ is on the throne of our lives, we can experience an abiding hope and joy through all circumstances.

Read Philippians 4:11–13. Write a prayer offering God the areas of your life in which you're experiencing frustration and discontentment. Ask Him for strength to find true contentment, whatever your current circumstances.

_____

_____

_____

_____

3. *Those who are right with God derive the benefit of everyone's labor.* Ecclesiastes 2:26 says, "For to a person who is good in His sight He has given wisdom and knowledge and joy, while to the sinner He has given the task of gathering and collecting so that he may give to one who is good in God's sight. This too is vanity and striving after wind."

People may labor for a variety of selfish reasons, but God ultimately uses the products of their labor to carry out His perfect plan. Romans 8:28 says that all these things, even the labor of the unrighteous, "work together for good to those who love God, to those who are called according to His purpose." We must be cautious here. This isn't the same as saying believers will necessarily benefit in financial or materialistic ways, but God's unfolding plan is to ultimately bless His people and make them a blessing. He uses all means—including the labor of unbelievers—to accomplish this. As far as the laborer is concerned, this leads to futility, for God's plan ultimately trumps human exploits and turns things around for the benefit of His people.

One example of this would be the labor of the Romans, who built a vast network of roads for military conquest and political control. Ultimately these roads were used by God to spread the gospel throughout the empire in a single generation. Even the evil labor of other anti-Christian governments that concentrated their efforts on persecuting Christians ultimately led to the benefit of believers, as their faith and perseverance increased and these persecuted believers reaped spiritual blessings.

Name three things produced by the labor of the world—either negative or positive—that ultimately advanced God's purpose or blessed His people.

1. _____

_____

_____

_____

2. _____

_____

_____

_____

_____

3. _____

_____

_____

_____

_____

~

Believers living in the world perform a precarious balancing act. On the one hand, we find the fallen world to be a frustrating, painful place. That's reality. On the other hand, we have the promise of a glorious and meaningful existence because we have a personal relationship with God. The tension lies in the fact that we're living in the midst of both realities. The old, earthly reality will one day pass away, but we wake up to it every morning. The new, heavenly reality could arrive at any moment, and we experience it by the gifts God has given us through His Spirit. But there are certain aspects of our heavenly reality that we still cannot fathom (1 Corinthians 13:12; 1 John 3:2).

As we live life on the ragged edge, teetering between frustration and fulfillment, and with all the traffic of the world headed toward desperation, it would be easy for us to lose our way on our journey. We don't want to end up like Solomon, announcing, "I hate life!"

More than ever, we must learn to read the signposts provided by Scripture. We're called to turn away from an empty pursuit of self-fulfillment and to receive God's indescribable peace and contentment. Pain and hardship won't cease on this side of eternity. But our perspective on them can align with that of the promising future rather than that of the disappointing present or the disillusioned past. Where are you finding your fulfillment today?

5 Do You Know What Time It Is?
[ECCLESIASTES 3:1–11]

There's a four-letter word that many of us can't stand to hear. Some cringe when it's spoken; others begin to sweat at the thought of it. Yet we talk about it regularly and think about it constantly. This four-letter word controls our lives, and there's simply no escaping it. What is this irritating utterance?

Time.

Time both fascinates us and frustrates us. We wear it on our arms, carry it in our pockets, and hang it on our walls. We're obsessed with being on time and stressed when we're late. Like a vicious taskmaster, time enslaves us with its strict demands: "Meet me at noon!" "Arrive before ten!" "Don't be late!"

Long before this second-by-second rationing of time began to characterize our world, King Solomon realized the central role that time plays in our lives. In the first several verses of Ecclesiastes 3, he recorded some of his thoughts about the timing of human events. Through a series of contrasting snapshots covering the span of life, Solomon set forth several principles about time intended to transform our outlook on life and deepen our relationship with God.

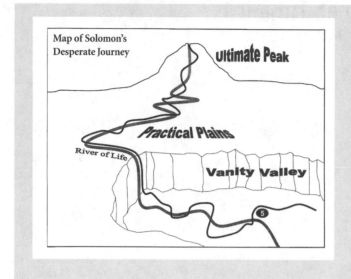

Map of Solomon's Desperate Journey

Ultimate Peak

Practical Plains

River of Life

Vanity Valley

5

TIME: A FEW PERTINENT QUESTIONS

Before turning to Solomon's documentary of life under the sun, let's answer a few difficult but necessary questions.

What is time? One dictionary defines it as "the measured or measurable period during which an action, process, or condition exists or continues."[1] It includes a series of events and our ability to measure or track those events. Think about the characteristics of photographs versus films. In photographs, the images are still and stationary—nothing about them ever changes. They are timeless. However, films capture the element of time in that images change and develop. When God created the material universe out of nothing, He created time as part of His perfect plan.[2]

Why is time so important? Among the many responses we could give, one stands out: time is significant because it's completely irretrievable. While science fiction writers have offered a variety of clever plots in which people travel through time to change the past, present, or future, we know that tampering with the past is impossible for us here on earth. Once a unit of time has been used, it can't be recaptured or reversed.

When will time end? Since time and space are inseparable, time would theoretically end if the physical universe ceased to exist and all perceivable events came to a halt.[3] In one sense, events will continue to proceed in logical order even in the new heaven and new earth (Revelation 21:1–22:5).

In another sense, however, time as we know it will come to an end. The cycles of day and night will cease (Revelation 22:5), and clocks and calendars will lose their relevance. While the passage of events will continue, for humans the measurement of time will become obsolete.

How do the following verses say a Christian should spend his or her time in this world?

Romans 13:10–12 _____

_____

_____

_____

Ephesians 5:15–17 _____

_____

_____

_____

1 Peter 5:6–8 _____

_____

_____

_____

LIFE: MEASURED ACCORDING TO ITS EVENTS

At the start of a passage described as "one of the most ingenious parts of the Old Testament,"[4] Solomon began with the following summary statement: "There is an appointed time for everything. And there is a time for every event under heaven" (Ecclesiastes 3:1).

What follows this summary is a series of snapshots of real life, showcasing the all-pervading opposites of existence—good and bad, positive and negative. While most of us fill our photo albums with only the best photos, Solomon portrayed life in its stark reality. He included not only laughter and love, but hardship and pain as well.

Read Ecclesiastes 3:1–8.

GETTING TO THE ROOT

Solomon used two Hebrew words for "time" in Ecclesiastes 3:1. The first, *zeman,* means "appointed time" and occurs only three other times in the Old Testament (Nehemiah 2:6; Esther 9:27, 31). In each of these cases, this term refers to a predetermined time at which an event will occur. The second word Solomon used, *aēt,* is far more common, and it refers to the simple time of an event without necessarily pointing out that its occurrence was prearranged.[5]

All-Pervading Opposites (Ecclesiastes 3:2–8)

In Ecclesiastes 3:2–8, Solomon strung together fourteen opposite events grouped together into seven sets.[6] Donald Glenn writes, "The number seven suggests the idea of completeness and the use of polar opposites—a well-known poetical device called merism—suggests totality."[7] Let's flip through Solomon's vivid photo documentary of life, examining these seven couplets to discover their wisdom.

The first pair of opposites refers to the beginning and ending of life in both the animal and plant kingdoms: "A time to give birth and a time to die; a time to plant and a time to uproot what is planted" (Ecclesiastes 3:2).

Certainly, we have no control over the time or circumstances of our birth, and neither can we lengthen our lives beyond the time God has allotted to each of us. These events are in God's hands and occur according to His own time and sovereign plan.

If you've ever looked on the back of a packet of seeds, you know there's usually a chart listing the proper growing season for different regions of the country. In order for plants to bear fruit, the seeds must be planted in the proper season and harvested neither too early nor too late. Similarly,

God has planted each of our lives according to His plan and purpose, and He will uproot us according to the same plan. That is, God may sometimes make drastic changes in our lives that make us feel like we're being pulled out of the ground and replanted elsewhere.

Read 1 Corinthians 3:5–7. Who is ultimately responsible for the "planting and uprooting" of our lives? Does this knowledge bring you comfort or distress? Why?

_____

_____

_____

_____

The second pair of opposites Solomon described centers on the appropriateness of certain actions in specific situations: "A time to kill and a time to heal; a time to tear down and a time to build up" (Ecclesiastes 3:3).

Real life involves a strange mixture of battlefields and hospitals, mortality and medicine, demolition crews and construction workers.

According to the following passages, what are some examples of when it is time to "build up" or time "to heal"?

2 Corinthians 2:6–9 _____

_____

_____

_____

James 5:14–16 _____

_____

_____

_____

The third set of terms contrasts lamenting and celebrating, suggesting there is an appropriate time for both: "A time to weep and a time to laugh; a time to mourn and a time to dance" (Ecclesiastes 3:4).

Because God appoints certain times for both pleasure and pain, both of these elements of life must have a purpose in His plan. C. S. Lewis gave us a glimpse through the keyhole of pain into the chamber of God's purposes when he wrote, "God whispers to us in our pleasures, speaks in our conscience, but shouts in our pains: it is His megaphone to rouse a deaf world."[8]

Knowing that God can and does use pain for His purposes doesn't make it any less painful. However, knowing that in God's plan there's also a time for joy can give us the hope to endure the pain and suffering that characterize life. Perhaps you're experiencing the grief of a tragic loss or the pain of an unexpected trial. If you're not there now, you will be someday! Life offers few guarantees, but pain is one of them. The reality of life is that our suffering ultimately will end only with physical death. But God promises believers an ultimate experience of laughter and dancing in heaven that will far surpass any relief we could gain in this world (Revelation 21:1–4; 22:1–2).

The fourth of Solomon's seven sets refers to times of confrontation or punishment versus forgiveness and restoration: "A time to throw stones and a time to gather stones; a time to embrace and a time to shun embracing" (Ecclesiastes 3:5).

The time to gather stones can be likened to the time to embrace, while the time to throw stones can be equated with the time to shun embracing. In other words, there are occasions when we should affirm and encourage others. At other times, however, we may need to offer caring confrontation to hold others accountable for their attitudes and actions.

Read 1 Thessalonians 5:14–15. Are there people in your life who fit into these categories and need encouragement or confrontation? If so, how might you approach each person appropriately?

_____

_____

_____

_____

The fifth pair Solomon noted refers to holding on or letting go of things of the world: "A time to search and a time to give up as lost; a time to keep and a time to throw away" (Ecclesiastes 3:6).

Rescue teams constantly face the difficult decision of whether to continue a search for someone who is lost or to cease their search. There are times when we, too, desire to continue holding on to things we should release—things that are harmful, things that have outlived their usefulness, or things that are of much greater use to others than they are to us.

The contrast of seeking/keeping versus ceasing/releasing reaches beyond the realm of our material possessions. Sometimes we try to hold on to the past, recalling with nostalgia a "golden age" while we fail to appreciate today's blessings. Or we may harbor bitterness toward others for things that have happened in the past, failing to forgive and forget.

Are there pursuits in your life that you need to release because they may not be part of God's timing? If so, what are they? Are there other paths God has placed before you that you need to seek out? If so, describe these paths.

_____

_____

_____

_____

Solomon's sixth pair of phrases may refer to the theme of mourning and recovery from loss, both personally and in ministry to others: "A time to tear apart and a time to sew together; a time to be silent and a time to speak" (Ecclesiastes 3:7).

Read Job 2:11–13. How did Job's friends initially respond to his grief? When do you think it's best to respond with silence to others' suffering? When might it be more appropriate to speak words of encouragement to them?

_____

_____

_____

_____

The final set of polar opposites refers to some of the more extreme realities of human life: "A time to love and a time to hate; a time for war and a time for peace" (Ecclesiastes 3:8).

On one hand, we're expected to express love, grace, and forgiveness to others. On the other hand, certain events require the response of hatred toward injustice, oppression, sinfulness, and prejudice. On an international scale, love, grace, and forgiveness are characterized by peace, while taking a stand against injustice and oppression may sometimes result in war.

It's true that Christians should advocate peace (Romans 12:18; Hebrews 12:14; 1 Peter 3:11). However, we're living in the real world, where peace is not always possible. If history has taught us anything, it's that peace always comes at a price. Sometimes that price is war.

Compare Joel 3:9–10 with Isaiah 2:3–4. Why do you think war in this fallen world is a matter of when, not if? When is it necessary to "fashion swords," and when should we "fashion plows"? What is God's ideal?

_____

_____

_____

_____

Would you characterize yourself as a peaceful person on a relational level, or do you often find yourself involved in conflicts? How can you better promote peace in your family, home, church, workplace, and/or school?

_____

_____

_____

_____

All-Encompassing Questions (Ecclesiastes 3:9–10)

Two questions seem to leap from this section of Solomon's journal. One is stated explicitly, and the other is implied.

What's the profit? Ecclesiastes 3:9 asks, "What profit is there to the worker from that in which he toils?" If life is just a series of inevitable events, the timing of which is out of our control, why do we even work toward such an uncertain future? If our world is characterized now by pain, then by pleas-

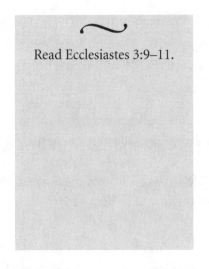

Read Ecclesiastes 3:9–11.

ure, today by life, tomorrow by death, why do we even go on? If that's the state of our lives, we're no better off than mice in a laboratory maze!

What's the purpose? Solomon wrote: "I have seen the task which God has given the sons of men with which to occupy themselves" (3:10). In other words, where is life headed? When will the roller coaster stop? As the seven pairs of opposites suggest, human life seems to go nowhere except up and down. We experience birth and death and have no control over either. So what makes us think that there is any value to be found in the rest of these events? We discover ceaseless cycles of love and hate, planting and reaping, building and destroying, laughing and crying. It's enough to drive us mad!

That's Solomon's conclusion as he looks at life under the sun. But what about life from God's perspective?

All-Important Conclusions (Ecclesiastes 3:11)

What is the profit and purpose of life from the divine rather than the human point of view? Does a shift in our world-view change things? Absolutely! After summarizing his analysis of life in Ecclesiastes 3:9–10, Solomon drew three important conclusions in 3:11:

1. *God has made everything appropriate in His time.* If you were a spider crawling along the ceiling of the Sistine Chapel, you'd think the world was just a chaotic mess of conflicting colors. Yet when you, as a person, view the stunning ceiling frescoes from the proper perspective, the entire panorama is seen in one glorious sweep. Similarly, human life may appear profitless and pointless if not observed in the light of God's revealed knowledge.

2. *God has put eternity in our hearts.* God created us with an insatiable curiosity about our future and an intense longing for eternal life. Augustine once wrote, "You [God] stir man to take pleasure in praising you, because you have made us for yourself, and our heart is restless until it rests in you."[9] Yet we won't be able to satisfy our hunger for eternity by our own means. We must approach eternity on God's terms—through faith in His Son, Jesus Christ.

3. *In this life we cannot discover God's eternal plan.* Until we reach eternity, "Man will not find out the work which God has done from the beginning even to the end" (3:11). Though God alone

knows His plan from beginning to end, He has graciously revealed enough of it in Scripture to allow us to find His purpose and meaning for our lives. Yet if we turn our eyes away from God's provision of wisdom through His Word and the Holy Spirit, we turn away from the illumination that puts this otherwise pointless world into a proper light.

Let's take a moment to consider eternity. Read the section of this workbook titled "How to Begin a Relationship with God" on pages 251–254, and then answer the following questions.

If you have already accepted God's free gift of eternal life through Jesus Christ, read 2 Corinthians 5:6–9. What was Paul's perspective on time in this world in light of His relationship with God?

_____

_____

_____

_____

_____

Does this perspective characterize your everyday actions and plans? Why or why not?

_____

_____

_____

_____

If you have not yet accepted Christ's payment for your sins, what is preventing you from doing this today?

_____

_____

_____

_____

Having flipped through the pages of Solomon's scrapbook of opposites, we are forced to come to one conclusion: from a strictly human perspective, life appears to be pointless and profitless. Change is the only thing that stays the same! Giving birth, dying, planting, uprooting, killing, healing, destroying, building . . . like a spinning carousel, life goes around and around in a dizzying cycle of uncertainty.

Yet from God's perspective, the events of history are like carefully woven threads of a tapestry, each appearing in its proper place at the proper time. We can turn to our Father for assurance of life's meaning and purpose in an otherwise dismal world. We can catch a glimpse of the breathtaking tapestry that will one day be made perfect. Are you living with eternity in view, or are you constantly enslaved by the drudgery of time?

6 Interlude of Rare Insight

[ECCLESIASTES 3:11–15]

A long time ago in a galaxy far, far away . . ." So begin some of the biggest blockbuster films of all time. Through his *Star Wars* saga launched in 1977, filmmaker George Lucas transported millions of moviegoers from dull, routine life on planet Earth to a fantasy galaxy filled with action and adventure. Having virtually set the standard for the "summer blockbuster," the *Star Wars* films inspired an entire genre of fantasy films that offer a temporary escape from the boredom of the world in exchange for a universe that tickles the senses.

Unfortunately, once the adventure ends, viewers find themselves again stuck on earth, surrounded by the same problems that plagued them and yearning to return to that alternate universe. Richard Winter writes, "The mass culture created by the entertainment industry in America now creates a fantasy world in which we aspire to live. The media create expectations for us, so ordinary life seems increasingly boring and we grow more dissatisfied. Thus we crave more of the media's sensational entertainment."[1] Reality on the horizontal plane can be transcended only temporarily, and even the stunning digital magic of *Star Wars* loses some of its enchantment the second time around.

So how do we end the cycle? What's needed is a proper perspective on earthly reality. Most people crave lives of fantasy because they fail to properly understand their lives and destinies from God's perspective. Yet a realistic, God-centered worldview doesn't come by way of some mystical, impersonal force from within us, but from the living God.

In the middle of Ecclesiastes 3, Solomon briefly shifted his focus from the human to the divine perspective, resulting in an insightful interlude that reveals how we can consistently enjoy life under the sun.

What do you think people either gain or attempt to avoid by watching movies and television these days?

_____

_____

_____

_____

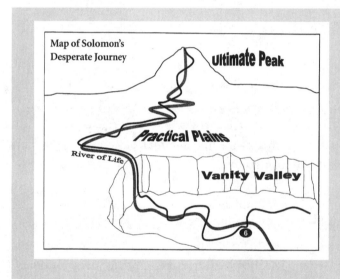

Map of Solomon's Desperate Journey

Ultimate Peak

Practical Plains

River of Life

Vanity Valley

6

ROAD MAP FOR THE JOURNEY #6

For the first time in his desperate journey through the Valley of Futility, Solomon crosses the River of Life—the divine source of wisdom—and shares an interlude of rare insight. God has given us simple things in life, he concludes, including the very desire for God (3:10–13), and He has ordered all of life's events so people will come to fear Him (3:11, 14–15).

LIFE WITHOUT GOD

Darth Vader, Obi-Wan Kenobi, Jabba the Hutt—these are just a few of the unusual characters in George Lucas's epic science fiction series. You won't find a single real person in the *Star Wars* universe—every character is fictional, played by actors. On the other hand, in King Solomon's universe, you won't find one work of fiction. Solomon didn't doctor his drab world with costumes, props, or computer graphics. He wrote about life on the ragged edge—not smoothing it over, but calling it like he saw it.

In Ecclesiastes' first two and a half chapters, Solomon declared that "all is vanity" (Ecclesiastes 1:2), that "there is nothing new under the sun" (1:9), and that all the work we do is a meaningless "striving after wind" (1:14). He said wisdom brings "grief, and increasing knowledge results in increasing pain" (1:18). He noted that pleasure-seeking is futile and profitless (2:1–2) and that both the wise and the foolish share the same fate of death (2:18–23). In short, Solomon said this world is boring and empty, profitless and purposeless. The wisest of all kings in the ancient world told the truth about life apart from God: it's a dry desert with no future and no hope.

DIGGING DEEPER

Common Grace

King Solomon concluded that life apart from God is boring, empty, profitless, and purposeless. Yet all of us have encountered unbelievers and even atheists who appear to experience happiness and excitement in life. Doesn't that contradict Solomon's conclusions?

The truth is that unbelievers will experience temporary enjoyment in life, even apart from a saving relationship with Christ. This is due to the gift of *common grace,* which is "grace that is available to all humanity. The benefits of common grace are experienced by all human beings without discrimination. It reaches out in a multitude of ways, promoting what is good and restraining what is evil."[2] Our loving heavenly Father extends a certain grace even to those who reject Him and His gift of eternal life through His Son. Several forms of common grace include revelation of God through nature (Romans 1:18–20); God's provision of sunshine, rain, and crops in due season (Acts 14:16–17); ordered human government (Romans 13:1–2); and the presence of truth and beauty in the world (Philippians 4:8).[3]

Though unbelievers may experience some blessing and joy in the present, justice and wrath are stored up for them in eternity. In contrast, while believers experience the common effects of a sinful world now, in the world to come they will receive the full blessings of salvation.

LIFE WITH GOD

After spending several pages in his journal describing a depressing life without God, Solomon abruptly changed his tone and perspective. Without warning, his desperate journey made a jump into hyperspace, taking us from an arid desert planet to a lush paradise, turning us from *human* activities to what *God* makes, gives, and does. Let's take a look at each of these.

Read Ecclesiastes 3:11–15.

What God Makes (Ecclesiastes 3:11)

When we begin to see life from a heavenly perspective, the first thing we discover is that God makes everything appropriate [or "beautiful"] in its time. The Hebrew word *yapheh* (translated in 3:11 as "beautiful" in some translations and "appropriate" in others) often refers to outward beauty, as in Genesis 12:11 and Song of Solomon 1:8. However, later Solomon used the term in 5:18 to mean "fitting," "appropriate," or "proper." In a sense, being appropriate is precisely what makes something beautiful. Scientists point to three traits of objective beauty: simplicity, harmony, and brilliance.[4] This is in accord with the view of philosophers, who believe that beauty is "that which has unity, harmony, proportion, wholeness, and radiance."[5] Seemingly chaotic events become beautiful when they are seen as essential parts of God's unfolding plan.

Now, let's be honest. Even though we know that God is working and that there will be a reckoning when all evil is destroyed, this promise doesn't stop the evil or erase the ugliness we see in everyday life. The new perspective on life doesn't always turn the wince of pain into a smile of delight— nor should it. At the same time, however, we must let the Word of God remind us that however excruciating and prolonged the pain may be, it will, like all things, come to an end. Even pain will be made "appropriate" in His time.

What evil and ugly things in your life are you experiencing today that seem like sour notes in God's symphony? Do you feel as though nothing good can possibly come of these things?

_____

_____

_____

_____

Read Romans 8:28–29 and answer the following questions:

What things "work together"?

_____

_____

_____

_____

Who works these things together?

_____

_____

_____

_____

What is the ultimate result?

_____

_____

_____

_____

Who are the recipients of this result?

_____

_____

_____

_____

The Bible clearly acknowledges that evil and ugliness exist, and it warns against those who call good evil and evil good (Proverbs 17:15; Isaiah 5:20). However, the Bible also clearly teaches that no wicked deeds can thwart God's eternal plan (Psalm 33:10–11; Isaiah 46:10; Hebrews 6:17). He is still in control and working *all* things for good.

Solomon also noted that God makes everybody curious about the future. Because God has set eternity in our hearts, we have an innate desire to see beyond today. But it is easy to despair about tomorrow when we lack hope. Only the Lord can supply the hope we desperately need in order to go on. In fact, He has made us in such a way that our thirst to know the future cannot be quenched until we place our trust in Him.

What God Gives (Ecclesiastes 3:12–13)

As Solomon continued to look on the world from a divine perspective, he observed four things the Lord gives us.

God gives the ability to rejoice and enjoy life. Ecclesiastes 3:12 teaches that there is nothing inherent in humanity that allows us to enjoy life. If people find any enjoyment or rejoicing in life, it's because God Himself grants it. By God's common grace, unbelievers may have short spurts of joy in response to positive events or material blessings, but believers can have an underlying joyous outlook on life regardless of their circumstances.

Read Philippians 4:11–13. How did Paul learn to have contentment in life? How might God be teaching you the same thing?

_____

_____

_____

_____

God gives us the ability to do good in our lifetime. True good deeds don't come from give-and-take motivation or a manipulative method of winning friends and influencing people. Truly good works cannot originate from sinful humanity but are themselves a gift of God's grace.

According to Ephesians 2:8–10 and Philippians 2:12–13, what is the ultimate source of our good works?

_____

_____

_____

_____

God gives us an appetite to eat and to drink. Solomon wrote, "Moreover, that every man who eats and drinks sees good in all his labor—it is the gift of God" (3:13). The ability to have basic needs met through our labor and to enjoy our meals—these are gifts from God, who gives us both an appetite for food as well as the ability to satisfy it.

Yet many of us believe that the necessities of life—food, clothing, and shelter—are things God owes us and that God's "blessings" are those extra things we want to make us feel good. We sometimes feel *blessing* means *bonus* and rarely consider that things as basic as our physical appetites are from God's gracious hand.

Read Matthew 6:25–34. In this passage, what things does God provide? Do you consider these a blessing or a right? How would you feel toward God if you were denied these necessities?

_____

_____

_____

God gives us the ability to see good in all our labor. The perspective of life under the sun says, "I deserve it because I earned it." As we spend that hard-earned money on food, clothing, rent, mortgage, entertainment, and luxuries, we begin to view them as things we earned and somehow deserve. But the above-the-sun perspective says, "I've been given what I never deserved and can never earn, not only the spiritual blessings of forgiveness, eternal life, and hope, but also the simple abilities to work, eat, sleep, and wake up in the morning."

If we adopt this perspective, the words of that great hymn will characterize our lives and our worship:

> Great is Thy faithfulness! Great is Thy faithfulness!
> Morning by morning new mercies I see;
> All I have needed Thy hand hath provided—
> Great is Thy faithfulness, Lord, unto me![6]

Read James 1:17. List some simple things in your life you take for granted, things you rarely, if ever, thank God for. Take a moment to thank Him for these blessings right now.

_____

_____

_____

_____

What God Does (Ecclesiastes 3:14–15)

There are four things about God's work that put life in perspective:

God's work is permanent. "Everything God does will remain forever" (Ecclesiastes 3:14). When God does something, it's etched in stone. In fact, when God *intends* to do something, it's as good as done. He's not flaky or fickle, fluttering from plan to plan like a butterfly collecting nectar. His decisions are firm, His plans unwavering, His promises secure.

God's work is thorough and complete. "There is nothing to add to it and there is nothing to take from it" (3:14). God doesn't do half the job and leave it for somebody else to finish. When a work is begun, He completes it regardless of the cost. His work is never too little and never too much.

What do the following passages say about the permanence and completeness of God's work in your life?

Romans 8:29–30 _____

_____

_____

_____

Philippians 1:6_____

_____

_____

_____

What work has God begun in you that you need to trust Him to complete?

_____

_____

_____

_____

God's work cultivates respect for Him. "God has so worked that men should fear Him" (Ecclesiastes 3:14). Romans 1:20 says that God's "invisible attributes, His eternal power and divine nature, have been clearly seen, being understood through what has been made." Though the natural response of fallen human beings is rebellion, the proper response to God's work is awe (Romans 1:21–23). By God's grace we respond to His works in wonder, praising Him and giving Him glory for the great things He has done (Psalm 150:2).

God patiently repeats His work until the lessons are learned. "That which is has been already and that which will be has already been, for God seeks what has passed by" (Ecclesiastes 3:15). Though by His works God proclaims His glory and majesty for all to see, because of humanity's sinfulness His clear message goes in one ear and out the other. But He doesn't let His children get away with ignoring His voice. Although we often walk away or let the things God places in our paths pass us by, God again brings them before our eyes until we learn the lesson. James Crenshaw suggests that Solomon "envisions God pursuing the past in order to bring it back into the present."[7] We may get weary of retracing the same steps over and over, and we may even run from Him, but God will work on our hearts until the light comes on.

Review the description of Jonah's attempt to flee from God (Jonah 1). Note the ways God stepped into Jonah's path. Have you been ignoring God's repeated pursuits and clear calling? What lesson may He be trying to teach you?

_____

_____

_____

_____

LIFE FROM GOD

In this interlude of rare insight in Ecclesiastes 3:11–15, we get a breath of fresh air in the midst of a depressing look at life on the ragged edge. Let's conclude with the thing that makes our horizontal relationships and our life under the sun come into full focus: life *from* God.

Life from God comes from outside this universe—not from within it. Positive thinking, further education, exciting movies, self-help books, or any other means under the sun cannot bring us the abundant, joyful, and content life that accompanies God's gift of eternal life (John 10:10). This life is found "above the sun," not in this world, not even in a faraway galaxy. True life comes from the true God, who transcends the universe.

Life from God results in supernatural power now and is not a vague force limited to a long time ago. God has been in the business of changing lives since the dawn of human history. His only Son, Jesus Christ, is the "author and perfecter of our faith" (Hebrews 12:2), who will see us through to the end. His Holy Spirit continually empowers and enables us. This power does not come from within us, but from Him who calls us and keeps us by His own power. We don't need to seek power in some arduous quest—He's available here and now.

Read John 1:12–13 and 14:6. Who is the source of eternal life?

_____

_____

_____

_____

According to 1 Thessalonians 5:23–24 and Jude 24–25, who is responsible for keeping believers blameless before God?

_____

_____

_____

_____

Have you been trusting in God alone for your spiritual growth, or have you been trusting in your own human abilities to earn His love or grow in His favor? Will you choose to place your trust in Him to receive all the blessings He has for you today?

In our desperate attempt to cope with the pressures and pains of the real world, it's easy for us to lose ourselves in fantasy, to seek an escape in a galaxy far, far away. Solomon provided such an escape from life under the sun, but not to a world of make-believe. Instead, he gave us a brief but glorious glimpse into life from God—the joy of His gifts and the benefit of His works. Rather than jettisoning us from reality, God's divine perspective grounds us in a proper view of the real world, where He provides meaning and purpose to an otherwise pointless life.

7 Confessions of a Cynic
[ECCLESIASTES 3:16–22]

Superheroes are more popular today than ever. Television programs, blockbuster films, toys, and books showcase an array of crime-fighting characters that the previous generation could find only on comic-book racks. Besides stunning special effects and exciting action sequences, something more profound attracts us to superheroes: the longing for justice.

In a world marred by compromising cops, unjust judges, crooked politicians, and greedy lawyers who give a black eye to otherwise noble professions, people long for a symbol of justice that transcends the weaknesses and corruption of the present world system. When police officers are unable to apprehend a violent criminal, we long for a caped crusader to swoop down and nab the fiend once and for all. When mad terrorists plot to destroy civilization, we want a team of superheroes to mete out instant justice with preemptive action.

This is why stories with tidy endings are so popular. It usually doesn't matter to us if the characters fall prey to harassment and hardship during the tale as long as right ultimately wins over wrong. A story doesn't even have to conclude happily as long as it contains a semblance of justice. We even put up with Humpty Dumpty's tragic demise because the king's men did everything they could to save him!

But life rarely includes fairy-tale endings. There are no real knights in shining armor or mighty superheroes. Even in human history, the greatest champions of freedom and justice have chapters in their biographies that disappoint us. In real life, viewed from a strictly earthly perspective, stories don't always end well. Sometimes it's the king's men who push Humpty Dumpty off the wall. Sometimes Cinderella's glass slipper shatters and a wicked stepsister marries the prince. Sometimes Pinocchio doesn't get to be a real boy but is chopped into kindling to warm Geppetto's feet. Sometimes life just isn't fair, and instead of "happily ever after," all we hear is an abrupt "The End."

Think of a recent example of tragic injustice in the news. What was the situation? How did it make you feel? If you were to rewrite the story, how would you end it?

_____

_____

_____

_____

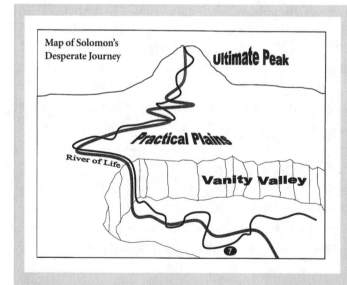

Map of Solomon's Desperate Journey

ultimate Peak

Practical Plains

River of Life

Vanity Valley

⑦

ROAD MAP FOR THE JOURNEY #7

Leaving the River of Life with a fresh perspective, Solomon's journey returns to an examination of vanity. Human "justice," he says, is inconsistent, and God's ultimate justice will come in a time and manner only He knows (3:16–17). Therefore, we must be content with the simple things in life (3:18–22).

Living with injustice long enough can cause a person to become cynical—that is, "contemptuously distrustful of human nature and motives."[1] King Solomon was an example of this. When looking at life from an under-the-sun perspective, he saw only barrenness. He observed the terrible effects of injustice, affliction, and suffering.

THE PROBLEM THAT CREATES CYNICISM (ECCLESIASTES 3:16)

Read Ecclesiastes 3:16.

The matter that sent King Solomon into his slump of cynicism is stated in various places throughout his journal: although people long for wrongs to be righted, our desire for justice often goes unfulfilled.

From the following passages, summarize the things that led to Solomon's cynical attitudes about justice:

Ecclesiastes 3:16 _____

_____

_____

_____

Ecclesiastes 4:1 _____

_____

_____

_____

Ecclesiastes 5:8 _____

_____

_____

_____

Nothing much has changed, has it? In our contemporary world, we witness the same things Solomon did: the poor are neglected, the guilty go free, sins go unpunished, and good is often unrewarded. In the face of such injustice, it's easy to get caught in the trap of cynicism.

69

Does Cynicism Have a Solution? (Ecclesiastes 3:17–21)

Read Ecclesiastes 3:17–21.

How can we cope with the reality of injustice and not become pessimistic and cynical in the process? Solomon proposed two potential solutions to the problem of cynicism, one founded in God, the other in humanity:

Realize that injustice will have only a temporary reign. In Ecclesiastes 3:17, Solomon said, "I said to myself, 'God will judge both the righteous man and the wicked man,' for a time for every matter and for every deed is there."

According to 2 Peter 3:7–10, why does God tolerate injustice for the time being? When will ultimate justice finally come?

_____

_____

_____

_____

Although it's true that God will ultimately put an end to injustice, this judgment never seems to come fast enough for human beings. We get impatient with what appears to be a timid God who tolerates evil. But He is actually a loving God who is granting opportunity for repentance. However, knowing that God will intervene on our behalf *someday* doesn't satisfy many of us. And it didn't satisfy Solomon, either, so he came up with an alternative "solution" to the problem of injustice.

Accept the fact that injustice reveals our beastlike nature and behavior. After entertaining a brief glimmer of hope in Ecclesiastes 3:17, Solomon was again distracted by the ragged world around him. Confronting the harsh reality of death, Solomon wrote, "All go to the same place. All came from the dust and all return to the dust. Who knows that the breath of man ascends upward and the breath of the beast descends downward to the earth?" (3:20–21).

DIGGING DEEPER

Natural Law and Justice

We all know when we've been treated unfairly. Humans have an innate moral sense of right and wrong that sets off an internal alarm when an injustice occurs.[2] Although imperfect, limited, and often numbed by sin, our conscience waves a red flag of warning when it detects a breach of moral judgment (1 Samuel 24:5; Romans 2:14–15).

> The Bible teaches that moral awareness is innate—everyone knows that there is right and wrong, though not all agree on precisely what. . . . And what a hell this world would be if God had not imprinted in man that moral likeness, however limited and blurred by sin.[3]

Even those who deny God or refuse to embrace an absolute moral standard can recognize within themselves a sense of justice:

> We find that even those who say that there is no moral order *expect* to be treated with fairness, courtesy, and dignity. If one of them raised this objection and we replied with, "Oh shut up. Who cares what you think?" we might find that he does believe there are some moral "oughts." Everyone expects others to follow some moral codes, even those who try to deny them. But moral law is an undeniable fact.[4]

It's ironic that Solomon pointed to the presence of injustice as evidence that humans are no better than mere animals; the fact that Solomon could perceive injustice at all shows he is above animals, which cannot! Solomon was viewing his world through a lens of pessimistic cynicism.

Adopting a proper attitude of optimistic realism enables us to see that our ability to discern good from evil, beauty from ugliness, is an indication that humans are made greater than animals. We are inherently more valuable because we have been blessed with a spiritual element.

> Ordinary people know instinctively that we are irreducibly different [from animals], vastly so. . . . We alone feel guilt, worship God, honor holiness of life, and experience the moral imperatives of conscience.[5]

Cont'd

Digging Deeper (Cont'd)

Depending on our perspective, we will either view the presence of injustice in the world as a sign that life is meaningless and that humans are no better than animals, or we will discern a purpose for humanity that goes beyond our present experiences, orients us toward a future age of righteousness, and points to a universal Lawgiver who is infinitely concerned about us. We must choose, sometimes even moment by moment, to look at life with this eternal perspective.

Have you ever experienced the kind of despair Solomon described as you look at the world around you? How did the world's wisest man come to this point? Let's take a closer look at his thought processes.

In what ways did Solomon say humans were like beasts in Ecclesiastes 3:19–21?

_____

_____

_____

_____

This passage has been misused by some to teach that there is no life after death for human beings, since Solomon said that there was no difference between humans and animals, and that nobody knew what happened to either one after death (Ecclesiastes 3:21). However, we must recall that Solomon was speaking here from a strictly under-the-sun perspective, the way things look apart from God's revelation of His reality and purpose. As Ray Stedman wrote, "From a human standpoint, a dead man and a dead dog look as if the same thing happened to both of them. But from the divine point of view that is not the case."[6]

Although this passage cannot be used to determine where the human spirit goes when people die, it does reveal to us something about real life under the sun: humans look like and can act like beasts. As sin eats away at our humanity, we yield more and more to beastlike behavior (Psalm 49:12–20; 2 Peter 2:12–13). So Solomon's solution to cynicism about injustice is, "Why expect more than beastlike behavior from beastlike people?" As Christians, however, we must reject this idea.

What are some examples from real-life experience that might make you conclude with Solomon that humans are nothing but animals? What are other examples that contradict this view?

_____

_____

_____

_____

Hope Beyond Cynicism (Ecclesiastes 3:22)

Read Ecclesiastes 3:22.

Solomon closed this entry of his journal with some closing thoughts on how to deal with injustice and mistreatment. What's his final answer? It's to press on in life, enjoying the things we can and leaving to God the unknown destiny of those who inflict injustice (Ecclesiastes 3:22). By allowing God to issue judgment on injustice in the future, we free ourselves from becoming obsessed with it in the present.

Solomon told us that God _will_ one day judge all people and deal out punishment for the injustices that are done (3:17). However, this may not happen in our lifetime. For the time being, God is patient with humans . . . and, therefore, the injustice on earth will continue.

After considering the options, Solomon didn't exhort us to try to understand our unjust circumstances, to retaliate with bitterness, or to retreat into our closets and suffer alone. What he _did_ suggest is that we reject self-pity and revenge, seeking out ways to find the hidden advantages in our disadvantages. In short, we may not be able to alter our lot in life, but we can change our response to it. This leads to a few very personal and practical questions that can help us reorient our hopeless cynicism to hopeful realism.

What is your unjust disadvantage? Is there a particular situation in which you feel you've been afflicted unfairly? Why is this unfair?

_____
_____
_____
_____

As you await God's intervention, are you wallowing in self-pity or responding to this disadvantage with active courage? If you're "wallowing," will you commit to an attitude change today?

_____
_____
_____
_____

How might you use your personal disadvantage to help or encourage those around you? What impact might this have? What specific people might you encourage, or what actions might you take to help others through your disadvantage?

_____
_____
_____
_____

Changing your attitude and actions concerning injustice doesn't make the evil go away. We shouldn't bury our head in the sand and pretend the world is fine. Neither should we brush off the nasty events of life with pat responses like, "Oh, well; God's in control" or, "God will get them in the end!" Those statements may be true, but they fail to tell us what to do as we struggle in the midst of the unfair and uncontrollable events of life on the ragged edge.

Romans 12:19–21 gives Christians some practical advice on how to live as we wait on the Lord to bring judgment and justice. Paul wrote:

Never take your own revenge, beloved, but leave room for the wrath of God, for it is written, "Vengeance is mine, I will repay," says the Lord. "But if your enemy is hungry, feed him, and if he is thirsty, give him a drink; for in so doing you will heap burning coals on his head." Do not be overcome by evil, but overcome evil with good.

These are hard principles to follow, aren't they? When we see injustice—especially toward us or our loved ones—our initial reaction is to respond in kind, stamp our feet, and bring the enemy to instant justice. But Paul had a different philosophy. He wasn't cynical. He didn't suggest we approve of evil. He instructed us to wait on the Lord to act, for though His judgment may be delayed, it's more certain than tomorrow's sunrise.

Below, write out the principle(s) you can glean from Ecclesiastes 3:22 and Romans 12:19–21. How can you apply these principles to your particular situation in order to move beyond cynicism to a realistic optimism?

Ecclesiastes 3:22
Principle: _____
_____
_____

Application: _____
_____
_____

Romans 12:19–21
Principle: _____
_____
_____

Application: _____
_____
_____

Have the injustices of life turned you into a cynic? Have you been scarred by the ragged edge of real life? Have you become numb to the touches of joy in life that come from God's grace? Are you nursing wounds, wallowing in disadvantages, or using suffering as an excuse for self-pity? Those are easy traps to fall into! Solomon warned us about the dangerous ditch of cynicism that lies on either side of the precarious path of life. It can pull us in and keep us bogged down when we should be facing the ugly realities of life head-on as well as enjoying the good things God has given us. Ask God to help you climb out of the ditch and get on the road again.

8 The Lonely Whine of the Top Dog

[ECCLESIASTES 4:1–8]

If you read the back of any bottle of liquor, pack of cigarettes, or household cleaner, you'll see a warning label that lets you know that improper use of the product can be harmful—even deadly. Even beneficial drugs are packaged with a warning to consumers and a list of potential side effects. Few of us would argue that such warning labels should be removed or that consumers should be left in the dark concerning the potential damage caused by abusing these products, right?

There's something else that ought to be labeled with a strong warning: the quest for success. Penned by an ancient king who had made it to the top tier of society several millennia ago, the wise insight buried in Ecclesiastes 4:1–8 ought to be shared with every man or woman who dreams of worldly gain. It ought to be required reading at the finest business schools, printed in every professional journal, and inscribed along the bottom of every diploma. Those who begin the climb toward the top ought to be warned far in advance that the dreams of power and wealth that wake them up in the morning will one day become nightmares. Like most things in the world's system, however, what ought to be isn't what is. Solomon's journal offers us insight into the inner workings of society and reminds us not to lose ourselves in the quest for worldly success.

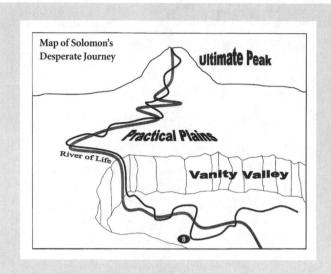

Map of Solomon's Desperate Journey

ROAD MAP FOR THE JOURNEY
#8

Still lingering in the Valley of Futility, Solomon concludes that since life's futile climb up the ladder of success results in oppression, competition, and loneliness (4:1–8), we should be content with the simple things God gives according to His own sovereign grace (3:22; 4:8).

Read Ecclesiastes 4:1–8.

A REALISTIC APPRAISAL OF SOCIETY

As Solomon considered his own society, he saw people who had reached the top as well as those who were still clawing their way up. He observed military officers, political leaders, and the other "top dogs" of his day, and then he recorded what he found. His appraisal of their lifestyles isn't pleasant to read, but it's nevertheless accurate—at least from the perspective of life "under the sun"—that is, life apart from the healthy balance and holy perspective infused by a relationship with God. He realized that climbing the ladder of success was all vanity and that the loneliest whine often came from the top dog.

Oppressive Conditions (Ecclesiastes 4:1–3)

As Solomon looked at society, he noticed various classes of people, which we'll diagram as tiers on a pyramid. The oppressed occupy the lowest rung (Ecclesiastes 4:1).

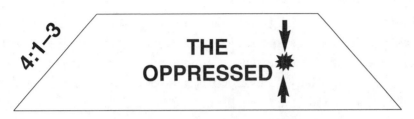

4:1–3

THE OPPRESSED

PYRAMID OF POWER—TIER 1

Solomon saw the plight of the oppressed, noting the conflict between the "haves" and "have-nots." Class conflict isn't just part of academic economic debates. It's an ancient reality that results from our selfish natures and lack of contentment.

In Ecclesiastes 4:2–3, Solomon described his reaction to the oppression he observed among the aching masses on the bottom of society's pyramid: "So I congratulated the dead who are already dead more than the living who are still living. But better off than both of them is the one who has never existed, who has never seen the evil activity that is done under the sun." Those are tough words! They sound more like something you'd hear from a sullen, black-clad rock band than from a passage of Scripture. Remember, these are the words of Solomon analyzing life from an under-the-sun perspective. The divine perspective will come later.

Have you or somebody close to you ever been to the point at which life seemed so cruel and unfair that death seemed more attractive than life? If so, what circumstances led to that point?

_____

_____

_____

On the other hand, could you be guilty of the sin of oppression in your own areas of leadership and influence? Take a moment to pray about and consider whether you may be contributing in some way to another's misery and disappointment in life.

Competitive Determination (Ecclesiastes 4:4–6)

Solomon observed another social group, one that managed to climb above the level of the oppressed masses, or at least was trying to escape that predicament. In this second tier are the "competitive edge-ers" who achieved status through hard work, perseverance, education, and knowing the right people. Others in this group, because of parents or family background, never had to work their way up and have no firsthand knowledge of the condition of those who feel oppressed by society. Yet this doesn't mean they're free from the curse of the invisible pyramid, for their tier is also characterized by its own trials—namely, unhealthy comparison, competition, and conflict.

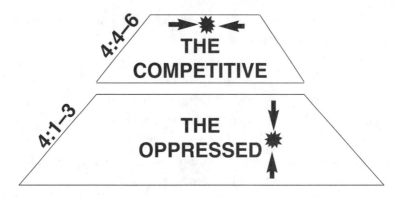

PYRAMID OF POWER—TIERS 1 AND 2

Solomon began his description of interpersonal competition in the following terms: "I have seen that every labor and every skill which is done is the result of rivalry between a man and his neighbor. This too is vanity and striving after wind" (Ecclesiastes 4:4).

Of course, Solomon wasn't concerned about the healthy competition that makes games enjoyable and challenging. Nor was he worried about ethical competition of a free-market society in which the competition between corporations benefits consumers through lower prices and better products and services. The competition Solomon had in mind was the one-on-one rivalry of pushing, fighting, and backstabbing—the meanspirited and self-destructive determination of people to outdo each other at any cost. According to Solomon, this kind of aggressive competition was empty and pointless.

Are you caught up in unhealthy competition? How might James 4:1–3 apply to your situation?

_____

_____

_____

_____

Is anything preventing you from changing your competitive attitude right now? If not, what changes can you make?

_____

_____

_____

_____

Competition does, however, indicate one virtue worth nurturing: a healthy work ethic. This is where we need to maintain balance. A healthy work ethic avoids laziness, but an overzealous work ethic produces the equally harmful extreme of workaholism. Solomon emphasized the need for balance when he wrote, "The fool folds his hands and consumes his own flesh. One hand full of rest is better than two fists full of labor and striving after wind" (Ecclesiastes 4:5–6).

Most of us tend toward extremes rather than maintaining a healthy balance of work and rest. If you tend toward laziness, read the following passages and summarize their warnings:

Proverbs 12:24; 19:15; 24:30–34 _____

_____

_____

_____

If you tend toward working so hard that you have very little relaxation, read the following passages and summarize their warnings:

Proverbs 15:16–17; 16:8 _____

_____

DIGGING DEEPER

Workaholism and The World

One definition of a *workaholic* is "an individual who has a dependence on overwork, a dependence which has a noticeable disturbance on the rest of his life."[1] Common characteristics of workaholics include the following:

- They have long working hours.
- Their accomplishments are frequent topics of conversation.
- They cannot say no and therefore amass a large number of projects and tasks.
- They are driven by a consuming need to perform in life's basic endeavors.
- They have trouble relaxing, always thinking or worrying about work.[2]

While workaholism has a variety of causes, including guilt, perfectionism, and debt, more often than we like to admit, the workaholic may be driven by simple greed.

In Luke 12:16–21, Jesus told a parable that illustrates the tragedy and futility of workaholism as a means of finding satisfaction for what are really *spiritual* needs. As you look at this passage, note the workaholic tendencies of the main character:

- He was already rich (v. 16).
- He took on extra projects to maintain his excess (v. 18).
- His plans pointed to enjoyment in the future rather than contentment in the present (v. 19).
- He was focused on earthly treasures instead of heavenly treasures (v. 21).

Material gain will never satisfy our spiritual hunger. Neither will power, prestige, or success. If we pursue these things with the passion of a workaholic, we might gain the world for a time, but we could be forfeiting blessings in eternity (Matthew 16:26).

Personal Disillusionment (Ecclesiastes 4:7–8)

After describing the lowest level of the oppressed and the middle tier of the competitive, Solomon concluded his portrayal of the great pyramid scam with an examination of life at the pinnacle. In Ecclesiastes 4:7–8, we see a perfect picture of somebody who became a slave to the pursuit of success. Even though he had no family to provide for, he continued to work long hours and amass more wealth. He never took the time to step back and ask himself one of the most important, life-changing questions: "Why am I doing this?" Having achieved top-dog status, the workaholic who fought his way up sits as king of the hill with a heart as empty and a life as pointless as those dwelling at the bottom level of the pyramid.

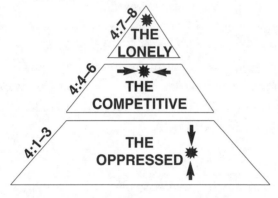

PYRAMID OF POWER—TIERS 1–3

Once they spend most of their lives getting to the top of the pyramid of success, many top dogs go through what is commonly called a "midlife crisis." James Dobson describes it this way:

> [A midlife crisis] is a time of intense personal evaluation when frightening and disturbing thoughts surge through the mind, posing questions about who I am and why I'm here and why it all matters. It is a period of self-doubt and disenchantment with everything familiar and stable. It represents terrifying thoughts that can't be admitted or revealed even to those closest to us. These anxieties often produce an uncomfortable separation between loved ones at a time when support and understanding are desperately needed.[3]

Don't overlook the implications of Dobson's last observation: a top dog who grapples with these questions tends toward separation from loved ones and friends, ending up in isolation. That's why the title of this chapter is "The Lonely Whine of the Top Dog." Top dogs tend to do this. They've stepped on everyone else to get where they are, and now there's nobody left. Isolation and loneliness are often the sorry results of climbing the ladder of success. Solomon was saying, "It's not worth it! It's all vanity."

Jesus had similar views regarding this lifestyle. He wasn't concerned about getting to the top; He was focused on serving those at the bottom. Remember the words of Jesus in Matthew 20:26–28: "Whoever wishes to become great among you shall be your servant, and whoever wishes to be first among you shall be your slave; just as the Son of Man did not come to be served, but to serve, and to give His life a ransom for many."

To Jesus and to Christians, love must come first. Relationships are what count. Don't lose sight of this in your search for meaning and quest for answers.

Even if you're not in your middle years, do Dobson's words describe you? Is your mind filled with probing questions about the purpose of your life and your labor on this earth? If not, perhaps you've found the contentment in Christ that many are still seeking. Or perhaps you've simply avoided asking the deep, important questions of life. It may be time to do so now and to seek answers, not in this world under the sun, but in the God who dwells far above it.

A Penetrating Analysis

Solomon has pegged our modern society well, hasn't he? Let's face it, most of us are taught that if we work hard and compete fiercely enough, we'll make it to the top of our profession and there we'll find relaxation, peace, contentment, and happiness.

But the truth is that if we're not content and satisfied where we are, then we'll never be satisfied. When we look up the pyramid of success and examine the lives of those at the top, do we really find many happy, carefree people? Not at all. If we listen long enough, we'll hear their whines of loneliness, disillusionment, and despair.

If we're going to avoid an emotional and philosophical crisis as we look back over our life's pursuits, now is the time to sit back and ask ourselves that question: Why am I doing this?

Where are you in the pyramid of success? What level are you trying to reach?

_____
_____
_____

Why are you doing what you're doing?

_____
_____
_____
_____

TWO HAUNTING QUESTIONS

Two questions emerge that demand soul-searching answers. You may want to mull over these questions, pray about them, or discuss them with your spouse, family members, close friends, or members of a group from church.

Are you telling yourself the truth about possessions? Solomon and Christ agree: material prosperity will never satisfy. Only a saving relationship with the Lord will fill your deepest needs.

What warning did Paul give in 1 Timothy 6:9–11 to those who seek to climb the pyramid toward riches?

_____
_____
_____
_____

What warning did Paul give in 1 Timothy 6:17–19 to those who have already achieved wealth?

_____
_____
_____
_____
_____

Are you heeding God's warning about priorities? The Lord must be given first place in our lives. We must adopt *His* priorities above ours. Only then will true satisfaction and contentment characterize our lives, no matter where we are in society's pyramid.

What comes first in the following passages about priorities? What comes second?

Matthew 6:24
First: _____

_____

_____

_____

Second: _____

_____

_____

_____

Matthew 6:31–33
First: _____

_____

_____

_____

Second: _____

_____

_____

_____

Philippians 2:3
First: _____

_____

_____

_____

Second: _____

_____

_____

_____

~

After going through this chapter, you may consider yourself exempt because you have no problem with the love of money, you're not a workaholic, and you keep your priorities straight. Good for you! Others of us may be wondering what can be done.

The answer is not to drop out of society, quit our jobs, or run away from our responsibilities like carefree hippies from yesteryear. The answer is Jesus Christ. Seek His kingdom first, and all other things will fall into place (Matthew 6:33). This process of escaping the great pyramid scam begins with a decision to make Jesus Christ the Lord of your life today and to present yourself to Him as a living sacrifice, no longer conformed to the pattern of this world, but transformed by His power (Romans 12:1–2). Will you do this today?

9 One Plus One Equals Survival
[ECCLESIASTES 4:9–12]

*D*esolate—it's a word that describes the lives of millions of people. It's the forlorn condition of the isolated, the abandoned, the widowed, and the orphaned. It describes those who have lost their closest companions and those who are too caught up in the vanities of life to have ever found a friend. Gary Inrig sums it up well:

> The world is filled with lonely people, and there are many Christians who find themselves in that position. We are surrounded by people whom we know, but not many of them could we consider genuinely close friends. And that is not a problem reserved for one age group. . . . At every stage of life, we need to know how to build solid friendships.[1]

In the last chapter we looked at Solomon's description of the grim scene of the top dog—successful, but alone. Next, Solomon zoomed in on the issue of loneliness itself. If we take his counsel to heart, we'll discover one of the most down-to-earth truths in Scripture: two are better than one. It may seem obvious to some, but in our individualistic, Lone Ranger society, the desire—indeed, the *need*—for companionship has been neglected.

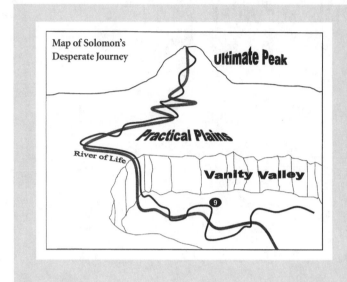

ROAD MAP FOR THE JOURNEY
#9

After several twists and turns along the Valley of Futility, Solomon now revisits the River of Life with a reflection on God's gift of human companionship. In order that we learn humility (4:13–16), share the joy of life's benefits with others (4:9), and survive the ragged edges of life (4:10–12), God has graciously given us friends that stand by us through thick and thin.

COMMON CRIES OF THE LONELY

If we were to stop and listen to the lonely people around us or search our own heart for that desperate cry of dereliction, we might hear something like the following:

"Why don't people love me and help me out of my problems?" This cry emerges from a heart of blame. But to have companionship in times of need, we must cultivate friendships *before* a crisis begins. Difficulties don't attract friends, but true friends remain through difficulties.

"If only others realized how difficult things are!" This is the lament of self-pity. Few responses will ruin a relationship more quickly than this one. In fact, it's an attention-getter that rapidly wears out another person's patience.

"Nobody really cares! I'm all alone in this!" These are the words of a self-proclaimed martyr. Of course, if people don't know about our heartache, we certainly can't blame them for not responding in a helpful manner.

All three of these cries of desperation come from people who have not cultivated a circle of true friends who know them intimately and care for them unconditionally. To prevent us and others from getting to this point, we need to tackle the issues of loneliness and companionship head-on.

To what things do individuals often turn to satisfy their need for companionship? In lieu of people, what do we use to fulfill this need?

_____

_____

_____

_____

Read Genesis 1:31. How did God describe the completed work of creation?

_____

_____

_____

_____

In Genesis 2:18, how did God describe Adam's condition?

_____

_____

_____

_____

What was God's solution to the problem? (See Genesis 2:19–22).

_____

_____

_____

_____

SURVIVAL COUNSEL FOR THE LONELY

Bemoaning the fact that we're lonely won't help us. Instead, we need to recognize that true companionship is the solution to our feelings of alienation, isolation, and abandonment. Although God is the ultimate fulfillment of our need for companionship, one way He has chosen to meet that need is through other people. Just as God made Adam with a need for the companionship of Eve, each of us is created with a need for relationships with other people and the ability to meet others' needs.

Read Ecclesiastes 4:9–12.

Does somebody come to mind when you think of a close, lifelong friend? If so, how has this person helped you through difficult times? How have you helped that person?

Statement of Fact (Ecclesiastes 4:9)

Ecclesiastes 4:9 says, "Two are better than one because they have a good return for their labor." This passage doesn't specifically refer to marriage but to friendship in general. Solomon said that it's better to share our life with another person than to try to go it alone, taking on all of life's troubles as if we were the last person on earth. Existence under the sun can be wearisome, frustrating, grievous, and sometimes treacherous. Having a friend at our side can enable us to survive even our most troubling challenges.

GETTING TO THE ROOT

In Ecclesiastes 4:9, the phrase translated "good return for their labor" can also be translated "a good outcome from their trouble."[2] The word *amal* (labor) often means "trouble" in the Old Testament, as in Genesis 41:51; Job 5:6–7; and Jeremiah 20:18. One commentator notes, "It is not *toil* which rescues these men from danger, but the fact that, being two together, they can *help* one another."[3]

Why Two Are Better Than One (Ecclesiastes 4:10–12)

Why does a faithful companion make our trek through life easier and more enjoyable? In Ecclesiastes 4:10–12, Solomon revealed three reasons that friends are a necessity in life.

A companion provides mutual encouragement when we are weak, "for if either of them falls, the one will lift up his companion. But woe to the one who falls when there is not another to lift him up" (Ecclesiastes 4:10). Solomon used the analogy of a journey to represent our course through life.[4] When we stumble, we need a companion who won't walk away but will stay and lift us up. This truth is illustrated beautifully near the climax of J. R. R. Tolkien's *Lord of the Rings* trilogy. As Frodo crawls up the slopes of Mount Doom, into which he must cast the accursed ring of power, his strength fails him and he can barely complete the desperate quest. Yet his faithful companion, Sam, not permitted to bear the ring himself, comes to his aid as Frodo collapses under the weight of the burden.

> Sam looked at him and wept in his heart, but no tears came to his dry and stinging eyes. "I said I'd carry him, if it broke my back," he muttered, "and I will!"
>
> "Come, Mr. Frodo!" he cried. "I can't carry it for you, but I can carry you and it as well. So up you get! Come on, Mr. Frodo dear! Sam will give you a ride. Just tell him where to go, and he'll go."
>
> As Frodo clung upon his back, arms loosely about his neck, legs clasped firmly under his arms, Sam staggered to his feet; and then to his amazement he felt the burden light.[5]

Do you have a self-sufficient attitude that refuses help from others even when you need it? In light of Ecclesiastes 4:10, what should be our attitude toward help in times of trouble?

_____

_____

_____

_____

Do you have a companion who needs lifting up? How can you do this today?

_____

_____

_____

_____

Friends give us mutual support when we are vulnerable. Ecclesiastes 4:11 illustrates that point: "Furthermore, if two lie down together they keep warm, but how can one be warm alone?" Because Solomon was using an analogy of companions on a journey, this is not to be taken as a reference to marriage.[6] This illustration points to the need for companionship in situations when we would be vulnerable alone—when our individual resources are not enough to get us through tough times. One author writes, "In the wilderness of loneliness we are terribly vulnerable."[7]

 When in your life have you felt most vulnerable and unable to handle tough situations on your own? Perhaps it was the start of a new job or a move. How did others help you get through it? If you had nobody to help you, describe how you handled your vulnerability.

_____

_____

_____

_____

An ally supplies mutual protection when we are attacked. Solomon's example of the need for a companion on life's journey is found in the first part of Ecclesiastes 4:12: "And if one can overpower him who is alone, two can resist him." The ability of two people to ward off physical assault is greater than that of one individual. Yet the illustration of two people on a journey points to more than just physical dangers. In everyday life, a companion can help thwart vicious rumors launched against us as well as support our spiritual stand against sin and temptation.

Solomon's Final Comment on Companionship (Ecclesiastes 4:12)

The hard reality of living on the ragged edge is that sometimes even our closest friends will let us down. Throughout our lives we'll encounter the betrayal of a Judas, the abandonment of a John Mark, or the harsh, insensitive words of Job's friends. This is why the principle of "two are better than one" is meant to be multiplied. Solomon wrote, "A cord of three strands is not quickly torn apart" (Ecclesiastes 4:12). His point is that we should seek to cultivate more than one friendship, for the more committed companions we have, the less likely we are to suffer the devastating effects of loneliness. Is companionship a failsafe solution to life's problems? Of course not, but its blessings are illustrated all around us.

BIBLICAL EXAMPLES, PRACTICAL PRINCIPLES

To help us apply Solomon's principles, let's look at a few men and women of the Bible who illustrate Solomon's wise counsel of companionship.

Elijah and Elisha

The friendship of Elijah and Elisha illustrates the principle that *companions calm the troubled waters of our souls.* After Solomon's reign, a prophet named Elijah arose to call Israel back to God. Elijah's ministry brought him hunger, hardship, and harassment from the kings of Israel (1 Kings 17:1–7; 18:16–40). In response to wicked Queen Jezebel's threat to have him executed (1 Kings 19:2), Elijah fled alone into the wilderness and was so discouraged that he wanted God to take his life (19:3–4). In the midst of these troubled waters, Elijah needed a companion to calm his soul.

Read 1 Kings 19:16–21. How did God help Elijah in his ministry? How does 2 Kings 2:1–6 illustrate Elisha's commitment to Elijah?

_____

_____

_____

Is there someone in your life who will stand by you no matter what? If so, who? Is there somebody for whom you need to step up and be an Elisha?

_____

_____

_____

_____

_____

Naomi and Ruth

From the poignant story of Naomi and Ruth we have another principle about friendship: *companions build bridges of hope and reassurance when we are vulnerable, exposed, and self-conscious.* After her husband and two grown sons died in a foreign land, Naomi decided to return to her homeland of Canaan. She urged her two widowed daughters-in-law—Ruth and Orpah—to stay and remarry (Ruth 1:3–5, 8–13). Yet Ruth's unfailing commitment to her mother-in-law stands as a timeless example of unconditional loyalty in the midst of loss, vulnerability, and confusion. Ruth was for Naomi a solid bridge over raging waters.

Read Ruth's promise to Naomi in Ruth 1:16–17. In what ways did her commitment go well beyond the obligations of a daughter-in-law? How would your own relationships with your family and friends change if you exhibited greater loyalty and commitment?

_____

_____

_____

_____

David and Jonathan

The friendship of David and Jonathan illustrates a third principle: *companions take our part when others try to take us apart.* After the young shepherd David had slain the giant Goliath, his popularity grew while King Saul's popularity waned, stirring up the king's hatred toward the young man (1 Samuel 17:1–49; 18:6–9). Although God had anointed David as the next king over Israel, he had to flee from the wrath of Saul for several years until the king's death (18:28–31:6). During this terrible period of his life, David found a close friend in the most unlikely place—Jonathan, the son of King Saul. The Bible says that "the soul of Jonathan was knit to the soul of David, and Jonathan loved him as himself" (1 Samuel 18:1). Even though his own father sought to rip David apart, Jonathan took David's side.

How would it make a difference in your life to know you had somebody like Elisha, Ruth, or Jonathan at your side?

_____

_____

_____

_____

Take a minute to think of one or two close friends. When was the last time you expressed your appreciation for and commitment to them? Write their names next to one or more of the following suggestions, or come up with your own way of demonstrating your gratitude.

Express your gratitude and commitment verbally or in writing._____

_____

_____

Show your appreciation and loyalty by a gift, favor, or some other act of friendship.

_____

_____

_____

Pray for your close friends, thanking God for them and renewing your commitment to them before God. _____

_____

_____

Plan more time in your schedule to meet with your close friends regularly for mutual encouragement and accountability. _____

_____

_____

Seek out current needs of your friends and find ways to meet those needs, even if it means sacrificial acts on your part._____

_____

_____

Other: _____

_____

_____

~

Gary Inrig tells a moving story about the commitment of two friends that transcends life and death:

> They had enlisted together, trained together, were shipped overseas together, and fought side-by-side in the trenches. During an attack, one of the men was critically wounded in a field filled with barbed wire obstacles, and he was unable to crawl back to his foxhole. The entire area was under a withering enemy crossfire, and it was suicidal to try to reach him. Yet his friend decided to try. Before he could get out of his own trench, his sergeant yanked him back inside and ordered him not to go. "It's too late. You can't do him any good, and you'll only get yourself killed."
>
> A few minutes later, the officer turned his back, and instantly the man was gone after his friend. A few minutes later, he staggered back, mortally wounded, with his friend, now dead, in his arms. The sergeant was both angry and deeply moved. "What a waste," he blurted out. "He's dead and you're dying. It just wasn't worth it."
>
> With almost his last breath, the dying man replied, "Oh, yes, it was, Sarge. When I got to him, the only thing he said was, 'I knew you'd come, Jim!'"[8]

Jesus said, "Greater love has no one than this, that one lay down his life for his friends" (John 15:13). Christ set this example of self-sacrificial friendship when He died on the cross to pay for our sins and have eternal fellowship with us. If true friends are willing to die for their companions, they must also be willing to live for them. Are you a true friend for others?

10 What Every Worshiper Should Remember
[ECCLESIASTES 5:1–7]

As we read Solomon's journal of his desperate journey, we find several "oasis encounters" that snatch us up from his ruminations on the mundane life under the sun and give us a glimpse of life from God's perspective. Have you ever experienced something like this—a time when you get a brief moment of clarity? While these islands of hope don't transform the severity of the desert around us, they do provide perspective, allowing us to face the ragged edge of life refreshed by the nourishing Spirit of God, who strengthens us through His Word and reminds us of the great God whom we worship and serve.

In this chapter we will study an "oasis" in Solomon's journal, a time when he shifted his focus upward rather than inward or outward. He focused on proper worship. Because much of what Solomon suggested regarding worship hinges on having a reverence for God and obeying His voice, let's take a careful look at the primary way God causes us to grow in reverence and obedience: through His Word. The Scriptures teach us about God's character, His holiness, His desires for our lives, and how we can conform our lives to His plan. It is absolutely essential to know the God of the Bible if we are to worship Him in spirit and in truth.

The Word of God: Hope for Our Times

God's Word is the cool, freshwater spring in the middle of an oasis. It nourishes life's travelers, washes them, and refreshes their souls. In the hectic complexity and confusion of life, we need to be reminded that the Bible provides the only infallible counsel on how to connect with the Lord in a meaningful way. Among the biblical writers, the author of Hebrews most succinctly expressed the relevance and power of God's Word, telling us what it does and how it works.

What God's Word Does

Hebrews 4:12 says, "For the word of God is living and active and sharper than any two-edged sword, and piercing as far as the division of soul and spirit, of both joints and marrow, and able to judge the thoughts and intentions of the heart." Scripture does two things. First, it *pierces,* cutting through the excuses we give, the rationalizations we manufacture, and the barriers we raise. Second, the Word of God is able to *judge,* exposing the truth about our innermost thoughts and motivations and leaving nothing in our lives untouched. Zane Hodges writes, "The inner life of a Christian is often a strange mixture of motivations both genuinely spiritual and completely human. It takes a supernaturally discerning agent such as the Word of God to sort these out and to expose what is of the flesh."[1]

GETTING TO THE ROOT

Several words are used in Hebrews 4:12 to describe the activities of the Word of God. First, it is "living." The Greek words *zaō* (to live) and *zōē* (life) are connected with the Word of God in several New Testament passages (Matthew 4:4; 1 Peter 1:23; Philippians 2:16), pointing to its life-giving work. Second, the Greek word translated "active" in this passage is the Greek word *energes* from which we get the word *energy.* It refers to the effective power of God's Word, which "performs its work in you who believe" (1 Thessalonians 2:13). Lastly, the phrase "able to judge" comes from the Greek word *kritikos,* from which we get our word *critic.* It indicates the deep probing nature of the Word's activities. In the hands of the Holy Spirit, the Word of God is alive, energizing, and discerning.

According to Ephesians 6:17, who is behind the power of the Word of God?

_____

_____

_____

_____

Why God's Word Works

Why is it that the relevance of the Word of God cuts across thousands of years of time, transcends cultures, and addresses people of all ages at once? First, Scripture is *universal in scope.* As Hebrews 4:13 notes, "And there is no creature hidden from His sight." Second, it's *limitless in its exposure.* Hebrews 4:13 concludes, "But all things are open and laid bare to the eyes of Him with whom we have to do." The most personal secrets hidden in the deepest recesses of our minds are completely open to the eyes of God.

Which areas of your life is God exposing today? Before moving on to the next section, ask Him to probe your life and reveal any strongholds of sin and rebellion that need to be addressed through His Word.

_____

_____

_____

GETTING TO THE ROOT

In Hebrews 4:13, the Greek word for "open," *gumnos,* literally means "naked," and *trachēlizō,* "laid bare," is related to the Greek word for "neck," from which the word *trachea* is derived. The throat, having little protection, is the most vulnerable target of attack. When we say somebody "had him by the throat" or "went for the jugular," we mean he attacked another at his weakest point. Likewise, when the Spirit aims His sword at the soft spot of our souls, we cannot escape His swift and precise strokes. He pinpoints areas of our lives He wants to sharpen, cutting away the rough edges and making us more like Christ.

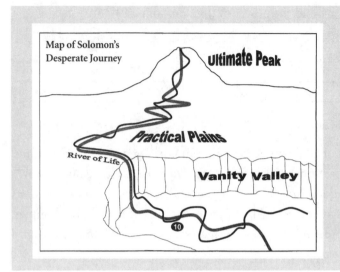

Map of Solomon's Desperate Journey

Ultimate Peak

Practical Plains

River of Life

Vanity Valley

10

**ROAD MAP FOR THE JOURNEY
#10**

In another reflection at the River of Life, Solomon warns that because we are prone to foolishness in word and deed (5:2), we must guard ourselves in worship by wisely approaching God in fear (5:1, 6–7), focusing on Him rather than on ourselves.

THE WORSHIP OF GOD: TRUTH FOR OUR MINDS

Turning abruptly from the secular to the religious realm, from the sphere of work to the sphere of worship, Solomon said in Ecclesiastes 5:1, "Guard your steps as you go to the house of God." Corporate worship ushers us spiritually into the very throne room of God. Before we dive into Solomon's truths, take a moment to consider the following question:

What are your current attitudes toward worship? Have you been experiencing refreshing cor-

porate worship, or has your worship become stale and routine? What things in your life contribute to this condition?

_____

_____

_____

_____

Read Ecclesiastes 5:1–7.

If we're feeling weary of worship, we must address this condition immediately rather than wait to see if it gets better on its own. Based on Ecclesiastes 5:1–7, we can glean four specific instructions on how to conduct ourselves in worship, along with four corresponding reasons for heeding these instructions.

1. *Draw near and listen well, because God is communicating.* Solomon wrote, "Draw near to listen rather than to offer the sacrifice of fools; for they do not know they are doing evil" (Ecclesiastes 5:1). The phrase "sacrifice of fools" probably refers to fruitless and irrelevant talk during worship (1 Samuel 15:22; Hebrews 13:15). Solomon tells us to close our mouths, refraining from unnecessary chatter that distracts our attention from hearing the Word being presented through music, prayer, and preaching.

2. *Be quiet and stay calm, because God hears the inaudible and sees the invisible.* Solomon warned that worshipers must not "bring up a matter in the presence of God" either in word or thought (Ecclesiastes 5:2). God, who dwells in heaven, sees the mental scribbling we construct during worship; He listens to the whispers between spouses or friends that nobody else can hear. Because of this, we must keep our words and unrelated thoughts at a minimum, as they take our focus off worship and indicate irreverence for God (Ecclesiastes 5:3, 7).

Does your mind wander during worship? Do you bring the concerns of the world with you and mull over them as you sit passively in the pew, letting the Word of God pass in one ear and out the other? You may want to try some of the following ways to keep your mind and heart on worship:

❏ Take notes during the teaching of the Word.

❏ Close your eyes as you participate in worship through song.

❏ Follow along in your Bible when Scripture is being read.

❏ Establish a "no-chatting" rule with those who worship with you.

❏ During worship through prayer, actively pray rather than simply listen.

Read Psalm 46. How does the psalmist find peace and calm in the midst of natural disasters and political upheavals?

_____

_____

_____

_____

Name some situations or events in your life for which you need the calming presence of God. Based on Psalm 46, on what will you determine to meditate when these concerns bombard your thought life?

_____

_____

_____

_____

3. *Keep your commitments, because God accepts them and doesn't forget them.* In our age of trivial divorces, defaulted loans, deceptive advertising, and broken campaign promises, commitments aren't taken seriously enough. The warnings of Solomon to keep our vows to God are serious. God has no delight in those who foolishly make and break vows (Ecclesiastes 5:4), and it's better to make no vows at all than to fail to fulfill what was promised (5:5).

In our New Testament church context, vows or commitments we make in response to God's prompting may involve a variety of things: our weekly offering in the collection plate, a pledge to support a missionary or missions organization, or a commitment to meet with God each day, to stay morally pure until marriage, or to place our family at the top of our priority list. We should make these decisions prayerfully and carefully. Once we've made these vows before God, only a fool would back out.

Obedience is a serious commitment to God. Vows include not only the vows we take in marriage or in a public dedication of our children, but also what we commit quietly when He's spoken to us about an action we're to take.

WINDOWS TO THE ANCIENT WORLD

Vows in Worship

Making vows to God was a common part of worship at the ancient Hebrew temple. Fulfilling a promise of this kind often consisted of making a sacrificial or monetary offering to God primarily in response to answered prayer (Psalms 50:14; 76:11).[2]

Vows played a prominent part in the lives of Israel's men and women. A vow was one way to show how seriously they took their need of God. In times of emergency they used vows to underline their prayer requests. A barren woman who longed for a son, a frightened soldier under enemy attack, an innocent person accused of serious crime each might vow to offer a special sacrifice to God if he would deliver him or her from the predicament.

How easy it was to vow, and how hard to pay! That was the tendency Ecclesiastes criticized. Apparently one way to get out of the vow was to tell the priest (here called "the messenger") that it was a mistake. [3]

Although the making of an oath or vow before God was voluntary, once it was made it was binding and irrevocable (Deuteronomy 23:21; Numbers 30:2). Solomon underscored the gravity of such promises, cautioning that they should only be made solemnly and reverently.

List the commitments you've made before God either privately or publicly. Are you fulfilling each of these, or are you neglecting your promises?

Commitment	Fulfilled	Neglected

4. *Don't decide now and deny later, because God doesn't ignore decisions.* This was the negative of the third principle. Solomon wrote, "Do not let your speech cause you to sin and do not say in the presence of the messenger of God that it was a mistake. Why should God be angry on account of your voice and destroy the work of your hands?" (Ecclesiastes 5:6). We must avoid trying to worm our way out of commitments we've made.

There's a tendency in our day, as there was in Solomon's, to rationalize or diminish the significance of tough decisions. Consider these common excuses:

- "I made a mistake. I married the wrong person."

- "Oops, I shouldn't have said I would rearrange my priorities to spend more time with my family."

- "I was pretty young when I promised God that He could have this part of my life."

- "I made a mistake when I said I'd stay morally pure until marriage—God knows, I'm only human!"

If you have made commitments that you are neglecting, what is preventing you from fulfilling them? Whom might you need to contact to recommit to fulfilling that commitment or seek forgiveness for your inability to do so?

_____

_____

_____

_____

The Warning of God: Strength for Our Lives

Solomon wrapped up his instruction concerning worship with a solemn warning: "Fear God" (Ecclesiastes 5:7). David Allan Hubbard's words are appropriate here:

> Better to bribe a judge than to ply God with hollow words; better to slap a policeman than to seek God's influence by meaningless gestures; better to perjure yourself in court than to harry God with promises you cannot keep. The full adorations of our spirit, the true obedience of our heart—these are his demands and his delights.[5]

DIGGING DEEPER

Are Vows and Oaths Allowed Today?

Some Christians maintain that Jesus sought to abolish the Old Testament practice of making vows and oaths. In support of this, they point to Matthew 5:33–37, where Jesus appeared to speak against the practice as "evil":

Again, you have heard that the ancients were told, "You shall not make false vows, but shall fulfill your vows to the Lord." But I say to you, make no oath at all . . . but let your statement be, "Yes, yes" or "No, no"; anything beyond these is of evil.

Yet elsewhere in the New Testament the taking of oaths is regarded as neutral, or even something that God Himself does (Acts 18:18; Hebrews 6:13–18). How should we understand and apply Christ's warning about making vows?

In Matthew 5:33–37, Jesus was challenging a widespread practice among the Pharisees that violated and softened the Old Testament instruction on oaths. They taught that only vows made directly to God or spoken in His name were binding. Thus, swearing by heaven, earth, Jerusalem, or the hairs on one's head became a means to renege on a promise without violating the law of oaths.[4] Christ rejected this kind of legal hairsplitting and restored the heart of the law: keep your word and fulfill what you promise!

Proper worship of God requires that we humbly recognize His holiness and serve Him with our whole hearts.

We shouldn't pretend to worship while we're really chattering or daydreaming, making hasty commitments or backing out of obligations. In short, Solomon warns us not to treat God like a chump just because we can't see Him. Remember that the sword of the Spirit is living and active and will cut through all of our false fronts and fake devotion. Are you fearing God in your worship and devotion and honoring Him in your commitments?

11 Straight Talk to the Money-Mad

[ECCLESIASTES 5:8–20]

Three thousand years ago, a famous queen paid a visit to an extremely rich king. She had heard rumors of his immense wealth, renowned wisdom, political savvy, architectural feats, musical talent, and religious commitment. That queen doubted the accounts of his fame and with heightened curiosity departed for his kingdom to see for herself if the reports were true.

After surveying the splendor and majesty of that famous king, she discovered the stories she had heard were, in fact, inaccurate—but not in the way she had expected. She said to that monarch, "I did not believe the reports, until I came and my eyes had seen it. And behold, the half was not told me. You exceed in wisdom and prosperity the report which I heard" (1 Kings 10:7). The famous king was Solomon, and the curious queen was the queen of Sheba. What she witnessed was a king who had become "greater than all the kings of the earth in riches and in wisdom" (1 Kings 10:23).

If anyone could have bought happiness with riches, it would have been Solomon. If anyone had a definitive perspective on the pursuit of affluence, it was that grand king. Yet Solomon learned that peace, joy, and contentment were gifts that no amount of wealth could acquire. We see his perspective outlined in Ecclesiastes 5:8–20, where Solomon recorded both the sickness and the cure of the money-mad, providing wise insights and practical applications for those of us who are constantly exposed to the malady of greed.

What would you do if you had so much wealth that you could literally do anything you wanted? How do you think such affluence would change your lifestyle? How do you think it would affect the people around you?

_____

_____

_____

_____

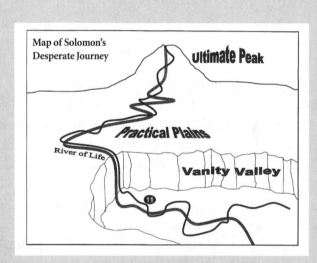

ROAD MAP FOR THE JOURNEY
#11

As Solomon nears the end of his trek through the Valley of Futility, he explores the issue of wealth, warning us that God will not permit people to have happiness through riches apart from His grace (5:10–17). However, Solomon notes that God *does* grant the enjoyment of the simple things in life so we never forget that He is sovereign and that all good things come from Him (5:18–20).

PROVERBIAL PRINCIPLES TO LEARN

Solomon's first statements regarding wealth suggest three proverbial principles that illustrate profound truths about the deceptiveness of riches. These deal in turn with oppression, dissatisfaction, and frustration.

Read Ecclesiastes 5:8–12.

Oppression (Ecclesiastes 5:8–9)

Solomon observed that *the rich tend to take charge, and their power intimidates and offends the poor.* An abundance of money frequently brings its possessors a greater degree of power and prestige, which often leads to their gaining control of more money, land, and enterprises.

Why do you think money and power often produce chains of hierarchy and bureaucracy as described in Ecclesiastes 5:8–9? Who benefits from such a system? Who suffers?

_____

_____

_____

_____

The rich and powerful at the top of the bureaucracy are in positions from which they can either oppress those below them or act in ways that benefit the common good. Solomon noted, however, that more often than not, money and power produce oppressive regimes rather than philanthropic saints. The red tape of bureaucracy becomes so thick and sticky that the poor and oppressed no longer have a voice.

Dissatisfaction (Ecclesiastes 5:10)

Solomon noted that *greed and materialism have no built-in safeguards or satisfying limits.* He wrote, "He who loves money will not be satisfied with money, nor he who loves abundance with its income. This too is vanity" (5:10). When somebody is asked, "What do you want?" the answer is almost always the same: "More." People want *more*—more money, more time, more space, more vacation days. Rarely will people answer that they have all they need, and never will somebody ask that the good things they have be taken away. The myth of being happy with just "a little more" is powerful, and Solomon wisely pointed out that even the very wealthy are not content with what they have.

Frustration (Ecclesiastes 5:11–12)

Finally, Solomon concluded that *with increased money and possessions comes an accelerated number of people and worries.* Wealth is a people magnet (Ecclesiastes 5:11). As people grow richer, they find themselves surrounded by a sudden "fan club." Everybody wants to be close to the one who can buy anything. They all want a piece of the pie, which, Solomon said, also brings more anxiety (5:12). Worries linger over losing assets, attracting frivolous lawsuits, maintaining an upper-class lifestyle, or even catching the attention of thieves or greedy friends and relatives.

Read Ecclesiastes 5:12. Have you ever lost sleep over financial worries? What kinds of anxieties can affect both those who have little and those who have an abundance?

_____

_____

_____

_____

How would you describe a "simple life" that keeps financial stress to a minimum? What are your challenges to living a simple life?

_____

_____

_____

_____

Grievous Evils to Remember (Ecclesiastes 5:13–17)

As Solomon continued, wisely reflecting on the insatiable appetite for wealth, he reminded us of two evils that riches can bring.

The first evil is that *those who have clutched can quickly crash* (Ecclesiastes 5:13–15). Our material possessions will not be ours forever. It makes no difference how well we manage them or how tightly we hoard them. We will either lose them during this life by some unforeseen tragedy or irreversible error, or we will ultimately leave them behind as we pass from time into eternity. Either way, every cent in our pockets and every item that we own will one day become completely irrelevant.

Read Ecclesiastes 5:13–17.

Take a moment to list five material possessions that you prize above all other things God has given you to enjoy.

1.

2.

3.

4.

5.

Read Job 1:13–21. How would your response compare to Job's if you were to lose in one day the five things you listed above?

_____

_____

_____

_____

The second evil is that *those who live high often die hard*. Solomon described a despairing image of a wealthy recluse, the ultimate end of someone who has been driven mad by the lust for money. He concluded, "Throughout his life he also eats in darkness with great vexation, sickness and anger" (Ecclesiastes 5:17). Few people in recent history illustrate this better than billionaire Howard Hughes, the wealthiest American in the 1960s and '70s.

Howard Hughes was one of the richest men in the world, with the destinies of thousands of people—perhaps even of governments—at his disposal, yet he lived a sunless, joyless, half-lunatic life. . . .

Why was Hughes so isolated and so lonely? Why, with almost unlimited money, hundreds of aides, and countless beautiful women available to him, was he so unloved?

Simply because he chose to be.

It is an old axiom that God gave us things to use and people to enjoy. Hughes never learned to enjoy people. He was too busy manipulating them. His interests were machines, gadgets, technology, airplanes, and money—interests so consuming as to exclude relationships.[1]

The untouchable materialist who lives in earthly opulence isn't as well off as he or she might seem. Such people quickly discover that money can't buy happiness, contentment, or peace. In fact, their insatiable drive for wealth usually fills their lives with futility, resentment, and pain.

GOOD AND FITTING GIFTS TO CLAIM (ECCLESIASTES 5:18–20)

While money and wealth in and of themselves are not evil, the *love of money* and the *vain pursuit of wealth* ultimately will lead to emptiness and disaster. To help inoculate his readers from the disease of "affluenza," Solomon concluded his straight talk to the money-mad with a shift from a human and worldly perspective to God's perspective. He revealed three God-given gifts that are available for us to claim and enjoy if we adopt God's balanced view of riches.

Read Ecclesiastes 5:18–20.

The first prevention against money-madness is to *claim the gift of enjoyment in your life.* Solomon wrote that it's "good and fitting" to eat, drink, and enjoy the fruit of one's labor for the "few years" of life given by God (Ecclesiastes 5:18). This approach emphasizes being content with what one has rather than pursuing what one doesn't have. The ability to find peace and joy in the simple things of life is a God-given grace not to be taken lightly. If we fail to view all of life as God's gift or provision for our enjoyment, we run the risk of becoming grim, negative, bitter, and resentful, always wanting more and never having enough.

DIGGING DEEPER

Is Money the Root of All Evil?

One of the most popular misquotes of Scripture is, "Money is the root of all evil." An improved, though still deficient, version is, "The love of money is the root of all evil." You may have heard 1 Timothy 6:10 quoted this way or may have even quoted it this way yourself.

In the original Greek, the word *rhiza*, "root," actually appears as the first word in the sentence for emphasis. Also, the word "all," *pas,* often means "all kinds" or "varieties" (Matthew 23:27; 1 Corinthians 6:18).[2] A literal order of the words in English would be: "A root of all kinds of evil is the love of money." So, although the love of money is not the *only* source of *all* evil in the world, it's a *major* source of *all kinds* of evil. One author writes, "The history of the human race, and perhaps especially that of modern Western societies, cries out in support of Paul's point."[3]

What does it mean that the love of money is a root of various types of evil? Concerning this metaphor, one commentator writes, "The hidden root is the source of life. If one is to rid a garden of weeds, the roots must come out. Similarly, Paul's hearers must not simply treat the problem caused by greed. They must tear out the root that produces the problems."[4] As we examine the problem of sin in society and in our own lives, we will discover that many sins—far too many to overlook—are vicious weeds sprouting forth from that single root of greed.

According to 1 Timothy 6:6–10, what are the negative causes of and positive solutions to greed?

Negative Causes   Positive Solutions

_____   _____
_____   _____
_____   _____
_____   _____

Is your life characterized by the causes of or the solutions to greed? Please explain.

_____

_____

_____

_____

A second immunization against money-madness is to *claim the gift of fulfillment in your work* (Ecclesiastes 5:19). You may ask, "But didn't Solomon say labor and toil are futile?" Yes, he did, but only if we approach work strictly from an under-the-sun perspective. When we view our labor as a gift from God, our perspective changes. Many of us don't discover fulfillment in our labor because we're too busy complaining about our current job, dreaming of better employment, or plotting our course up the corporate ladder. Always moving is never enjoying.

Look up the following verses and write down what each says our attitude should be toward work.

1 Corinthians 10:31 _____

_____

_____

_____

Ephesians 4:28 _____

_____

_____

_____

Ephesians 6:7 _____

_____

_____

_____

Are you exhibiting these attitudes? Where are you falling short?

_____

_____

_____

_____

The third vaccination against becoming money-mad is to *claim the gift of contentment in your heart.* Regarding the one who enjoys the gifts God has given him, Ecclesiastes 5:20 says, "For he will not often consider [remember] the years of his life, because God keeps him occupied with the gladness of his heart."

> When people discover the richness of life which God has provided, they do not much think of the past, or even talk about it. They do not talk about the future either, because they are so richly involved with savoring life right now.
>
> How good it is to know the Living God, to know that he controls what comes into your life. He expects you to make choices; Scripture always encourages that. But rejoice in the wisdom of a Father's heart, and richly enjoy what is handed you day-by-day. That is the secret of life.[5]

God gives us the ability to work and acquire material possessions. There's no reason to feel guilty for what God has given you freely by His grace. And there is no reason to feel ashamed if God has gifted you with fewer possessions than you'd like. In both cases, God also offers the gift of contentment.

Read Philippians 4:11–13. Which of Paul's categories are you in now? Are you approaching your current situation with God-given contentment, or do you need to ask Him for this gift today?

_____

_____

_____

_____

When the queen of Sheba witnessed Solomon's tremendous wealth, she exclaimed, "The half was not told me" (1 Kings 10:7). She was right. To play on her words, the other half of the story was that someone who attained to the ultimate level of wealth, fame, and honor could regard it all as pointless and vain. As Solomon's life attests, a person who has everything in the world can be completely empty inside. As we reflect on the pursuit of riches and contemplate our priorities in life, we must also remember that the world only tells us half of the story. Solomon's journal of a desperate journey records the other half for us: "He who loves money will not be satisfied with money, nor he who loves abundance with its income" (Ecclesiastes 5:10). Are you at peace with what you have now, or are you pursuing the crash course of the money-mad?

12 The Few Years of a Futile Life
[ECCLESIASTES 6:1–12]

Imagine we are standing in the middle of a long hallway lined with vivid portraits—word pictures painted by the great sage Solomon. They are true-to-life frescoes of reality under the sun. As we stroll through Solomon's gallery, we come upon a poignant portrait described in Ecclesiastes 6:1–12. This one's painted in dark, drab colors that communicate inner turmoil, conflict, and pain. As we examine it more closely, we realize it's a self-portrait of a disillusioned monarch. This moment of Solomon's introspection may be troubling, for it will force us to examine our own lives both in the dim light of the world under the sun and the bright illumination of God's perfect revelation.

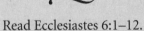

Read Ecclesiastes 6:1–12.

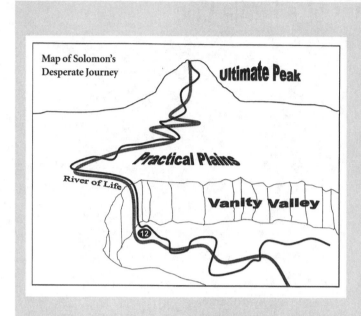

Map of Solomon's Desperate Journey

Ultimate Peak

Practical Plains

River of Life

Vanity Valley

12

ROAD MAP FOR THE JOURNEY
#12

Before finally climbing out of the Valley of Futility, Solomon looks back along his path and paints a portrait of his own life as a concrete example of futility apart from God (6:2, 9). He shows that worldly wealth, wisdom, labor, and possessions will never satisfy (6:1–9). Only God, who controls all things and cannot be controlled, is able to provide true meaning and purpose (6:10–12).

An Enlargement of a Single Portrait

In Ecclesiastes 6:1–12, Solomon provided his own life as an example of futility, an example all of us need to consider as we come to terms with reality.

The Situation (Ecclesiastes 6:1–2)

When Solomon referred to one whose riches, wealth, and honor were given to a foreigner to enjoy (Ecclesiastes 6:1–2), he was likely talking about himself. The phrase "riches and wealth and honor" in verse 2 is found elsewhere in the Old Testament only in 2 Chronicles 1:11–12, where God spoke to Solomon with the same terminology. In Solomon's specific case, many of the things for which he labored in life were given after his death to a "foreigner": Jeroboam the Ephraimite.

How could such a godly king be stripped of the enjoyment of his power and possessions—especially such a king as Solomon, to whom God gave not only great wisdom but also abundant riches and honor (1 Kings 3:5–14)? When he began his forty-year reign, Solomon "loved the LORD, walking in the statutes of his father David" (1 Kings 3:3). But as Solomon's reign progressed, he drifted away from the close relationship he had with God.

GETTING TO THE ROOT

"Yet God has not empowered him to eat from them, for a foreigner enjoys them" (Ecclesiastes 6:2).

Although in most instances the Hebrew word *nakheriy* refers to literal foreigners from another nation (Deuteronomy 29:21; Ezra 10:2), in wisdom writings it can sometimes have a figurative meaning, for example, one who is "like a foreigner" or "stranger" (Job 19:15; Psalm 69:9; Proverbs 2:16; 5:10).[1] In Ecclesiastes 6:2, the meaning is likely "one of another family—not a regular heir."[2]

First Kings 11:4 says, "For when Solomon was old, his wives turned his heart away after other gods; and his heart was not wholly devoted to the LORD his God, as the heart of David his father had been." To appease his foreign wives, Solomon built altars so they could worship their gods. Although Solomon personally never forsook God, his heart of disobedience reached such a state that God eventually raised up adversaries to discipline him.[3] In the end, God told Solomon that his son would only reign over the land of Judah, while the rest of Israel would be given to another (1 Kings 11:1–13).

As we read Ecclesiastes 6:1–12, we see Solomon reflecting on the reality of God's pronouncement: "A man to whom God has given riches and wealth and honor so that his soul lacks nothing of all that he desires; yet God has not empowered him to eat from them, for a foreigner enjoys them" (Ecclesiastes 6:2). It appears Solomon later returned to the Lord, regretting his time of disobedience and admonishing all those who would come after him to "remember also your Creator in the days of your youth" (12:1).

The application of the general principle Solomon illustrated through his autobiographical snapshot is much broader than his own life. Applying this to our own situations, we could all think of a "foreigner" in our lives that could potentially rob us of our enjoyment. It may not even be a literal person but an invasive event or circumstance. As in the case of Solomon, our "foreigner" could also be the result of our own foolishness. It may be something out of our control, such as a debilitating illness or a natural calamity. The principle is still the same: we may work all our lives and be robbed of our enjoyment of the planned benefits, either by our own folly or the frustration of "fate."

Given the broad application of "foreigner" above, what unavoidable disappointment or tragedy would you say constitutes a "foreigner" in your life today?

_____

_____

_____

_____

A Few Added Details (Ecclesiastes 6:3–9)

As we examine Solomon's drab self-portrait more closely, we discover faint traces of color that can give us hope. By sharing his story, Solomon could at least serve as a bad example and thereby lead his readers to make wiser decisions than he. We ought to listen carefully to his warning, as many of these details apply just as well to us.

Solomon tried to invest his life, wealth, and honor in something many people try today: a large family (Ecclesiastes 6:3). Don't misunderstand, children are a gift from the Lord and we should seek to establish a strong family (Psalm 127:3; 1 Timothy 5:8). However, like any good gift from God, even families can become an object of idolatry if we place our hope and trust in them for happiness and fulfillment.

Are you trying to find ultimate happiness and fulfillment through your family? How could unavoidable disappointments or tragedies destroy this misplaced hope?

_____

_____

_____

_____

In this passage, Solomon also considered that long life would add to meaning and fulfillment (Ecclesiastes 6:2, 6). Yet upon reflection Solomon concluded that even a two-thousand-year life span would be miserable if one did not have his or her priorities straight enough to enjoy the good things in life as a gift from God (6:6).

In what ways do people try to prolong life today, diminishing the effects of aging or sheltering themselves against disappointments and tragedies? In Solomon's thinking, what makes these efforts ultimately futile?

_____

_____

_____

_____

Revisiting themes he touched on previously, but now applying them personally, Solomon noted that using hard work to relieve depression would fail (6:7), as would a good education, wise living, and riches (6:8). Instead, he concluded, "What the eyes see is better than what the soul desires. This too is futility and striving after the wind" (6:9). Solomon was saying, "Latch on to reality: the real things you see, the simple things you have now, are better than all the dreams you could hope for." We can put it into a common saying: "A bird in the hand is worth two in the bush."

It's important to have a vision and to pursue your dreams—the technological advances we've seen could never have happened without that. But alongside the dreams, we need to embrace reality as well as have the wisdom to let go of vain pursuits and foolish idealism that can lead to frustration. Solomon recognized that dreams and goals can be unexpectedly intercepted by "foreigners" at any time, so he said it's wise to enjoy what we have in the present.

Are you holding on to any dreams or ideals that rob you of contentment with what God has given you to enjoy? If these dreams were derailed by unavoidable events, would the time and energy you've invested be wasted? Why or why not?

_____

_____

_____

_____

We must constantly evaluate our dreams and ideals in light of the reality God has ordained in our lives, the gifts He has given us, and our own human limitations. We cannot begin to discover contentment with God's will for our lives until we accept these realities.

Solomon's Realistic Observations (Ecclesiastes 6:10–11)

As we study Solomon's self-portrait, let's step back and grasp the big picture, examining what Solomon's warnings tell us about the reality of life as he learned it by experience. He conveyed three realistic observations in Ecclesiastes 6:10–11.

God is sovereign (6:10). In Scripture, the act of naming something is a sign of control over that thing, just as Adam's naming of the animals expressed his God-given responsibility to rule over the earth (Genesis 1:26–28; 2:19–20). Scripture tells us that everything—even the acts of evil people against us—are under God's perfect, all-knowing control and that nothing catches Him by surprise or thwarts His plan (Genesis 50:19–20; Daniel 2:20–23; Acts 4:27–28). However, when our own plans are frustrated by the unexpected events in our lives, we may tend to doubt God's sovereignty. This assumes our plans were in alignment with His in the first place! We wrongly believe that our plan for our life's course is better than His. But He promised us that all things would work together for good to those who love Him (Romans 8:28). By saying "whatever exists has already been named," Solomon acknowledged that God is in control.

According to the following passages, over what things does God have control by naming?

Genesis 5:2 _____

_____

_____

_____

Psalm 147:4 _____

_____

_____

_____

Does this include our negative circumstances and unexpected tragedies? Why is this often difficult to accept?

_____

_____

_____

_____

Humankind is not sovereign (Ecclesiastes 6:10). Although God has control of all things, Solomon noted that "it is known what man is." As created beings, we humans have only limited authority. Isaiah 45:9 states it this way:

> Woe to the one who quarrels with his Maker—
> An earthenware vessel among the vessels of earth!
> Will the clay say to the potter, "What are you doing?"
> Or the thing you are making say, "He has no hands"?

That is, we must accept God's sovereign plan or be frustrated and discontent all the days of our lives.

Disputing with God is a waste of time and effort (Ecclesiastes 6:10–11). Simply stated, God is God, and we are not. We are wasting our breath to argue with Him, to question His goodness and wisdom. It's futile and foolish to complain to Him when our own plans are set aside to make way for His better plan.

Read Isaiah 45:9–12; Daniel 4:35; and Romans 9:20–21. What do these reveal about God's will compared with man's will?

_____

_____

_____

_____

Do you tend to accept your circumstances, or do you usually react against them? What could you do to become more accepting?

_____

_____

_____

_____

A Look at Our Own Portrait (Ecclesiastes 6:12)

The words that put the final touches on Solomon's self-portrait prompt us to take a closer look at our own lives. He wrote, "For who knows what is good for a man during his lifetime, during the few years of his futile life? He will spend them like a shadow. For who can tell a man what will be after him under the sun?" (Ecclesiastes 6:12). The implication is that *God* knows what's best for us, that our lives are far too short for us even to approach the eternal perspective He has, for we can't see how our "futile" lives will affect future lives as His plan unfolds. Based on this passage, take a moment to evaluate your perspective.

Does life seem futile to you? It does to almost all of us at times. And when we become frustrated, bewildered, and discontent, we often argue with God rather than acknowledge our utter ignorance compared to His infinite wisdom.

Read the following passages and summarize what they reveal about God's thoughts toward you.

2 Corinthians 4:16–18 _____

_____

_____

_____

Ephesians 1:3–4 _____

_____

_____

_____

James 1:12 _____

_____

_____

_____

1 John 3:1 _____

_____

_____

_____

In the midst of futility and frustration, does it help you to know that your life, though short, plays a part in God's unfolding plan? How would you explain this to a fellow believer who asks you why God is allowing him or her to go through an unexpected loss or tragedy?

_____

_____

_____

_____

Are you fearful about the future? None of us knows what our future holds or what will happen on earth after we've gone. However, Christ has assured us that if we build our lives on Him, whenever the inevitable storms of life come we will stand (Matthew 7:25–27). The future may hold disaster by the world's standards, but when our hearts are relying on God as the foundation, we can trust in His wisdom and power even when His goodness isn't evident to our limited observation.

Read James 4:13–15. If the person described in this passage failed to make a profit or encountered tragedy along the way, how do you think he would respond if he had submitted it all to God's will?

_____

_____

_____

_____

Are there specific elements of your own life that you need to release to His sovereign control and guidance? Write a prayer that turns these things over to Him.

_____

_____

_____

_____

Ecclesiastes 6:1–12 paints a painfully realistic portrait, one more in a long series of "under-the-sun" scenes. It's the tragic picture of a man, old and weary, full of regrets and disappointments, who had arrived at the sunset years of his life. Long shadows had fallen across his memory as he stared out the window at his past and sketched in words the dim image he saw. From this picture, however, he hoped to share a simple message with his sons and those who would dwell in this futile world after him: God is God, and we are not. Are you surrendering your plans to His sovereignty, even if His purpose is not always evident?

13 Wise Words for Busy People
[ECCLESIASTES 7:1–14]

hate life!" Whether they were muttered, whispered, or screamed, the chances are that you've heard someone say these words before. They may have come from a teenager struggling with peer pressure and the challenge of dangerous, life-altering decisions. They may have been uttered by an adult devastated by a lost dream, rejection in a relationship, perceived personal failure, or simply the trials of life.

Perhaps you've said these words yourself. Maybe you've received a negative medical report, a pink slip from your employer, or divorce papers from an unfaithful spouse. Maybe you've gotten yourself into hot water through a chain of bad decisions and now you're drowning in the consequences of your actions. You may be recovering from a severe loss, railing from shocking news, or just worn out by the stress brought on by fear, anxiety, and the frantic juggling act of life. You've shaken your clenched fist toward heaven and shouted, "I hate life!"

Often the busyness of life is the very thing that catches up with us and makes us want to throw our hands in the air. We rush around, scurrying to and fro . . . and for what purpose? It seems futile. People who reach this level of frustration are in good company. In the distant past, wise King Solomon, surveying his great worldly accomplishments, looked around and admitted, "I hated life" and "I hated all the fruit of my labor" (Ecclesiastes 2:17–18).

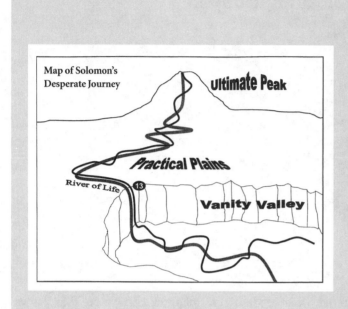

Road Map for the Journey #13

Finally climbing the steep walls out of the Valley of Futility, Solomon now begins to reflect on the wisdom he learned from his ragged-edge journey, following the winding River of Life across the Practical Plain. Because God gives and takes away according to His own will (7:13–14), Solomon first calls people to focus their attention on the simple and important things in life rather than the temporary and trivial (7:1–12, 14).

Solomon's conclusion in the first half of his journal is that all things apart from God are "futility and striving after wind" (2:17). Yet, having come to a dead end in his journey, Solomon didn't simply stare at the wall of futility and sink into the depths of depression. He did what all of us must do. He shifted gears and turned around.

Have you ever felt as though you were at a dead end in your life and didn't have the energy to turn around and start over? What brought you to that point? What did you do about it?

_____

_____

_____

_____

A Change of Scenery

In the first six chapters of Ecclesiastes, Solomon provided evidence for his hypothesis that life under the sun is futile. Without God, ragged-edge reality is meaningless. As we studied Solomon's expedition into excruciating emptiness, we were grateful for the few sparks of light he offered along the way, but overall the mood was dark. From chapter 7 onward, however, the focus of Ecclesiastes becomes less man-centered and descriptive and more God-centered and prescriptive. In the second half of his journal, Solomon ceased reflecting on the pointlessness of life and his own drifting from the Lord and turned his attention instead to his slow but steady voyage home.

Some evidence of this change is the more frequent occurrence of verses addressing wisdom. If we compare the number of verses in Ecclesiastes 1–6 addressing vanity with those addressing wisdom, we see an emphasis on the futility of life. However, in Ecclesiastes 7–12 the emphasis shifts, with more verses dealing with wisdom than vanity. The following chart illustrates this change of focus in Solomon's book.

Also, Ecclesiastes 7 opens with a string of proverbs that offers a wise perspective on dealing with life. In light of the evidence and experience of futility he described in chapters 1 through 6, Solomon began to make some general conclusions about wise living in chapter 7. These pithy observations offer nuggets of perspective to those in the crunch of busyness.

Comparison of the Number of Verses
Addressing Vanity and Wisdom in Ecclesiastes

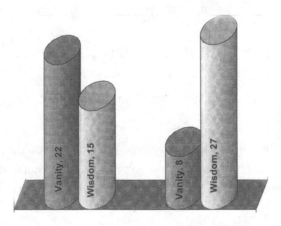

Chapters 1–6   Chapters 7–12

Write your own definition or draw a picture representing wisdom, from your perspective. What is it? Is wisdom something you are, know, or do, or a combination of these?

_____

_____

_____

_____

COUNSEL FOR THOSE IN THE CRUNCH (ECCLESIASTES 7:1–10)

Let's take a moment to explore Solomon's proverbs to glean some guidance for our own journey through life.

Read Ecclesiastes 7:1–10.

1. *"A good name is better than a good ointment"* (Ecclesiastes 7:1). The principle here is that an excellent reputation is more valuable than any external enhancement we might apply. Our physical impression on others is not unimportant, but it is certainly less important than our character and integrity.

Read 1 Samuel 16:7 and 1 Peter 3:3–4. Is your life characterized by an overemphasis on appearances to the neglect of the heart, or are you maintaining a healthy balance? What attitudes or actions might you need to adjust to conform to God's standard?

_____

_____

_____

_____

2. *"The day of one's death is better than the day of one's birth"* (Ecclesiastes 7:1). This may sound pessimistic, but when believers reflect more deeply on this proverb's meaning, we can understand its implications. Depending on your relationship with God, you may respond to this proverb in a couple of ways.

First, if you're a believer walking with the Lord, you'll view death as an ultimate deliverance

DIGGING DEEPER

Proverbs

A proverb has been described as "a pithy saying, especially one condensing the wisdom of experience."[1] It's a brief, practical generalization of truth that helps us approach life wisely, a "sound bite" of wisdom for living. The proverbs in the Bible, like most Hebrew poetry, are characterized by parallelism,[2] the three most common types of which are summarized below:

Type of Parallelism	Description	Key Words	Examples
Contrastive	Second line contrasts with the first	*but; nevertheless*	Proverbs 13:1, 10
Completive	Second line completes the first	*and; so*	Proverbs 14:10, 13
Comparative	Second line compared with the first	*better . . . than; like/as . . . so*	Proverbs 25:24–25

In Ecclesiastes 7:1–10, Solomon set forth seven comparative proverbs that illustrate for us things in life that are "better than" others. As we explore his insights, however, we must understand that Hebrew proverbs are meant to convey general truths. One author describes the use of proverbs this way:

> They boil down, crystallize, and condense the experiences and observations of the writers. . . . They tell what life is like and how life should be lived. In a terse, no-words-wasted fashion, some statements . . . *relate* what is commonly observed in life; others *recommend* or exhort how life should be lived. And when advice is given, a reason for the counsel usually follows.
>
> Many of the proverbial maxims should be recognized as guidelines, not absolute observations; they are not ironclad promises. What is stated is generally and usually true, but exceptions are occasionally noted.[3]

from the pain and struggles of this world. You may respond in joyful agreement that the day of death is better than the day of birth because of the glory that awaits you after death.

Second, for believers who aren't walking in close fellowship with God, this verse may remind them of the truly important things in life. Throughout our earthly lives we celebrate birthdays, honoring a person's past and anticipating their future. However, on the day of a person's death we are given a unique opportunity to reflect on the person's entire life. We ponder what impact their accomplishments might make on future generations, what their earthly life was like, whom they loved, their character and reputation, and also the ultimate brevity of life. Contemplating the finality of death forces us to reflect on our own life and work.

Can you relate to Paul's words in Philippians 1:21–24? How does your current relationship with God affect your perspective on this verse?

_____

_____

_____

_____

3. *"It is better to go to a house of mourning than to go to a house of feasting"* (Ecclesiastes 7:2). This proverb completes its thought with what seems to be a strange assertion: "Because that is the end of every man and the living takes it to heart." Similar to the previous proverb, in which Solomon emphasized reflection on the profundity of one's funeral over the frivolity of one's birthday, here Solomon was more explicit. He prodded us to consider death, to move beyond the superficial and temporary things in daily life to the significant matters that will affect the final significance of our existence. In doing so, we take a crucial step toward living wisely.

In what ways does our culture handle death? Do you personally tend to dwell on death or to avoid it? Why?

_____

_____

_____

_____

In light of 1 Thessalonians 4:13–18, what should be the proper Christian response to death? What enables Christians to respond this way?

_____
_____
_____
_____

4. *"Sorrow is better than laughter"* (Ecclesiastes 7:3). Solomon didn't advocate a life of tears and frowns but a life of authentic reflection, one that handles the realities of the ragged edge with a confidence that transcends the superficial. A quick laugh is easily forgotten. It can distract us from reality for a flash, but inside we can remain miserable. Yet Solomon said the opposite could be true: "For when a face is sad a heart may be happy" (7:3). If we reflect on the brief trajectory of our lives from the divine perspective, we are better able to cope with the real sorrows of life without forfeiting an inner joy. In fact, those who avoid dealing with death and instead live their lives pursuing pleasure as a means of escape are foolish (7:4).

Read Psalm 90:10–17. In the midst of affliction, discipline, and sorrow, what does the psalmist request from God?

_____
_____
_____
_____

What do you tend to request in similar circumstances?

_____
_____
_____
_____

5. *"It is better to listen to the rebuke of a wise man than for one to listen to the song of fools"* (Ecclesiastes 7:5). "Fools," or people who deny God's relevance in their daily lives, are often fun to be around, but their entertainment-oriented lifestyle is empty (4:6). The wise, however, can sometimes seem harsh and unloving when they urge us to face reality and call us to a higher standard. We need to be careful whose counsel we follow, for even a discerning individual can succumb to the pressures of adversity or be tempted by the promise of prosperity (7:7).

Read 2 Timothy 4:1–4. When you make decisions, do you seek counsel from those who tell you what you want to hear or those who aren't afraid to be honest even if it means hurting your feelings? Do you know someone personally who falls in the second group?

_____

_____

_____

_____

6. *"The end of a matter is better than its beginning"* (Ecclesiastes 7:8). When we reach the end of a novel or film, the whole story often makes sense. Even the seemingly fragmented pieces of the Bible's story come together in Christ and are summed up at the end of history. The same is true in our own lives. Grand plans and idealistic dreams may abound at the beginning, but the actual course of our lives only becomes evident at the end. As we step into eternity and catch a glimpse of God's perspective, our joys, pains, struggles, and triumphs will begin to take shape as a miraculous work of God.

Can you recall a period of trial or suffering that made little sense at the time, but later its purpose became clear? How did this knowledge change your perspective on the process? How does this prepare you for the unknown challenges of the future, including trials that we won't understand until the end of our lives?

_____

_____

_____

_____

_____

7. *"Patience of spirit is better than haughtiness of spirit"* (Ecclesiastes 7:8). On our journey from birth to death and beyond, one of God's purposes is to transform us into the likeness of Christ, replacing our pride with humility (7:8). Solomon noted in these verses that impatience can lead to anger, and anger can lead to foolish acts that we'll regret later (7:9). He warned against dwelling on the past so much that we become dissatisfied with the present (7:10). This blind nostalgia may also stem from impatience, bitterness, or pride. Haughtiness, anger, bitterness, and regret—these things stay on the minds of fools rather than the wise.

WHAT MAKES WISDOM SO SPECIAL? (ECCLESIASTES 7:11–14)

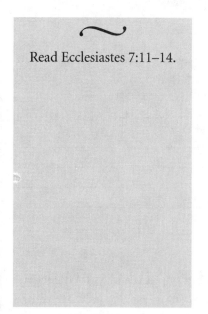

Read Ecclesiastes 7:11–14.

Solomon's numerous comparisons of wisdom and folly might prompt us to ask, is wisdom really all its cracked up to be? If wisdom is so great, why does the Bible need to promote it? Or, as Solomon once reasoned, don't both the wise and the fool end up the same—dead (Ecclesiastes 2:14–15)? In order to balance this under-the-sun mentality with a proper perspective on life, Solomon pointed out two major benefits of wisdom, regardless of circumstances.

Wisdom preserves our lives from human pitfalls (Ecclesiastes 7:11–12). While many things are out of our control—including natural disasters, the way others treat us, and the gifts and blessings of God—wise living can protect us from one of our worst enemies in life: ourselves. Sound instruction and practical insight help us avoid such traps as pride, impatience, disillusionment, and resentment.

Are you dealing with problems that were caused by your own foolishness, either because of impatience, pride, or anger? Often these are the very qualities that blind us to resolution. Take a moment to ask God to soften your heart and open your eyes to your own folly. He longs to restore you. Write these problems in the space provided, and ask God what wise course of action you can take to turn them in the right direction.

_____

_____

_____

_____

Wisdom provides our lives with divine perspective (Ecclesiastes 7:13–14). Wisdom turns our attention from ourselves to consider "the work of God" (7:13), to realize that, while there are circumstances that wise living can avoid, all things are in God's hands and we can't argue with Him or change His course (7:13). Such an attitude frees us to enjoy the prosperity He gives and to accept the challenges He uses to mold us into the people He wants us to be. Both good times and adversity come from His hand (7:14).

Take a moment to consider the growth you've experienced or the lessons you've learned through prosperity (the bright days of life) and adversity (the dark times).

Through prosperity	Through adversity
_____	_____
_____	_____
_____	_____
_____	_____

Go to the Source

In our busy world in which so many decisions are made at a moment's notice (and with little reflection) and in which stressful circumstances can lead us to say "I hate life," we need to keep two things in mind: *we dare not make a major decision without asking for wisdom from God.* He has the past, present, and future in His hands, and failing to approach Him for insight will lead to frustration.

This leads to the second point: *we can't see the whole picture without drawing on wisdom from God.* Our perspective will be limited to certain details, while God's perspective includes the big picture. As we seek His wisdom for our decisions and our responses to everyday life, proper attitudes and actions will become clearer.

In chapter 7 of Solomon's journal, he shifted from the negative to the positive, from gathering data and reflecting on the futility of life under the sun to summarizing some of his conclusions in stimulating, insightful, and provocative proverbs. He may have not yet come to the ultimate conclusion about what is *best* for people living in the fallen world, but he did let us know some things that are *better* than others. In the busy twenty-first century where everything seems urgent and the truly important things are often forgotten, such wisdom is long overdue.

14 Putting Wisdom to Work
[ECCLESIASTES 7:15–29]

W e're living in an age when it seems like everything in the world is "extreme." We can engage in extreme sports, extreme vacations, and extreme politics. Different diets advocate completely opposite extremes: high carb, low carb, high protein, low protein, no fat, good fat. Any major bookstore offers guides to a cornucopia of lifestyle extremes, from having it all to spending it all to investing it all to getting away from it all.

Sometimes Christians also tend toward extremes. We want to avoid worldly influence, so we stop going to movies. Or we want to be culturally relevant, so we go to lots of movies. We want to grow spiritually, so we read nothing but the Bible. Or we want to be informed, so we read everything else and try to squeeze in the Bible. We want to affect our world, so we throw ourselves into worthwhile political or social causes. We want to count for eternity, so we eschew all such involvement and only evangelize.

God knew that in many areas of life we might swing toward one extreme or another. And He provided an antidote for undue extremism: His wisdom. Wisdom from God brings balance to the Christian life. It provides strength and the ability to handle challenges with insight and prudence. Recall Solomon's words in Ecclesiastes 2:24–26, which tell us that wisdom, knowledge, and joy are all "from the hand of God." The life of wisdom is a gift, and putting wisdom to work is a blessing from the sovereign God.

An Analysis of Wisdom

Solomon's perspective was rather dim in the first six chapters of Ecclesiastes as he examined the futility of life without God at the center. However, in chapter 7, Solomon began to use the wisdom he gleaned from his exploration of the world. In this chapter we'll see Solomon's perspective come into clearer focus as he described the outworking of wisdom—that is, how wisdom is fleshed out in a balanced and stable life of insight.

GETTING TO THE ROOT

The definition of biblical wisdom could be summed up as the God-given ability to see life objectively and to handle life with stability. In Hebrew thinking, wisdom *(chokhmah)* "is intensely practical, not theoretical. . . . Stemming from the fear of the Lord . . . , it branches out to touch all of life."[1]

To explore the contrast between divine wisdom and human wisdom, turn to 1 Corinthians 2:4–16. In these verses, who receives divine wisdom? How does it differ from the wisdom of the world?

_____

_____

_____

_____

The Outworking of Wisdom

How does wisdom from God work itself out in our lives? Solomon addressed this question in Ecclesiastes 7:15–29. He pinpointed three characteristics produced by divine discernment and indicated several areas in which wisdom can perform its work of maturing us.

The Balance Wisdom Gives (Ecclesiastes 7:15–18)

First, Solomon said wisdom gives *balance.* He began this discussion with an example from his observations of life under the sun. But he didn't end there. He moved toward application of the principles he had learned.

Read Ecclesiastes 7:15–29.

How might the injustices described in Ecclesiastes 7:15 affect people who don't approach life with divine wisdom?

_____

_____

_____

_____

In response to his observation in Ecclesiastes 7:15, Solomon didn't throw up his hands and say, "What's the point of living, when the wicked thrive and the righteous perish?" Instead, given this all-too-common set of circumstances, he determined what would be the wisest course of action. Here's his prescription on how to put wisdom to work in the midst of a world of contradictions and frustrations: "Do not be excessively righteous and do not be overly wise. Why should you ruin yourself? Do not be excessively wicked and do not be a fool. Why should you die before your time?" (7:16–17).

In other words, we should be careful not to go to extremes. Thinking that wise living and righteousness are guaranteed to bring blessing from God, we may strive with all our might to be excessively prudent and pious. Then, when our attempts at getting God's favor are cut down by the ragged edge of life, we might go to the opposite extreme: we throw in the towel and give up completely, thinking, *Well, if good things don't come from being wise and righteous, I might as well just give up.*

Solomon called for balance, not extremes. Aiming to live a life of righteousness and wisdom has its blessings, but even that's not foolproof or without risk. It's easy to fall into the trap of pride or to believe that our good deeds will earn God's favor. We should also avoid foolishness and wickedness in favor of a humble and balanced life before God.

If you're in a phase of life in which you're sacrificing other areas of your life in an effort to succeed in work or trying hard to make yourself seem good to God, read the following passages and note the warning involved in each:

Genesis 3:17–19 _____

_____

_____

_____

Luke 18:9–14 _____

_____

_____

_____

If you've already "been there; done that" and given up on doing your best, read the following passages and note the warnings:

2 Thessalonians 3:10–13 _____

_____

_____

_____

2 Timothy 2:15 _____

_____

_____

_____

Solomon completed his call to live a balanced life with a final exhortation: "It is good that you grasp one thing and also not let go of the other; for the one who fears God comes forth with both of them" (Ecclesiastes 7:18). Balanced living in the fear of God allows us to walk the tightrope of life without falling either to the right or the left.

In which areas of life do you think people in the world are most unbalanced? How has this affected your own quest for balance in the Christian life?

_____

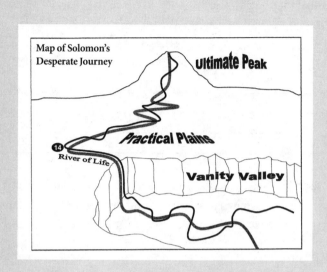

Map of Solomon's Desperate Journey

ultimate Peak

Practical Plains

14
River of Life

Vanity Valley

ROAD MAP FOR THE JOURNEY #14

Having escaped from the Valley of Futility and now following the River of Life across the Practical Plain, Solomon begins a series of journal entries dealing with living wisely in the fallen world. In this section Solomon urges us that, in light of God's unalterable and unknowable will and man's sinfulness (7:23–24, 29), a balanced approach to life in the fear of God is the best solution (7:19–22, 26).

The Strength Wisdom Produces (Ecclesiastes 7:19–22)

Besides producing balance, the gift of divine wisdom also brings us strength to handle unpredictable and difficult areas of life. Solomon wrote, "Wisdom strengthens a wise man more than ten rulers who are in a city" (Ecclesiastes 7:19). Now that's strength! Let's take a look at a few areas Solomon focused on to show how wisdom produces strength in everyday life.

Divine wisdom produces strength to handle the painful tensions. Perfectionists need to hear Solomon's words: "Indeed, there is not a righteous man on earth who continually does good and who never sins" (Ecclesiastes 7:20). Many people have a hard time accepting this truth. All of us stumble from time to time, and this state of imperfection will continue all our lives. At the same

145

time, God's standard of holiness cannot be compromised. This creates an uncomfortable tension that can easily lead to frustration and imbalance.

According to 1 Corinthians 1:30–31 and 2 Peter 1:2–3, what is our only source of holiness and godliness?

_____

_____

_____

_____

Do you have high expectations of yourself (set by you or by somebody else) that you can't reach? How has this produced frustration, insecurity, apathy, or other negative emotions? What can you do to wisely adjust these expectations to more realistic goals without compromising excellence?

_____

_____

_____

_____

Divine wisdom gives strength to avoid the pitfalls of gullibility. Solomon wrote, "Also, do not take seriously all words which are spoken" (Ecclesiastes 7:21). When we receive lavish praise, we shouldn't let it inflate our egos. Divine wisdom allows us to keep our feet anchored in reality, even while the praises of people may be lifting us into a dream world. It's okay to appreciate kind words spoken to you, but don't be fooled into believing you are better than others.

Read Romans 12:3. What is Paul's solution to the problem of an inflated ego?

_____

_____

_____

_____

WINDOWS TO THE ANCIENT WORLD

The Spirit as Wisdom

In the Old Testament, the gift of wisdom was associated with the gift of the Holy Spirit, so that wisdom was not something learned or a lifestyle adopted but a result of being led by the Spirit of God (Exodus 31:3; Isaiah 11:2). In the New Testament, the same idea is emphasized, though the Spirit who brings true wisdom comes to us through faith in Jesus Christ, who is the perfect example of wisdom (Acts 6:3; 1 Corinthians 1:24, 30; Ephesians 1:17; Colossians 3:16).

In the early church, while the teaching of the apostles was still ringing in pastors' ears, the abstract concept of "wisdom" was clearly linked to the person of the Holy Spirit. Theophilus, pastor of Antioch around AD 180, referred to the Trinity as God, the Word, and Wisdom—that is, Father, Son, and Holy Spirit.[2] At about the same time, Irenaeus, pastor of Lyons in modern France, said God created all things "by Himself, that is, through His Word and His Wisdom."[3]

It was important in the ancient church to emphasize that wisdom is not a set of principles but is personified in the Holy Spirit and exemplified in Jesus Christ. As we think about wisdom today, we should realize that it comes not from us, nor from the world of experience and learning, but from God the Father, who works in His people through His Son and His Spirit.

Divine wisdom provides strength to resist criticism (Ecclesiastes 7:21–22). While we shouldn't let extreme praise inflate our egos, we should also take extreme criticism with a grain of salt. Don't ignore criticism—especially by those who love and care for you—but always consider the source, the motives, and the limited perspective of those who criticize. This takes wisdom.

How does an examination of your own criticism of others help you balance another's criticism of you? Are you always fair and wise in your criticism, or do you sometimes exaggerate or even criticize unjustly?

_____

_____

_____

_____

The Insight Wisdom Offers (Ecclesiastes 7:23–29)

Having discussed the balance and strength wisdom imparts, Solomon next mentioned three insights into divine wisdom.

We cannot understand ourselves, nor can we make ourselves wise (Ecclesiastes 7:23–24). Solomon began his career as king of Israel by asking God for wisdom before anything else (2 Chronicles 1:7–10). Wisdom is a gift from God; no human being can manufacture it. No amount of psychology, self-analysis, education, or life experience can unveil all that we are and all that we're not. Like Solomon, we must ask God for wisdom in all things (James 1:5).

Intimate relations are compelling but often unsatisfying. It takes a lot of insight in today's sex-driven world to accept the truth that the one-night stands and clandestine affairs that ensnare so many men and women end in tragedy. Solomon had a thousand women available to fulfill his every desire, but they did not bring him the contentment he sought.

Review Ecclesiastes 7:25–28. Why do you think the snare of adultery is "more bitter than death?" Why do so many who fall into this trap believe they will come through unscathed?

_____

_____

_____

_____

In the context of his immoral affairs, why do you think Solomon warned his readers about trying to find wisdom from intimate relationships? How do you think a faithful marriage to one partner could have changed his perspective?

_____

_____

_____

_____

Our basic problems are not outside of us but within us (Ecclesiastes 7:29). Wisdom provides us with the ability to see that "God made men upright, but they have sought out many devices" (7:29). Although God created humans in a state of untested innocence with freedom to love and serve Him, after the Fall, all of humankind became creatively deceptive and destructive toward themselves and others (Genesis 1–4; Romans 1:18–32). Wisdom from God teaches us that we have nobody to blame for our sin except ourselves (James 1:13–17). And we have nobody to praise for our righteousness other than God, who works in us by the Holy Spirit to produce fruit pleasing to Him (Ephesians 2:8–10).

Read Galatians 5:19–26.

What is the cause of our sin?

_____
_____
_____
_____

What is the cause of our righteous deeds?

_____
_____
_____
_____

After thinking through these carefully, circle your answer to each of these questions:

Is wisdom guarding you from a life of extremes?   Yes   No

Is wisdom enabling you

- to avoid perfectionism?   Yes   No

- to avoid the gullibility of too much praise?   Yes   No

- to avoid sponging up undue criticism?   Yes   No

Is wisdom clearing your mind to see

- that balance, strength, and insight are gifts of God?   Yes   No

- that immoral relationships are unsatisfying?   Yes   No

- that sin comes from your own flesh?   Yes   No

If you answered no to any of these questions, follow the advice of James 1:5 now. Write a prayer to God on the lines that follow.

_____

_____

_____

_____

_____

_____

_____

_____

~

Wisdom is not merely a theoretical concept to be written about and stored on our shelves to collect dust. Neither is it the result of our own ingenuity, education, or experience. The Lord gives us wisdom so we can view life with objectivity and handle it with stability. Those of us who have placed our faith in Christ alone for forgiveness have access to that wisdom from God through the Holy Spirit (1 Corinthians 1:30). Have you received God's gift of wisdom by the Holy Spirit through faith in His Son? Are you putting wisdom to work?

15 The Qualities of a Good Boss
[ECCLESIASTES 8:1–9]

Being a good leader is neither easy nor accidental. Exceptional effort is not required to be a *lousy* president, CEO, parent, supervisor, pastor, teacher, or coach. But to lead with excellence is a challenging feat.

All too often, bosses tend toward one of two extremes. Some are *incompetent.* They're not qualified for the jobs they do and are therefore frustrating to work for. They can be negative and discouraging rather than positive and encouraging. Other bosses are *intolerant.* They may be qualified and knowledgeable, but they can be almost impossible to please. These bosses are rigid perfectionists, usually demanding more from others than what's reasonable.

It's easy to see how a lack of the wisdom we discussed in the previous chapter comes into practical play in the matter of leadership. Without *balance,* a person will end up going to extremes in his or her leadership style. Without *strength,* either praise or criticism can cause instability. Without *insight,* leaders may be paralyzed by fear and indecision. Wisdom and leadership go hand in hand.

Who are the people in your life in direct authority over you?

_____

_____

_____

_____

Who is under your authority, looking to you for leadership?

_____

_____

_____

Keep these people in mind as you answer the questions in this chapter.

Characteristics of a Wise Leader (Ecclesiastes 8:1–8)

As we have seen, the first six chapters of Ecclesiastes record Solomon's exploration and observations of the futility of life under the sun. Chapter 7 contains a series of proverbial principles based on his conclusions. In chapter 8, Solomon painted a picture of those principles personified, illustrating in verses 1–9 the traits of a wise leader.

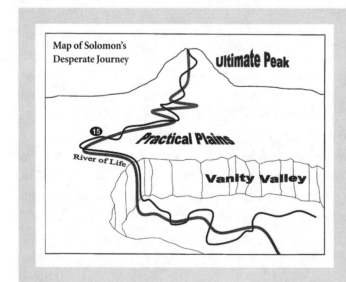

Map of Solomon's Desperate Journey

Ultimate Peak

Practical Plains

River of Life

Vanity Valley

ROAD MAP FOR THE JOURNEY #15

Continuing his trek across the Practical Plain, Solomon now argues that God has ordained all things in this world—including those rulers in authority over us (8:6–8). Therefore, he says we should wisely submit to their authority since God will hold them accountable and honor us as well (8:2).

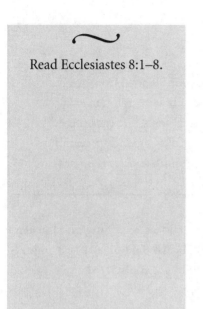

Read Ecclesiastes 8:1–8.

Notice that Solomon was looking at leadership from the follower's perspective. It is precisely this point of view that good leaders need. Because Christians are called to be servant-leaders (Mark 10:42–45), starting from the perspective of those we lead is not only permissible; it's required. Solomon's words speak not only to the issue of the king's authority but also to various types of leaders. From Ecclesiastes 8:1–8, we can glean at least five qualities of a good boss.

Describe the qualities of a good boss or leader from the world's perspective. What would the world be looking for on a résumé for a supervisor position? How do you think this compares with the qualities God looks for in a leader?

_____

_____

_____

_____

A wise leader has a clear mind (Ecclesiastes 8:1). Solomon wrote, "Who is like the wise man and who knows the interpretation of a matter?" A wise person exhibits the type of insight Solomon discussed in Ecclesiastes 7:23–29. A wise leader asks the "why" questions, not just the "what" and "how" of a matter. Good leaders know where they stand philosophically and theologically. They don't just follow the trendy, pragmatic, reactionary approach to leadership but are able to think through things clearly before making a decision. After all, clarity at the top is necessary if there's to be defined purpose and fulfilled responsibility at the bottom. When confusion and uncertainty characterize the leader of an organization, home, business, or church, that same perplexity will trickle down to every level.

GETTING TO THE ROOT

The word translated "interpretation" in Ecclesiastes 8:1 is the Hebrew word *pēsher*, which means "solution." Likely a word loaned from Aramaic, it occurs in literature from the Dead Sea Scrolls with reference to "the interpretation of the hidden meanings in biblical texts."[1] It is also used in Daniel approximately thirty times with reference to the interpretation of dreams (Daniel 2:4). It therefore refers to the hidden, secret, or not-so-obvious explanation of something.

Take a moment to consider or discuss your ideas regarding good leadership. Jot down principles you think should be lived out in any type of leadership role. One suggestion has been given to get you started.

1. *Leadership should reflect honesty and integrity in relationships.*

2.

3.

4.

5.

When you complete this chapter, revisit your list of principles to see how many match those discussed in this study.

A wise leader has a cheerful disposition (Ecclesiastes 8:1). Solomon completed his previous thought by saying, "A man's wisdom illumines him and causes his stern face to beam" (8:1). Fewer things are more contagious than cheerfulness. When leaders are happy and optimistic, their positive outlook rubs off on their followers. When bosses are negative and critical, their employees will reflect this same dour mentality. If you're greeted with a scowl at a store or restaurant, the chances are good that the manager is a grump.

Do you reflect the attitudes of those in authority over you? Are these attitudes positive or negative? How do your own attitudes in leadership affect those under you?

_____

_____

_____

_____

A wise leader has a discreet mouth (Ecclesiastes 8:2–4). This passage addresses primarily the responsibility of those under a leader's authority to submit to that authority, but it also teaches us the importance of a leader's words.

According to Ecclesiastes 8:2–4, how are those under authority to respond to their bosses?

_____

_____

_____

_____

Is your attitude toward authorities in harmony with 1 Peter 2:13–15 and Colossians 3:22–25? Where do you think it may need correcting?

_____

_____

_____

_____

Because God calls Christians to submit to earthly authority (except where that authority is abused or goes against His commands), Christian leaders carry a huge responsibility to speak with wisdom and discretion. The application of Ecclesiastes 8:2–4 is obvious: the speech of superiors has a direct effect on the loyalty and cooperation they receive from their subordinates. Just as overbearing parents can "exasperate" their children (Colossians 3:21), bosses can drive those under them to frustration and even rebellion. Leaders who exercise authority with tact, diplomacy, sensitivity, and compassion will generally receive the benefit of a supportive and loyal staff.

Based on the following proverbs, what are some positive and/or negative effects a leader's words might have on those they lead?

	Positive	Negative
Proverbs 12:18		
Proverbs 15:2		
Proverbs 18:21		
Proverbs 25:11–13, 23		

A wise leader has keen judgment (Ecclesiastes 8:5–7). In these verses we find four ways leaders exhibit keen judgment. First, wise leaders acknowledge the "royal command" (8:5); that is, they realize that their positions are ultimately given by the sovereign hand of God, not by their own personal achievements and merit. Second, effective leaders can map out and execute a successful plan because they know "the proper time and procedure" (8:5–6). Third, bosses with keen judgment are able to remain stable under pressure (8:6). Difficult situations don't cause them to panic; instead, they continue to think clearly and remain calm (8:6). Fourth, insightful leaders have strong intuition, so they're able to sense the attitude of their followers and make plans accordingly (8:7).

A wise leader has a humble spirit (Ecclesiastes 8:8). Since we are unable to control natural occurrences or even the timing of events in our lives, Solomon pointed out that leaders should have a realistic view of their abilities and limitations. Regardless of how gifted, skillful, or influential we may be, none of us can do whatever we want whenever we want. Good leaders express this knowledge through a humble attitude. They draw on the strengths of those under them, giving their employees a sense of importance and dignity. This kind of humility also causes good bosses to depend on God—not on their own abilities—to accomplish their tasks.

It's unlikely that you include in your résumé a section titled "Limitations and Weaknesses," but it's important for you to know what they are. In order to gain a proper view of yourself the way God made you, write a short paragraph that describes your God-given weaknesses and limitations. This exercise will help you develop godly humility as well as show you what complementing qualities to look for in your teammates.

_____

_____

_____

_____

Read Ecclesiastes 8:9.

TWO WARNINGS TO THOSE IN AUTHORITY (ECCLESIASTES 8:8–9)

After describing five character traits of good leaders, Solomon shared two warnings for all who are in leadership positions.

It is inexcusable for leaders to take unfair advantage of those under their charge (Ecclesiastes 8:8). Superiors may try to abuse and oppress their workers. They might even rewrite the rules or ignore them altogether. Yet their reprehensible conduct and rationalizations will not be excused by God, who will hold all leaders accountable.

Leaders who take unfair advantage of their followers hurt themselves more than they hurt those under their authority (8:9). People who initiate unjust policies and practices will not get away with it. The Lord says they will reap what they sow—in this life, the next one, or both (Ecclesiastes 12:14; Amos 8:4–14; Matthew 12:36–37; 2 Corinthians 5:10).

DIGGING DEEPER

Should I Submit to Government?

By reciting the Pledge of Allegiance, citizens of the United States promise loyalty to, responsibility for, and support of their nation. It's a serious commitment—one that Christians in the U.S.A. should not regard lightly.

A strong commitment to our nation, whether or not we formalize it with a pledge, is biblical. God established the system of human government and its authority to punish wickedness to prevent the world from spiraling into the kind of chaos characterized by the days of Noah before the Flood (Genesis 9:5–6; Romans 13:3–4). In the New Testament, Christians are instructed to submit to governing authorities at every level (Romans 13:1; 2 Peter 2:13). The purpose of this biblical instruction is not only for our own good (Romans 13:3), but also to silence those who unjustly persecute believers (1 Peter 2:15).

As we consider what the Bible says regarding a Christian's responsibility to submit to governing authority, it's important to understand the full effect of this New Testament command on believers in the early church. Some of them were being persecuted unjustly by the government, yet Christ instructed His followers to pay taxes even to the pagan Roman Empire—a government that oppressed the Jews and used their taxes to build temples and enforce the worship of Caesar (Matthew 22:21). How much more should we who enjoy political and religious freedom respect our government out of submission to God?

The Bible never suggests that rulers will be perfect. Though a system of government has been established by God to prevent anarchy and promote civil and criminal justice, God does not necessarily endorse particular rulers, nor does He approve of particular laws that are in defiance of Him. Commenting on Solomon's words in Ecclesiastes 8:9, which states that some rulers abuse their power, Ray Stedman notes:

Evil in government arises from the evil in fallen man, living in a fallen world. Who of us is free of evil? Who of us can claim absolute innocence for all we do? No one. There is none righteous, the Searcher found, there is no one who does not do evil. There is no government, therefore, that does not have evil within it.[2]

Cont'd

Digging Deeper (Cont'd)

When a ruler or nation becomes too corrupt, God may send another nation to bring judgment against it (Isaiah 10:5–12). Or He may deal directly with a particular ruler (Acts 12:21–23).

Because of the sin in human government, believers often find themselves in difficult situations in which they must choose whether to obey God or men (Daniel 6; Acts 5:29). In cases where God has clearly given His people a command, such as to share the gospel or to avoid idolatry, believers must obey God . . . and suffer the consequences of their civil disobedience.[3] One author notes, "Certainly, our circumstances vary greatly from those Daniel and Peter experienced, and we must examine our motives and circumstances very carefully before standing against our leaders. But the principle is a scriptural one, and we ignore it to our own detriment."[4]

Clearly, our responsibility to submit to human government and our response to the evils of that same government are matters we must approach prayerfully. The answer is neither to follow the godless mandates of a dictator in the name of blind patriotism, nor to wage war against the government from behind a walled compound. Only God-given wisdom can keep our submission to authorities balanced.

Personal Appropriation of These Qualities

Being a good boss is neither easy nor accidental. Most of us have been called to positions of leadership in some capacity—whether in the home, school, workplace, or church. At the same time, we also have people in positions of authority over us. As we meditate on how to apply to our own lives the characteristics of a good leader, let's remember two important things.

We must never forget the value of being a role model. Like the proverbial bull in a china shop, high-achieving, hard-charging leaders often overemphasize the finished product while abusing the people who are helping them meet their goals. In the end, this leadership style can leave people exhausted and frustrated. But effective leaders realize that successfully accomplishing a job must be balanced with providing a good model for those under their leadership. The influence we have on the lives of others will outlive the memory of our achievements.

Think of people in your life who are or have been your role models. What character and leadership qualities stand out as you reflect on the influence they had on you?

_____

_____

_____

_____

We must never lose the vision of seeing a cycle. One day our positions will be taken over by other individuals. In fact, good superiors seek to train others who can take over when they're gone. Regardless of whether this cycle turns in a home, church, or office, the cultivation of new leaders is a significant task. By modeling wise leadership and teaching others to become godly leaders, we influence the future more than we may ever know.

How would you want those under your leadership to someday describe your influence on their lives? What can you do today to begin building this legacy?

_____

_____

_____

_____

Being a godly and wise boss is not easy. It takes a conscious effort, years of work, and a large dose of faith in God, who alone grants the wisdom necessary to maintain the balance, strength, and insight that turns a mere boss into a model leader. And being a godly and wise leader is not automatic. In fact, the opposite is true. By doing nothing, you're guaranteed to fail.

Will you take up the challenge to be a good leader today? If you're an employee, will you apply yourself to becoming a faithful and diligent worker? Both tasks are demanding. Both require God-given wisdom. But both bring great rewards not only in this life but also in the life to come.

16 Mysteries That Defy Explanation

[ECCLESIASTES 8:10–17]

People love mysteries. TV shows explore the unexplained, films guide us through unexpected plot twists to surprise endings, and whodunit novels tempt readers to flip to the final pages and peek at the resolution. Mysteries of the universe attract the curiosity of scientists. While science has taken great strides in answering many questions, each discovery seems to create a new list of challenging questions that force us to reexamine earlier conclusions and theories. Yet the innate curiosity about the inner workings of things keeps scientists trekking through the micro- and macrocosms of God's creation in search of that place where no one has gone before. Yes, people love mysteries—at least *some* kinds of mysteries.

Other mysteries people hate. Nagging questions about the perplexities of life can be excruciating: Why did I come down with this incurable disease? Why isn't this marriage counseling working? Why did my child die so young? Why is there evil in the world? Why do bad things happen to good people? These questions represent some of the mysteries of life that can cause us to question the very goodness and sovereignty of God.

In Romans 11:33, Paul wrote, "Oh, the depth of the riches both of the wisdom and knowledge of God! How unsearchable are His judgments and unfathomable His ways!" Although he was well educated and widely traveled, the apostle Paul didn't hesitate to acknowledge and exalt the mystery of God's knowledge and wisdom.

Do you think people are comfortable with mysteries in the Christian faith that no pastor or scholar can answer? Why or why not?

_____

_____

_____

_____

Hundreds of years earlier, in the eighth chapter of Ecclesiastes, Solomon came to a similar understanding after considering some puzzling observations of the fallen world and the Lord who rules over it. Before digging into Solomon's discussion about a few mysteries of the world under the sun, we need to orient ourselves to the different types of mysteries we find in the Bible. This will help us gain a better understanding of Solomon's comments and their application to our lives.

The Mystery about Mysteries

Some questions about life can be cleared up through simple education: the mysterious world of childhood loses its enchantment as we grow older and wiser. Then, there are other questions that can't be answered through human learning but are understood only as God illuminates the mind and heart (Ephesians 1:7–8, 18; 1 John 5:20). One example in this category would be the gospel of Jesus Christ: salvation comes as a free gift by believing in Jesus's finished work on the cross as payment for our sin.

There are other mysteries that humans can't know and will never know. These are truths of such profound and infinite depth that our created minds will never be able to comprehend them, including the nature and intricate purposes of God (Job 11:7–11; Isaiah 55:8–9; Romans 11:33-36). Just as Einstein would be incapable of explaining relativity to a preschooler, we can't expect to fully understand all the mysteries of God.

In the following passages referring to "mysteries," what is revealed and to whom is it revealed?

GETTING TO THE ROOT

Our English word "mystery" comes from the Latin *mysterium,* which is derived from the Greek *mustērion.*[1] In the New Testament the word refers to the thoughts and plans of God that are hidden from the natural man and must be made known by divine revelation to whomever God chooses.[2] In the Old Testament, the word *raz* corresponds to *mustērion* and is found only in the book of Daniel.[3] It refers most often to dreams or secrets about things that can't be known except by special revelation from God. Daniel said to King Nebuchadnezzar regarding the interpretation of his dream, "As for the mystery about which the king has inquired, neither wise men, conjurers, magicians nor diviners are able to declare it to the king. However, there is a God in heaven who reveals mysteries" (Daniel 2:27–28).

Matthew 13:11 _____

_____

_____

_____

Ephesians 1:9 _____

_____

_____

_____

Ephesians 3:4–6 _____

_____

_____

_____

Colossians 1:26–27 _____

_____

_____

_____

Before diving into the issue of mysteries God has *not* revealed, pause now and thank God in prayer for those mysteries above that He *did* reveal to us through Christ and by the Holy Spirit. If you'd like, write your prayer below.

_____

_____

_____

_____

_____

SOLOMON'S MUSINGS ON MYSTERIES

It's probably best to start our study of Ecclesiastes 8:10–17 by doing what some readers of sleuth novels do: flip to the end and see how all the pieces of the puzzle will eventually fit together. Ecclesiastes 8:16–17 gives us a twofold outlook on divine mysteries. Although this conclusion doesn't answer all our questions, it does put our questions in a proper perspective.

Read Ecclesiastes 8:10–17.

God's mysteries defy human explanation. No matter how hard we try in our own human strength—even if we were to stay up night and day searching—we couldn't explain the infinite workings of God. Even the brief glimpses of purpose that pierce the dark storm clouds of life like beams of insight are beyond explanation.

God's mysteries go beyond human intellect and wisdom. Not only can we not explain what God is doing, we lack the intellect and wisdom to grasp it. If God wants us to know even part of His infinite mind, He must reveal it to us by His Spirit, who expresses that revelation in Scripture.

Of course, the sheer volume of unsolvable mysteries of life can frustrate us and challenge our faith. It would be easy to throw up our hands and shout, "Vanity of vanities; everything is vanity!" Sometimes if answers are what we're after, futility is all we'll find. As humans who lack wisdom of our own, we often respond wrongly to God's mysterious ways.

If you could ask God to solve any mystery of life for you, what would it be? How has this particular mystery troubled you in the past?

_____
_____
_____
_____
_____

In his exploration of God's unexplainable ways, Solomon mentioned three mysteries that can be particularly troubling to us: unjust triumph, unfair consequences, and untimely pleasure.

The Mystery of Unjust Triumph (Ecclesiastes 8:10–13)

Solomon said that the evil deeds of men are often forgotten (8:10), resulting in a repetition of the same evils from generation to generation. We could easily point to the extreme examples of people like Hitler or Stalin, whose heinous atrocities are sometimes repeated to varying degrees in our own day. Yet their evil deeds have been forgotten by many or perhaps never even learned. On a smaller scale, most of us have been to the funeral of a person who was meanspirited and unloving in life, but whose memorial service and obituary portrayed him or her as a saintly parent or loving spouse. Why do people gloss over wickedness and sometimes even forget it?

To make matters worse, Solomon pointed out that wicked people often escape punishment from the legal system, only to live long, prosperous lives (8:11–12). Failing to punish sin in society leads to a downward spiral as criminals intensify and multiply their evil with less and less fear of

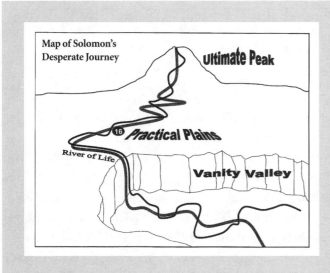

Map of Solomon's Desperate Journey

Ultimate Peak

16 *Practical* Plains

River of Life

Vanity Valley

ROAD MAP FOR THE JOURNEY #16

As he harvests more fruit of wisdom along his journey through the Practical Plain, Solomon tells us that although there's injustice in the world that results in futility (8:10–11, 14), God will still ultimately judge all according to His sovereign rule (8:12, 16–17). Therefore, we should submit to His perfect plan, hope for justice in the future, and enjoy God's simple gifts in the present (8:15).

being captured and brought to justice (8:11). Solomon was particularly frustrated because he knew that things should be better (8:12–13).

Why is punishment a vital operation of human government? If the government didn't punish people for their crimes, what would our society look like?

_____

_____

_____

_____

Imagine that a fellow Christian asked you to explain Proverbs 11:20–21, wondering, "If this is what God promises to do to the wicked, why do so many evil people go unpunished?" How would you respond to this mystery?

_____

_____

_____

_____

The Mystery of Unfair Consequences (Ecclesiastes 8:14)

Although God established human government to exercise justice (Romans 13:1–7), it's understandable that governments can become corrupt and fail to carry out their God-given duties. However, Solomon described another mystery in which it appears that God Himself allowed the righteous to suffer while the wicked prospered (Ecclesiastes 8:14). We see this all too often. Why are godly missionaries martyred while brutal murderers keep their freedom? Why does an irresponsible drunk driver walk away from an accident without a scratch while the Christian family he hit dies in the collision? Why must a hardworking, godly woman barely scrape enough money together to provide for her children's necessities while vicious drug dealers are able to live in luxury? For those of us who believe in an all-good and all-sovereign God, these questions raise issues that we're unable to fully understand. Phillip Yancey writes:

Consider the most common curse word in the English language: "God" followed by the word "damn." People say it not only in the face of great tragedy, but also when their cars won't start, when a favored sports team loses, when it rains on their picnic. That oath renders an instinctive judgment that life *ought* to be fair and that God should somehow "do a better job" of running his world.[4]

Have you ever questioned either God's goodness or His sovereignty after observing a good person suffer unjustly? Have you ever been the victim of what you considered injustice from the hand of God? How did these things make you feel?

_____

_____

_____

_____

The Mystery of Untimely Pleasure (Ecclesiastes 8:15)

A third mystery goes beyond the crook who escapes punishment and the saint who is targeted for calamity. In Ecclesiastes 8:15, Solomon described his response to the mysterious injustice and unfairness of the world:

> So I commended pleasure, for there is nothing good for a man under the sun except to eat and to drink and to be merry, and this will stand by him in his toils throughout the days of his life which God has given him under the sun.

In reaction to the mysteries of injustice, Solomon didn't encourage us to indulge in a carnal, hedonistic lifestyle; rather, he advised us to enjoy life and to trust God even in the face of unsolved mysteries. Such a response of joy and contentment in the midst of raw futility is itself the greatest mystery of them all. The "natural" response would be to become resentful, pessimistic, and increasingly wicked in reaction to unjust triumphs and unfair consequences.

Can you think of people who endured extreme injustice or the unfairness of life with patience and contentment? What effect did these people have on you?

_____

_____

_____

_____

Ways to Handle Life's Mysteries

We hate to be out of control. We want to feel that we're on top of life—or at least that we're not being dragged underneath it. We want mysteries to be solved and all the details of life to make sense. However, in order to cope with the distressing and disturbing mysteries that engulf us, we must let go of our hopeless quest for answers.

The perspective granted by God does not solve the mysteries of life, but it gives us confidence that God is still good and sovereign, that He has His own answers and purposes. The proper perspective on mysteries allows us to place our trust and hope in God, regardless of whether or not He reveals the mysteries to us.

Three final reminders will help round out Solomon's counsel for dealing with life's troubling enigmas. Remember, however, that even wise Solomon could not explain the mysteries of life; in fact, there may not be any answers we humans could even comprehend.

We must admit that we are only human. God is God, and we are not. It's a simple—almost cliché—truth, but one that humans have been forgetting ever since the temptation by Satan in the Garden of Eden (Genesis 3:5). There are just some things we can't discover and could never comprehend no matter how much information God poured into our comparatively tiny minds.

We must admit that we don't understand why, and we may never learn why while on this earth. When relating to people who are hurting, who are questioning God, or who are struggling with injustice and unfair consequences in life, we must resist trying to bandage them up with a quote, a quip, or a proof-text like Romans 8:28. Though these responses may be true, we often toss them out as answers when the reality is that sometimes there are no answers we could understand. We must become comfortable with acknowledging without shame or guilt our own ignorance of the mysteries of life. Jerry Bridges writes:

We are unwilling to live without rational reasons for what is happening to us or those we love. We are almost insatiable in our quest for the "why" of the adversity that has come upon us. But this is a futile as well as an untrusting task. God's ways, being the ways of infinite wisdom, simply cannot be comprehended by our finite minds.[5]

We must admit that there are some things we cannot change no matter how hard we try. Because we're not God, we can't always be Mr. or Ms. Fix-it. This is especially important for men to remember, for often their first reaction when confronted with a problem is to try to change things—to solve the problem and repair the damage.[6] But some things just can't be fixed. Only God can change them; only He can solve the mysteries of life in His own time and according to His own plan. In the meantime we must choose to fear Him, to enjoy His good gifts amid the mysteries of injustice and evil.

Revisit the answer you gave to the fellow Christian regarding Proverbs 11:20–21 on page 166. Having completed this lesson, would you change your answer?

_____

_____

_____

_____

In advising believers who are struggling with the tough questions of God's goodness and sovereignty, how would you communicate the importance of allowing God's mysterious will to remain a mystery?

_____

_____

_____

_____

_____

_____

All of us struggle with unsolved mysteries of life from time to time. The suffering of the righteous, the triumph of the wicked, the indiscriminate catastrophes of nature, and other unavoidable calamities of life often appear as sure signs that either God has completely lost control of the universe or He just doesn't care. But there's a better response to these mysteries than doubt and despair. By embracing God's goodness and sovereignty and by living with an attitude of contentment with the simple gifts in life, you'll struggle less with unexplained mysteries. Instead, you'll *become* an unexplained mystery to others.

17 Have a Blast While You Last!
[ECCLESIASTES 9:1–10]

From the very beginning of his journey, Solomon blasted away at the bedrock of man-made philosophies of life. He reminded materialists that possessions can't satisfy. He showed hedonists that pleasure is fleeting. He demonstrated to humanists that people can never be in control of their destinies. And to fatalists he warned that people will be held accountable for their evil deeds. In short, Solomon argued that man-made philosophies fail to provide meaning and fulfillment.[1]

Match the human philosophies on the left with their "bumper-sticker" mottos:

Philosophy	Motto
_____ 1. Materialism	a. "If it feels good, do it!"
_____ 2. Hedonism	b. "Life is a terminal disease"
_____ 3. Humanism	c. "He who dies with the most toys wins"
_____ 4. Fatalism	d. "Fulfill your human potential!"

Answers: 1-c; 2-a; 3-d; 4-b.

Examine your own lifestyle for a moment. Are any of the above philosophies guiding your decisions? Which ones?

_____

_____

_____

Solomon hammered away at all these philosophical foundations before building a balanced philosophy of life in Ecclesiastes 10–12. Chapter 9 is the final section in which he continues to take a wrecking ball to human wisdom, replacing the ideas he refutes with better ways of living.

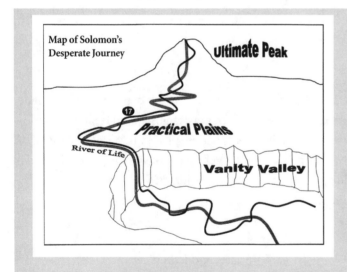

ROAD MAP FOR THE JOURNEY
#17

Halfway across the Practical Plain, Solomon tells us that because we're sinful (9:3) and the ultimate fate set by God for all people is death (9:1–6), we ought to enjoy God's gifts of food, work, clothing, family, and even luxuries during the few days we have in this world (9:7–10).

AN ALTERNATE PHILOSOPHY OF LIFE THAT WORKS

In the opening words of Ecclesiastes 9:1, Solomon reminded us that he had plumbed the depths of life's under-the-sun philosophies and found that none of them satisfied. However, during his search he unearthed the building blocks of a philosophy that *does* bring contentment. What is that philosophy? In Ecclesiastes 9:1–6, Solomon filled us in on four biblical perspectives.

Read Ecclesiastes 9:1–6.

The Sovereign Hand of God (Ecclesiastes 9:1)

In the second half of Ecclesiastes 9:1, Solomon asserted that nobody can escape God's sovereign hand. There's nothing out of His control or up for grabs. God is God, and we are not. Though God has a plan that we cannot alter, ours is not a blind, pointless fate. The universe is not ruled by a spiteful, malicious pantheon of reckless gods and goddesses, nor is it passively guided by a mindless energy force that has no love or concern for creation. The universe and all things in it are directed by the living, loving God, whose goodness is as infinite as His power.

If we don't fear and trust God, His sovereignty can be frightening and produce anxiety as we wonder what will come next and we fret over not having full control over our lives. But if we trust that whatever comes is under His control and that it will end in greater good for those who are His children, we can maintain a steady endurance in the midst of trials. Author Jerry Bridges writes:

Confidence in the sovereignty of God in all that affects us is crucial to our trusting Him. *If there is a single event in all of the universe that can occur outside of God's sovereign control then we cannot trust Him.* His love may be infinite, but if His power is limited and His purpose can be thwarted, we cannot trust Him.[2]

In the following sets of passages, what things are said to be under God's sovereign hand?

Proverbs 16:9; 19:21_____

Isaiah 40:23–24; Daniel 4:17_____

Jeremiah 10:13; Matthew 10:29_____

Isaiah 45:7; Lamentations 3:38_____

Job 2:3–7; Psalm 106:15_____

Is there anything in your life that lies outside of the above list? Is there anything for which you cannot trust God?

_____

_____

_____

_____

How does an awareness of God's sovereignty defeat the following man-made philosophies?

Humanism: "I am master of my own destiny." (Hint: Proverbs 19:21)

_____

_____

_____

_____

Fatalism: "Everything is determined by irrational cause and effect." (Hint: Ephesians 1:11)

_____

_____

_____

_____

The Absolute Certainty of Death (Ecclesiastes 9:2–3)

All but the severely despondent and depressed possess an innate desire to escape the fate of death. Solomon knew this well and reminded us of our own mortality.

Since the first sin of Adam and Eve, death has become an inescapable fact of human life (Genesis 2:16–17; 3:1–19; Romans 5:12). It makes no difference whether we are righteous or wicked, saintly or sinful. Deterioration of our physical bodies and ultimately physical death devour all people. Coming to grips with this fact can help us straighten out our priorities and live wisely with the time God has given us.

How does having an awareness of our own mortality and not knowing the appointed time of our death defeat the following man-made philosophies?

Materialism: "Money and possessions satisfy, so get all you can." (Hint: Luke 12:15–20)

_____
_____
_____
_____

Hedonism: "If it feels good, do it! You only live once!" (Hint: 2 Corinthians 5:8–10)

_____
_____
_____
_____

The Evil and Insanity of the Human Heart (Ephesians 9:3)

Like the dimming of twilight from evening to night, evil and insanity often blur together indistinguishably. It's tempting for people to see extreme expressions of evil, such as the Nazi holocaust or the terrorist attacks on the World Trade Center, and conclude that the perpetrators were insane. Most people are reluctant to admit that the same potential for evil deeds we see in those extreme instances lurks dormant in each of us. We'd much rather believe we're okay and they're crazy. But we need to remember the prophet Jeremiah's words about the unredeemed heart: "The heart is more deceitful than all else and is desperately sick; who can understand it?" (Jeremiah 17:9).

The fact is that each of us is born with a depraved heart and mind that can deteriorate toward uncontrollable evil if not for the restraining grace of God (Genesis 6:5; Romans 3:9–12). Those who have placed their faith in Jesus Christ have received a new heart (Ezekiel 36:26; John 3:5–6). However, we're still in the process of spiritual growth; we have hardly arrived (Colossians 3:10). As a result, each one of us is still susceptible to wickedness—sins that not only contradict God's principles but also put our lives, families, and jobs in jeopardy.

Are you dabbling in "minor" sins that, when viewed objectively, are damaging to relationships and potentially self-destructive? If so, take this moment of objectivity to present these to the Lord in confession and repentance.

_____

_____

_____

_____

Genuine Hope for the Living (Ecclesiastes 9:4–6)

The final realization that combats worldly philosophy is the genuine hope and joy we have in life in the midst of an awareness of God's sovereignty, our own mortality, and the evil of our hearts. God hasn't left us wallowing in the misery of sin and mortality. By His common grace He has provided gifts for all to enjoy, and by His special grace He has given believers spiritual gifts and the assurance of a destiny that transcends all earthly pleasures and pains.

To the extreme fatalist who might say that life is so pointless and the pain so disturbing that we're better off dead, Solomon responded with an old proverb: "A live dog is better than a dead lion" (9:4). Solomon said that we're better off struggling among the living than laid to rest with the dead. Why? Because the living have hope. They can look forward to enjoying things on the earth, but the dead have no such hope. Those who have passed on can no longer share in the joys of earthly pleasures.

How to Live Well 365 Days a Year

Having destroyed the foundations that support man-made philosophies sheltering those living under the sun, Solomon next gave an answer to the lingering question, how should we then live? Brace yourself—his answer may surprise some of the more "pious" among us.

Solomon began by calling his listeners to *do* something (Ecclesiastes 9:7). Go! Live life! Be active, not passive. We can summarize this approach to life: Have a blast while you last! If anybody has rea-

WINDOWS TO THE ANCIENT WORLD

Man's Best Friend?

The description "man's best friend" often conjures images of childhood pets, adorable puppies, or faithful guardians that make us feel secure. Names like Benji, Lassie, and even Snoopy may come to mind.

But this fond affection for the canine companion wasn't appreciated throughout history. In many ancient Near Eastern cultures, most breeds of dogs were regarded as unclean, useless, despicable creatures, perhaps not much better than a rat in our own culture.[3] The Bible refers to dogs as homeless scavengers (Psalm 59:6) that will eat everything from a corpse to their own vomit (1 Kings 14:11; Proverbs 26:11).

In contrast, the lion was regarded as "king of the jungle," as he is in much popular imagery today (2 Samuel 17:10). Thus, the contrast between the lion and the dog in Ecclesiastes 9:4 is striking. Commentator R. N. Whybray writes, "[The writer] is saying, then, that life, however wretched, is preferable to (better than) death."[4]

Read Ecclesiastes 9:7–10.

son to find joy in the good things God has given us under the sun—both physical and spiritual—it's the believer. How do we do this? The following four principles are God's counsel on how to experience a joyful life during your relatively few days on earth.

Live Happily Wherever You Are
(Ecclesiastes 9:7)

This is definitely uncommon advice in some Christian groups that try to maintain a narrow view, not only in their theology and morality (which is good), but even in their view of the blessings God has given them (which is sad). God approves of the enjoyment we receive from His simple material blessings of food and drink, for He graciously gave us the ability to enjoy the fruits of our labor (Ecclesiastes 2:24–25; 3:12–13; 5:18–19). The Lord is pleased when we find pleasure in His physical blessings and enjoy freedom from guilt as we partake of His benefits.

This is true in a spiritual sense too, for we know from the New Testament that believers stand approved before God based not on our own merit but on the merit of Christ (Ephesians 2:8–9). In this sense, we are called to richly and wisely enjoy freedom in the grace of Christ; we're no longer shamed by sin or bound by the rules and regulations of the Law (Galatians 5:1).

Walk in Purity and in the Power of the Spirit (Ecclesiastes 9:8)

We could interpret this verse in a physical sense as referring to the enjoyment of material blessings (having clean clothes and refreshing fragrances), rather than as presenting ourselves as super-righteous because we live a more spiritual life of humble means (Matthew 6:16–17). But in the spiritual realm, especially for us living in the New Testament age, white clothes symbolize moral purity and spiritual righteousness (Isaiah 1:18; Revelation 3:4–5; 7:9–14), and oil represents the ministry of the Holy Spirit (Isaiah 61:1; Acts 10:38). In today's words, Solomon encourages us to not live as ascetic prudes or as extreme hedonists, but to live by the wise guidance of the Holy Spirit in both the physical and spiritual realms. When we live a balanced life in this way, our contentment and joy will be contagious.

Enjoy Your Spouse (Ecclesiastes 9:9)

The third principle Solomon shared concerns the enjoyment of the joys and pleasures of marriage. The comforts, delights, and passions of a healthy marital relationship are to be expressed and relished by both the husband and the wife. After all, God has sanctioned marriage as an honorable relationship, and He considers the marriage bed to be undefiled (Genesis 2:24–25; Matthew 19:4–6; Hebrews 13:4). It's also important to note that marriage is intended to symbolize our spiritual relationship with Christ (Ephesians 5:22–33).

Even if our marriages disappoint us and we fail to enjoy the passion described by Solomon in Ecclesiastes 9:9, God loves and cherishes us above all things, and our relationship with Him through His Son is irrevocable. We can enjoy its spiritual benefits all the days of our fleeting life with the knowledge of a better life to come.

Throw Yourself Fully into . . . Whatever (Ecclesiastes 9:10)

Finally, Solomon instructed us to do whatever we do in this life with vim and vigor. Don't wait until you retire to start enjoying life. How do you know you'll make it that long? If you were to die today, would your family be left with memories or just material possessions?

We need to be active in pursuing the good gifts God has given us. To neglect His gifts or to pick at them delicately may show a lack of appreciation to the Giver. As we partake of God's blessings, we must also remember to do all things to the glory of God and in awe of Him (1 Corinthians 10:31; Colossians 3:17, 23). Wise living balances an enjoyment of the gifts with a love for the Giver, never forgetting that "from Him and through Him and to Him are all things" (Romans 11:36).

In the following chart, evaluate your personal application of the four responses to life by circling the appropriate answer, with 1 being the lowest and 5 being the highest.

	Never		Sometimes	Always	
I live joyfully wherever I am.	1	2	3	4	5
I walk in wisdom and purity by the Spirit.	1	2	3	4	5
I enjoy life with my spouse.	1	2	3	4	5
I embrace God's gifts to the fullest.	1	2	3	4	5

Based on your ratings, circle the response that needs the most work.

What specific thing can you do *today* to begin applying at least one of these four principles?

_____

_____

_____

_____

Near the end of his demolition project, Solomon leveled the false foundations of man-made philosophies such as materialism, hedonism, humanism, and fatalism. Like a wrecking ball smashing a condemned building, Solomon stated the inescapable reality of life: God is in control of all things. We may resist Solomon's conclusion and gasp at the go-for-broke attitude toward life proposed in Ecclesiastes 9:7–10, but we are hard pressed to offer a better plan, especially in light of the certainty of death and our tendency toward evil. Which philosophy of life will you choose?

18 An Objective View of the Rat Race
[ECCLESIASTES 9:11–18]

Webster's defines it as "strenuous, wearisome, and . . . competitive activity or rush,"[1] and it has often been summed up in three words: *hurry, worry,* and *bury.* It replaces living with survival, regards relaxation as a waste of time, and considers leisure activities as luxuries. It's the rat race—speeding along the ragged edge of reality at full throttle, trying desperately to catch the horizon before the sunset of life.

In the fury of the chase, Ecclesiastes 9:11–18 invites us to pull over to the side of the road and step back for an honest, objective look at the rat race that captivates so many of us. These few verses provide us with divine counsel on how we can live with a more balanced perspective and why the race can never be won.

VARIOUS WAYS TO VIEW LIFE

Faced with living on the ragged edge, people often construct systems of coping with the chaos of life. Let's focus on four of the most popular ways people handle life from a human perspective. These aren't philosophical approaches like humanism, nihilism, or materialism, but rather practical approaches to life that people often adopt without thinking. The problem with each of these is that they cause us to be self-centered. They turn our attention to our own strengths, weaknesses, knowledge, and power rather than God's.

Optimism. Those who view life optimistically look at it through rose-colored glasses. They have big dreams and expectations that often ignore or downplay the sharp edges of life under the sun. *Optimists lack reality.*

Pessimism. Contrary to optimists, pessimists view life as gloomy and humorless. Convinced that if something bad can happen it will, they often scowl, complain, and scoff at any attempt to turn things around. *Pessimists lack joy.*

Suspicion. Suspicious people distrust everyone, even God. They think that everyone is out to get them and that the world is full of cheaters, liars, crooks, and perverts. Such people are often lonely, alienate others, and have difficulty accepting an act of grace from either God or people. *Suspicious people lack trust.*

Fatalism. As we learned in the last chapter, fatalists often resign themselves to life's circumstances in order to accept their lot in life. They feel that since all events are fixed by impersonal forces beyond man's control, their own existence is pointless and futile. *Fatalists lack hope.*

Why do people feel the need to approach life through the lens of optimism, pessimism, suspicion, or fatalism? Because life can be harsh, unjust, treacherous, and out of control—and in the end we die! How else will people cope with life when each day nudges them closer to falling over the ragged edge (Ecclesiastes 9:2)? In the midst of these approaches, God's realistic view of life crashes in, toppling all these unbalanced extremes like a bowling ball smashing a set of pins. In contrast to these views, God exhorts us to live with a perspective characterized by reality, joy, trust, and hope (9:7–10).

But if we take Ecclesiastes 9:10 seriously and do whatever our hand finds to do with all our might, doesn't that mean we should put the pedal to the metal and *live it up?* We could draw this conclusion if we aren't careful. This is why Solomon switched on the warning lights in Ecclesiastes 9:11–18, offering reality in the place of fantasy, gloom, paranoia, and passivity. It's the balance needed to save us from the rat race of the ragged edge.

Some Under-the-Sun Counsel

Our study of Solomon's desperate journey from futility toward a wise outlook from God's perspective has shown us that he believed in a realistic appraisal of life. Optimism, pessimism, suspicion, and

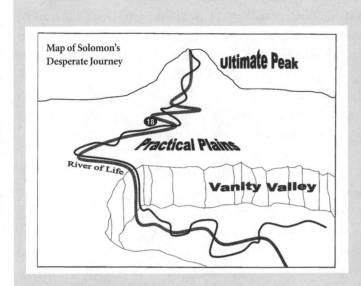

Map of Solomon's Desperate Journey

Ultimate Peak

18

Practical Plains

River of Life

Vanity Valley

ROAD MAP FOR THE JOURNEY #18

At this point in his journey across the Practical Plain, Solomon reminds us of his central thesis—God is God, and we are not—by asserting that God's sovereign plan supersedes all our labor, gifts, and abilities (9:11, 18). Because we can't know His purposes (9:11–12), we ought to live in wisdom and quiet fear of God, regardless of what the outcome may be in this world (9:13–18).

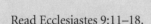

Read Ecclesiastes 9:11–18.

fatalism—and, indeed, all other human perspectives and philosophies—fail to present life as it actually is. At the close of Ecclesiastes 9, Solomon warned his readers against an unending cycle of competing harder, running faster, getting up earlier, neglecting family and friends, and making our jobs a top priority.

What characteristics or personality traits does society tell us are necessary in order to be successful at winning the rat race? Create a profile of the perfect "rat."

_____

_____

_____

_____

_____

The Rat Race as It's Being Run (Ecclesiastes 9:11–12)

We try all sorts of things to win the race, but Ecclesiastes 9:11 denies the right to build success by being fast, strong, wise, discerning, or capable. In short, life teaches us that we cannot attain meaning and joy by human effort or ingenuity. Instead, all people, no matter who they are or what they do, are subject to the all-powerful providence of God, to whom we must ultimately bow.

If you're in the rat race speeding down the highway at full throttle, remember that God's omnipotent hand still rules. He's like a traffic cop forcing us to slow down when we're headed for a spiritual wreck. The best example of this is found in the next verse.

The End of Every Life (Ecclesiastes 9:12)

Solomon likened the intervention of God's hand in a person's life to fish caught in a net or birds in a snare—a negative event that falls upon people suddenly. This could be death or some other life-altering occurrence that stops people in their tracks (Ecclesiastes 9:12). Death is a reality, and sudden cataclysmic change is real. We can't escape such events no matter how mighty, clever, or aggressive we are. It does us no good to deny our own mortality or to challenge God's sovereignty. We are only deceiving ourselves if we pretend to be immune to tragedy.

Has God ever gotten your attention by unexpected or drastic means? How did He do it? How did it make you feel?

_____

_____

_____

_____

The Nature of Those in the Race (Ecclesiastes 9:13–16)

In the next four verses Solomon tells a story that, though it may draw on real-life occurrences (2 Samuel 20), is probably a parable illustrating a general truth about real life.[2] Through this tale Solomon pointed out that the insignificant "poor wise man," who single-handedly saved a tiny city from destruction, was ultimately overlooked and forgotten. In fact, much of the time the wise words of the "insignificant" or "outcast" are ignored entirely (Ecclesiastes 9:16). If success were measured by fame—or at least by getting the kudos we deserve for a job well done—then wisdom in this story utterly failed to do the job.

Put yourself in the place of the poor wise man. Imagine that you discovered something that benefited humanity and saved a lot of lives, but you received neither recognition nor compensation for your discovery. How would you feel about your accomplishment? About your God?

_____

_____

_____

_____

Some Above-the-Sun Wisdom

Based on the verses we have covered so far and the last few verses of this chapter, we find at least five principles to take to heart as we resist the temptation of getting caught up in the rat race. Remember, Solomon began by warning us that "the race is not to the swift and the battle is not to the warrior" and that even the wise who actually do accomplish things of lasting significance are forgotten in the rampage of the race. Each of these five principles will help us face life realistically and handle it wisely as we reconsider our participation in the relentless drive for success.

Human ability cannot guarantee genuine success (Ecclesiastes 9:11, 15)

The common advice of the competitive world includes the following statements: "Keep your Christianity private." "Keep God out of the business world and your faith at home and in the church—they will only slow you down." "The law of the jungle and the Law of Christ simply don't mix." But this counsel is false! God is God, and we are not. Because God is in control, success ultimately comes from His hand, not ours.

Evaluate your profile of the perfect "rat" on page 183 against the wisdom of Ecclesiastes 9:11. How do they compare?

_____

_____

_____

Strength is more impressive, yet less effective, than wisdom (Ecclesiastes 9:16)

Remember that a poor wise man can deliver a city from vast military might—thus, wisdom can prevail over strength. However, people usually prefer power and might to wisdom or the counsel of God. How often do politicians or decision makers call on pastors and theologians to advise them of God's wisdom? Rarely. To bring it closer to home, how often do you turn to God's Word and the Spirit's wisdom to guide you in routine daily decisions regarding raising kids, workplace tasks, relationships, or personal finances? Godly wisdom is often put down or ignored . . . always to our own harm.

In what ways do you think wisdom is more effective than power and wealth at handling the inevitable pressures of life?

_____

_____

_____

_____

In your opinion, why is godly wisdom sometimes one of the last places people turn when dealing with decisions and challenges?

_____

_____

_____

_____

Wise counsel is never popular, rarely obeyed, and seldom remembered (Ecclesiastes 9:16)

Yes, wisdom is ultimately better than power, but Solomon didn't paint a picture of life as it ought to be. He scratched out a realistic sketch of the way things really are. Be wise, but remember that in the world's eyes wise living won't receive the lauds and honor it deserves. Seek God's will and walk by the Spirit in the home and the workplace, but don't expect to be patted on the back.

Though we may never receive honor on earth for doing the right thing, what biblical promises can we cling to, based on the following passages?

Jeremiah 17:7–8, 10 _____

_____

_____

_____

Matthew 6:6 _____

_____

_____

_____

James 1:12 _____

_____

_____

_____

Think of someone you know who exemplifies godly wisdom. How can you personally honor that person in some way today?

_____

_____

_____

_____

Human rulers will always outshout wise counselors, and fools prefer the former (Ecclesiastes 9:17)

Our world is filled with propaganda, flashy advertising, and advice motivated by money and greed. In politics, mudslinging is often the norm, and the one with the blackest dirt and farthest throw will often end up on top. The quiet, reasonable, wise person who gently dispenses godly counsel is often trampled underfoot because the rat race isn't won that way. You see, people often prefer the loudest authority or the latest self-help fad to the wise counselor who calmly speaks the unpopular truth.

Are you struggling with ethics in your workplace, fighting against immorality in your relationships, or wrestling with marital or family conflict at home? If so, where are you turning for advice and counsel for these things?

_____

_____

_____

_____

What do the following passages suggest regarding our source of life-changing truth and godly counsel?

Psalm 1:1–2 _____

_____

_____

_____

Proverbs 13:10 _____

_____

_____

_____

2 Timothy 3:16–17 _____

_____

_____

_____

2 Timothy 4:2–5 _____

_____

_____

_____

Constructive words of wisdom are no match for destructive weapons of war (Ecclesiastes 9:18)

As Solomon put it, "Wisdom is better than weapons of war, but one sinner destroys much good" (Ecclesiastes 9:18). A foolish, reckless lifestyle that fails to heed God's warning signs concerning the rat race can ruin many lives. The pursuit of success can drag us down and lead us away from God's Word and Spirit—our unerring guides for life. It can cause us to ignore godly counselors who seek to reveal to us His wisdom. Only by stepping out of the rat race of life will we begin to experience real success and satisfaction on God's terms, not ours. We do this by changing our attitudes toward achieving the futile goal and altering our actions in a way that places emphasis on the important things in life rather than vain pursuits.

Do you feel like you're on the proverbial treadmill, jogging frantically but getting nowhere, running at top speed but stuck in one place? *That's the rat race.* Or do you feel like you're searching for just the thing that will make you happy, but with every turn you get even more lost in the frustrating maze of real life? *That's the rat race.* Solomon invited us to step out of the race and take an objective view, to conclude with him that it's better to listen to God's quiet voice of wise counsel than to get caught up in the endless and fruitless pursuit of success based on the world's rules for winning an unwinnable game. Will you accept his invitation?

19 Be Sensible!
[ECCLESIASTES 10:1–11]

Toward the end of his search for meaning in the seemingly endless halls of human philosophy, Solomon realized that there he could find nothing but futility—nothing that truly satisfied. Having gleaned a handful of practical principles from a realistic examination of everyday life under the sun, Solomon began to calmly and logically build the case that "the fear of the LORD is the beginning of wisdom" (Proverbs 9:10). He would ultimately conclude that every person must "fear God and keep His commandments" (Ecclesiastes 12:13), regardless of the unexpected punches life sometimes throws.

In Ecclesiastes 10, Solomon again called on his readers to look "above the sun" and seek wisdom rather than folly. He described this lifestyle in a series of loosely connected proverbs, but they can all be summed up in one exhortation: be sensible!

A CONTRAST: WISDOM AND FOLLY

As a final warning concerning life under the sun, Ecclesiastes 10 makes a transition into the two concluding chapters of the book. Here, Solomon associated folly with the futility of the world under the sun and wisdom with the proper above-the-sun perspective on earthly life.

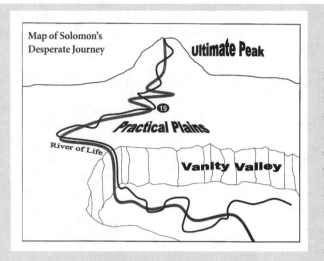

Map of Solomon's Desperate Journey

ultimate Peak

Practical Plains

River of Life

Vanity Valley

ROAD MAP FOR THE JOURNEY
#19

At this point in his desperate journey, Solomon's path is beginning its steady climb from the Practical Plain to the Ultimate Peak, from which he will soon be able to look back on life and make his final conclusions. In this transition to the final ascent, Solomon illustrates living in the fear of God by contrasting wisdom with folly (10:1–3) and encouraging sensible, above-the-sun wisdom that considers and plans for the inevitable risks in life (10:8–11), regardless of the under-the-sun circumstances (10:4–7).

Advantages versus Disadvantages (Ecclesiastes 10:1–3)

This first set of proverbial contrasts between wisdom and folly deals primarily with the individual. Solomon began with a vivid statement illustrating a profound truth that many Christians need to be reminded of today: just as a few dead flies can ruin costly perfume, a little folly can cast a dark shadow over a life otherwise characterized by wisdom and honor (Ecclesiastes 10:1). We can all think of examples in which a person's lapse in good sense seriously damaged his or her reputation.

Make a list of a few people who look to you as an example. How would it affect them if your reputation were polluted by foolish or sinful choices?

_____

_____

_____

_____

_____

Be Sensible!

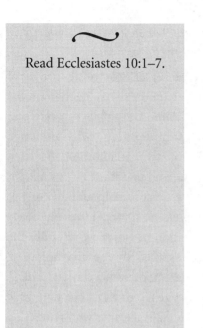

Read Ecclesiastes 10:1–7.

Living sensibly means weighing the consequences of our actions, considering the risks, always asking what the Lord's will is in a situation, and making right decisions moment by moment. Nothing is outside His concern or too small for dependence on the wisdom given by the Holy Spirit.

In the next verse (Ecclesiastes 10:2), we are told that a wise man directs his heart to the right rather than the left. Of course, this is neither a political statement nor a statement preferring right-handed over left-handed people. In the Bible, the right hand is a symbol for divine protection, power, and presence (Psalms 16:8; 110:5; 121:5–8; Colossians 3:1). This imagery tells us that a wise person will follow God's way, but the fool travels in the opposite direction. When people take a route leading away from the Lord's will, the result is always the same: they lack a sense of direction and demonstrate their foolishness to all (Ecclesiastes 10:3). Fools wander away from divine counsel because they fail to be sensible.

According to the following verses, how is a person's foolishness revealed to others?

Proverbs 12:23 _____

_____

_____

_____

Proverbs 18:2 _____

_____

_____

_____

GETTING TO THE ROOT

There are two related Greek adjectives translated "sensible" or "wise" in the New Testament, *phronimos* and *sōphrōn.* To be wise in the sense of these words is to be "thoughtful" and "prudent."[1] The wise and sensible person is the one who hears and obeys Christ's words (Matthew 7:24). The disciples are told to be "shrewd" *(phronimos)* as serpents, but innocent as doves (Matthew 10:16), and the same word is used in the parable of the ten virgins to describe those who were prepared for the bridegroom's coming (Matthew 25:1–13). Likewise, the leaders of the church and mature believers are to be "prudent" and "sensible" in their responsibilities (1 Timothy 3:2; Titus 1:8; 2:2, 5). As we can see from these passages, being wise, prudent, and sensible are not merely Old Testament commands but New Testament fruits of the life of faith.

Humility and Patience versus Popularity and Partiality (Ecclesiastes 10:4–7)

The second set of Solomon's proverbs focuses more on the social life than on the individual. Almost all of us can relate to the first example: living with patience under an impatient and hotheaded leader. Solomon advised that if the ruler's temper rises, a wise person maintains his or her own composure (10:4). This could apply to any situation in which we're under the authority of somebody else: an employer, a teacher, a parent, or even a church leader.

When we're faced with a hot-tempered person (especially a leader who's directing a foolish outburst toward us), it's easy to return insult for insult. However, what we really need to do is diffuse his or her offense with a patient spirit. Fools escalate conflict because they fail to be sensible.

What are the typical results of answering a hot-tempered person in a similar tone? How have you experienced this?

Be Sensible!

Read Proverbs 15:1; 15:18; and 25:15. According to these passages, what is the wisest way to deal with a hot-tempered person? Why do you think this is often difficult to do?

_____

_____

_____

_____

Another situation Solomon observed was incompetent people holding positions of authority and responsibility. He saw people who were unqualified to lead working in exalted places and those who should have been in leadership positions living like servants (Ecclesiastes 10:6–7). This is clearly a case of political inequality, and it's not something we find only in government. The politics of partiality and prejudice are everywhere! Solomon's words confront us with the fact that one's level of skill and discernment doesn't automatically guarantee a position of authority equal to his or her abilities. Instead, other factors—popularity, wealth, family ties, friendships—often win people roles that they are unqualified to fulfill.

How have you seen partiality exalt a fool while scorning a wise person? Have you experienced this personally? How did it make you feel?

_____

_____

_____

_____

Fools may demonstrate their lack of sensibility by promoting friends and family to positions of responsibility over those who are better qualified and more skilled. God calls wise people to base their decisions, not on emotional attachments or self-interest, but on wisdom and prudence—reflecting justice and equity.

How can playing favorites in your family, business, or personal relationships prove to be unwise? Who gets hurt?

_____

_____

_____

_____

If you think you've been unfair in your personal relationships, what can you do today to stop the inequity?

_____

_____

_____

_____

Read Ecclesiastes 10:8–11.

Inevitable Risks versus Inexcusable Stupidity
(Ecclesiastes 10:8–11)

In these verses, we find several similar situations that are united by a common theme: each seemingly neutral activity carries with it certain risks (Ecclesiastes 10:8–10). If you dig a pit, you run the risk of falling in. If you quarry stones, one may fall on your foot. Break through a wall, and you may be bitten by a snake. Chop wood with a dull ax, and you may chop yourself instead! These examples demonstrate that even the most mundane activities require wisdom, for there are risks involved in almost everything we do. Donald Glenn writes, "Solomon strung together four proverbs that set forth the potential dangers inherent in representative daily tasks . . . dangers which could only be averted by applying wisdom or prudence."[2] Fools fall victim to these avoidable injuries because they fail to be sensible.

Besides these obvious everyday activities, Solomon's words also apply to more profound matters of life. We must take into consideration the potential consequences of our actions as we plan our course. Wisdom quickly teaches us that fools who try to dig "pits" for others will end up getting hurt in the process. Fools who "break down walls" for their own advantage will end up being victimized themselves. We see examples of this during each political season, when desperate attempts to smear an opponent backfire and damage the attacker's reputation instead. In short, fools go through life using and abusing other people to their own detriment, yet the pain fools experience seldom leads to significant change in their lives.

Wisdom: Two Marvelous Advantages

From Ecclesiastes 10:10–11, we can extrapolate two advantages of wisdom. First, *wisdom prepares the way for success* (10:10). In a world that winks at folly and even rewards it by overlooking the wise for positions of prominence, we must constantly remind ourselves that fools may succeed for a season, but in the end their folly will be exposed and they will fail.

Second, *wisdom thinks ahead.* Unlike a snake charmer who fails to take the necessary precautions and then gets bitten, a wise person plans ahead, carefully considering the potential dangers (10:11). This approach affects not only how we go about accomplishing a task but also whether we even attempt it. Godly wisdom can steer our wills and actions in the proper direction.

Are there tasks you are currently trying to accomplish in your life that you jumped into without submitting to God's input? Select one or two and take a moment to consider whether you need to approach these tasks differently or not at all. Write your insights below.

_____

_____

_____

_____

Before making a final decision on this, be sure to work through the next section.

Gaining Wisdom According to Proverbs

How do we gain the wisdom that Solomon exhorted us to possess and practice? Where do we turn for the prudence and insight to set and achieve proper goals? According to James 1:5–6, we must ask God to give us that wisdom as a gift received through faith (1:6). However, this request is usually not answered through a sudden lightning bolt of wisdom striking our minds. In most cases, God uses various means to graciously teach us wisdom.

Because God is the source of wisdom, He gets all the glory. Though we respond to Him in obedi-

---

DIGGING DEEPER

Wisdom: From God or Us?

The theological problem of God's sovereignty and human responsibility is ancient and complicated, and we simply can't solve it here. However, the question of God's role and our own role in obtaining wisdom is one that we need to dig into a little deeper.

A basic biblical truth is that every good and perfect gift is from God (James 1:17), and this includes wisdom (James 3:17). Also, Christ is not only our righteousness and sanctification but also our "wisdom" (1 Corinthians 1:24, 30; Colossians 2:3). We receive all of these things from Him by grace through faith (Ephesians 2:8–10). Scripture also associates wisdom with the Holy Spirit, so that the Spirit is the personal agent by whom the gift of wisdom is lived out in the Christian life (Isaiah 11:2; Ephesians 1:17; Acts 6:3, 10).

The practical implication of this is that if we take credit for anything—even our wisdom and good works—we rob God of the glory, for He has illumined our minds, softened our hearts, and enabled our hands by His Spirit to exercise our wills in good works. On the other hand, if we sit back and wait for God to "zap" us with wisdom and good works, we're fooling ourselves. As difficult as it is to understand, God works through our own wills and efforts in order to accomplish His will in our lives (Philippians 2:12–13; Hebrews 13:20–21).

How do our own wills, responses, and choices harmonize with God's sovereign will and infinite knowledge? This profound mystery we may never understand, but we can still respond to this mystery by obeying Scripture's admonitions to do our part in seeking wisdom while always giving God the glory for what He accomplishes in, through, and sometimes in spite of us![3]

ence, His Spirit is the one who continually draws us, empowers us, and reveals the Father's heart to us (John 16:13–15). He teaches us this wisdom through various means, some of which are described in Proverbs 2:1–9, where David exhorted his readers to respond to God's work in faith and obedience.

According to Proverbs 2:1–9, how is God's gift of wisdom received?

_____

_____

_____

_____

If you feel your growth in wisdom is standing still, what part of Proverbs 2:1–9 applies to you most right now? What does your response need to be to grow in wisdom?

_____

_____

_____

_____

If you're growing in wisdom, how has God been working in your life to cause this growth? How can you specifically respond to God's revelation which equips you for wise living?

_____

_____

_____

_____

Are you sensible? Do you face the decisions and events of everyday life with prudence and wisdom, weighing the pros and cons and approaching all things with an above-the-sun perspective? It's not always easy, but it's well worth the effort!

While God will graciously grow us in wisdom if we ask in faith, the process He uses involves our own response to His Word. Solomon reminded us that God's wisdom will protect us and give us success. Are you ready to travel the road of sensibility?

20 A Fool's Portrait
[ECCLESIASTES 10:12–20]

When Scripture paints a life portrait, it doesn't remove the scars or blemishes or flatter its subjects with airbrushing or digital effects. Instead, what you see is what you get. There's something refreshing about the realism with which Scripture depicts the lives of those God uses to accomplish His will—but this realism also uncovers the truth about those who are constantly (but vainly) working at frustrating His plan. Ecclesiastes 10 is a good example of a realistic portrait of a fool. It's not a photograph of a particular person but a representation of general characteristics we encounter in life.

In the previous chapter, we saw that fools refuse to listen to rebuke and that their uncontrolled folly always makes its way into the open. While on the subject of the manifestation of folly, Solomon began adding colorful brush strokes to the pencil sketch set forth in Ecclesiastes 10:1–11. But the portrait that emerges by the end of chapter 10 is anything but delightful, especially for people who resemble its disturbing image. What begins as an almost comical sketch of the fool turns into a tragic and dangerous depiction. One thing is certain: being a fool is no laughing matter.

THE CHARACTER OF A FOOL

Let's first consider a couple of passages outside of Ecclesiastes from which Solomon seems to have drawn the colors used to paint his portrait of a fool. Among the many passages in Psalms and Proverbs exploding with colorful wisdom and practical advice, we find some dusty earth tones of the foolish.

GETTING TO THE ROOT

The Hebrew word often translated "fool" in Ecclesiastes is *sakhal,* from a verb root that means to be foolish in a "moral or spiritual sense."[1] In Psalms and Proverbs, the word used to describe the foolish is *nabal,* which means "the man who has no perception of ethical and religious claims."[2] Being a fool in the biblical sense doesn't necessarily mean somebody is stupid, uneducated, or ignorant, but that he or she lacks sense in spiritual and moral matters (Jeremiah 4:22; 5:21). As one dictionary puts it, "Men can be clever in mind, but at the same time be fools in spiritual matters."[3] We must not think this is a condition only for unbelievers, for Christians, too, can become foolish (Galatians 3:1, 3; Ephesians 5:17; Titus 3:9).

The Language in the Fool's Heart

Many images come to mind when we think of fools. We might imagine a mischievous prankster, a careless blunderer, or a lazy oaf who sits around all day. But Psalm 14:1 projects a different image of a fool: the person who believes there is no God to whom he or she is accountable (Psalm 14:1). Because this type of fool fails to live in light of the reality of God and His ultimate judgment of humankind, he or she routinely commits sins against God, offenses against other people, and sometimes even gross atrocities against humanity.

Read Psalm 14:1–3 and Romans 3:9–12. What does Paul's use of Psalm 14 suggest about the condition of all people apart from God?

_____

_____

_____

_____

A Fool's Portrait

The Bent of the Fool's Will

Although without God all human beings suffer from depravity and are fools, some manifest their foolishness to greater degrees than others. The book of Proverbs reveals at least four characteristics of the foolish. First, *fools traffic in deceit* (Proverbs 14:8). They habitually lie, mix truth with error, and sometimes can't even tell the difference themselves. Second, *fools mock sin* (Proverbs 14:9). They make light of wrongdoing, utter dirty jokes, and indulge in improper forms of entertainment. But whatever the means of expression, fools make it clear that they don't consider sin to be sinful. Third, *fools treat wickedness like it's a sport* (Proverbs 10:23; 15:21). They find great pleasure in committing sin and exhorting others to do the same (Romans 1:32). Finally, *fools rage against the Lord* (Proverbs 19:3). They sneer with malice and vindictiveness at God and His ways, often blaming Him for the mess they got into by their own unwise choices.

Obviously, fallen humans who are lost in sin and foolishness can't change their ways by themselves any more than a dead man can revive himself. Only God can revive the dead, and only He can transfer the fool from his realm of recklessness into the territory of responsibility. Foolishness is a deep problem of the heart, not simply surface attitudes or actions like the ones we all have from time to time. In realigning the fool's heart, the Holy Spirit must perform a complete overhaul.

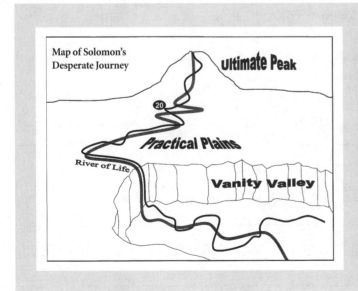

Map of Solomon's Desperate Journey

Ultimate Peak

Practical Plains

River of Life

Vanity Valley

ROAD MAP FOR THE JOURNEY #20

Solomon continues his climb in the foothills of the Ultimate Peak. From this vantage point, his perspective on the truth is coming into clearer focus. In the realm of wise living, this means that life apart from the fear of God is utter folly (10:12–20), as is life apart from an acknowledgment of God's sovereignty over our future (10:14).

Read Ecclesiastes 10:12–15.

The Actions of a Fool

We've seen what makes the fool tick: a sinful heart that has not yet been transformed by God's grace. This is not only the condition of an unbeliever whose heart is hardened to the things of God, but Christians, too, can become "dull of hearing," in need of God's transforming grace for their spiritual growth (Hebrews 5:11; Romans 12:2).

Now let's turn to Ecclesiastes 10:12–20 for an inspired painting of a fool's behavior. Here we'll see at least five ways fools manifest the internal folly of their hearts to everyone.

Their Harmful Verbosity
(Ecclesiastes 10:12–14)

In contrast to the speech of the wise, which brings them favor and honor, the speech of fools is self-destructive. Solomon noted that the undiscerning multiply words to their own harm (Ecclesiastes 5:3; 6:11). Their conversation is foolish from start to finish and can even border on madness.

Read Proverbs 4:23–24 and Matthew 15:18. According to these passages, what is the connection between our patterns of speech and our heart's condition?

_____

_____

_____

_____

In order to address sinful patterns in your speech, where does the change need to take place?

_____

_____

_____

_____

According to Ephesians 4:22–25, what are the effects of being renewed in the "spirit of your mind"?

_____

_____

_____

_____

Their Unpredictable Future (Ecclesiastes 10:14)

Fools are ignorant of the fact that "no man knows what will happen, and [no one] can tell him what will come after him" (10:14). Fools may make detailed plans for the future or live like there's no tomorrow. They may even miscalculate or fail to consider the damaging or disastrous effects their speech and actions could have on their lives and the lives of others. Their rebellious and reckless lifestyle may land them in the unemployment line, prison, a hospital room, or even the grave—and they could take a lot of people down with them.

Their Confusion and Stupidity (Ecclesiastes 10:15)

The often inefficient and unproductive lifestyle of fools causes them to become unable to follow directions. Solomon says they don't even know how to go to a city (10:15). Even if they have a destination in mind, they don't know the road to take to get there. The fool is pictured as wandering around in the wilderness, unwilling to seek the Lord for assistance in finding his way. In such a scenario the fool must be faulted for wandering from the right road in the first place.

Read Psalm 107:4–8. What was the condition of those wandering in the wilderness?

_____

_____

_____

_____

_____

What ultimately led to their rescue?

_____

_____

_____

_____

Their Destructive Leadership (Ecclesiastes 10:16–17)

Whenever fools are in positions of authority, the people they lead suffer. This stems from all the considerations we saw above—lack of control over their foolish speech, the inability to plan

Read Ecclesiastes 10:16–20.

ahead, and the lack of direction according to God's principles. In Ecclesiastes 10:16, Solomon wasn't describing a situation in which actual children were ruling, but a scene in which the political leaders are inexperienced, incompetent, and undisciplined like children. And unlike King Solomon, who knew he needed God to make him wise (1 Kings 3:7–9), foolish rulers reject God by their attitudes and actions.

A nation with such a ruler is in a sad state of affairs. So is a business with a foolish boss or a family with foolish parents. Throughout history Israel suffered under such leaders. Sometimes God even elevated fools to leadership as judgment against Israel's disobedience, as in 1 Samuel 8:10–22. In this case, the people refused to listen to the prophet of God and demanded a king like the other nations. They were given King Saul, who eventually turned against God.

In contrast, wise leaders are those who have not only been adequately trained for their positions but also possess the character and discernment necessary to faithfully carry out even the most mundane tasks in the fear of the Lord (Ecclesiastes 10:17). The people they lead are considered blessed, for they reap the many benefits of wise leadership.

In your own life, whom do you consider to be wise leaders? Which of their characteristics or actions have caused you to come to this conclusion?

_____

_____

_____

_____

Whom do you consider to be foolish leaders? Which of their characteristics or actions have caused you to come to this conclusion?

_____

_____

_____

_____

In your list, circle the characteristics you most need to develop in your own realms of influence. Make an X through those you need to eliminate. Pray that God would empower you to pursue these changes.

Their Procrastination and Poor Judgment (Ecclesiastes 10:18–19)

The final trait Solomon mentioned is that fools neglect their daily obligations because they are too distracted with merrymaking and fun. This is certainly a timely observation for our high-paced and entertainment-oriented culture. Because fools party, waste time, and seek fulfillment from things money can buy, they lead careless, undisciplined lives that fail to fulfill their essential responsibilities. These responsibilities may include maintenance of home, car, or other belongings. But more often than not, the fool neglects the more important but less obvious parts of his or her life: marriage, children, work, health, and spiritual development.

Which areas of your life are you letting "sag" by neglecting important things?

_____

_____

_____

_____

What does procrastination reveal about our true feelings? What does it reveal about our faith?

_____

_____

_____

_____

A Warning: Criticism and Confidentiality

Adding a finishing touch to his portrait of a fool, Solomon framed the image with a warning (Ecclesiastes 10:20). The idea behind this warning is that if you live under (or even with) a foolish leader, it's wise to keep your mouth shut, even in private. As we've studied in this lesson, we can't change a fool's heart on our own. Instead of trying to do so—either by words or actions—we need to pray that God would change the heart of the leader in His own time and by His own means. If all you do is criticize, you will be involved in foolish talk that sets you on a precarious path of dissatisfaction, joyless living, and frustration. Plus, as Solomon's counsel suggests, it's quite likely your words will eventually come into the open. If you think it's hard enough to deal with or live with a fool, wait until the fool finds out you've been talking about him or her!

Can you share a personal experience of a time when complaining or gossiping about others caused your attitude toward a boss or other leader to deteriorate? If so, how did it change the person you or others were complaining about? How did it change those who were complaining?

_____

_____

_____

_____

A Few Tips on Dealing with a Fool

As we pray that God would work to transform a person's heart, what should our role be when we interact with a fool? Surely we aren't supposed to sit back and let them destroy themselves or empower them to act on their foolishness without restraint. Whether he or she is an employer, minister, family member, or friend, Scripture specifies at least three steps we can take in handling a fool with integrity.

1. *If there is continued folly, isolation may be the most effective treatment.* Proverbs 14:7 says, "Leave the presence of a fool, or you will not discern words of knowledge." There's a point at which unlimited companionship with a fool will actually "fool-ize" the wise. Paul said in 1 Corinthians 15:33, "Bad company corrupts good morals." Some may think isolation is a terribly harsh response, particularly in marriage. After all, why not continue to try to reason with a fool and give him or her a chance to listen and change? Yes, honorable treatment is appropriate—for as long as one can remain sane and safe. But there's a limit. The fool's problem lies at a deeper level than words of reason can affect. Proverbs 23:9 even says, "Do not speak in the hearing of a fool, for he will despise the wisdom of your words."

In the case of marriage, the biblical prescription is for wives to win their husbands through their godly behavior (1 Peter 3:1–6) and for husbands to live with their wives in an understanding way (1 Peter 3:7). However, the extremes of life can sometimes make these general principles seem impossible to uphold, and people can feel like failures. When faced with an extremely unwise and ungodly spouse as described in this chapter, sometimes separation may be necessary. We're not talking about divorce, but a time when separation is needed for survival and the ultimate health of the marriage. To give a foolish husband or wife all the benefits of home and all the joys of happiness regardless of the godless lifestyle he or she is living doesn't make practical sense, to say nothing of biblical sense. In such cases, of course, we should seek godly counsel before we take action, and the separation should not be viewed as the first step toward divorce but as the first step toward healing and reconciliation.

The removal of important people from a fool's life may be the shocking experience needed for him or her to listen to God's voice and finally realize the consequences of reckless attitudes and actions. If God hasn't used your presence in a fool's life to get through to him or her, perhaps He wants to use your absence instead.

2. *If there is true repentance and brokenness, restoration is appropriate.* The process of restoration should begin when there's solid evidence that a fool has begun to wise up. God does not rush to rescue fools who are still steeped in rebellion (Psalm 107:10–12, 39–40); rather, He may allow them to experience the most extreme results of their disobedience (Psalm 107:17–18). Through this severe treatment God can get their attention and promote repentance, at which time He delivers and heals

them (Psalm 107:1–3, 13–14, 19–20). We are to follow the same example of restoring a fool to fellowship when there is genuine repentance (2 Corinthians 2:6–8). Dr. James Dobson wisely writes, "Our purpose must never be to hurt or punish the other person, even when retribution is deserved by him or her."[4]

3. *When there is restoration from folly, let there be proclamation.* This final point describes what we see as the result of Israel's restoration after repentance in Psalm 107:21–22. Today, churches need to hear the testimony of former fools, who at one time lived reckless and rebellious lifestyles but have been transformed by Jesus Christ, "the wisdom of God" (1 Corinthians 1:24).

Of the three steps described above, which do you think is the most difficult? Why?

_____

_____

_____

_____

Is there a relationship in your life right now to which you may need to apply God's counsel of isolation, restoration, or proclamation? What specific steps do you need to take to apply it?

_____

_____

_____

_____

Fools say in their hearts, "There is no God." Whether or not they are literal atheists, their lifestyles suggest they don't take seriously the reality of God's judgment or discipline. Sometimes they realize this far too late in life, after they've squandered the time and resources—and the people—God has given them. If we're "playing the fool," we need to turn from our foolish ways and ask God for wisdom in our own lives. And if we're close to fools who disregard God, we need to pray for them earnestly and take the necessary steps, allowing God to lead them to repentance.

21 Be Bullish!

[ECCLESIASTES 11:1–6]

Some people are stuck in a rut. They drive their vehicles down the straight, paved road of life, never changing lanes or switching gears. The air-conditioned ride in their luxury sedan is comfortable and predictable. They follow the main road and avoid the windy, unknown scenic routes because they're just "too risky." Gripping the steering wheel of certainty and security, they set their cruise control, put the CD player on Repeat, and stay in the center lane.

Occasionally, they catch a glimpse of different kinds of drivers, those who leave the main road to explore the countryside, risking a flat tire, a dent on the hood, or a nick in the windshield for a more ambitious route.

Interestingly, the older we get, the more cautious we become on our journey through life. With deliberate and careful concern, we study before we step, we ponder before we leap, and we hesitate before we move into the open. Under the guise of ripened wisdom, we often replace the risk of faith with a tedious, methodical lifestyle of fear that borders on boredom. What's the result? Often we become crotchety and set in our ways.

Are you stuck in the rut of life, using "creaking joints" to excuse inactivity, a "learned prudence" to support indecision, or a "fixed income" to defend miserly hoarding? Are you set in your ways, unwilling to budge? Even if you consider yourself too young to relate to some of these questions, you may well detect early signs that suggest you're headed in that direction.

The good news is that we don't have to live this way, no matter how old we get. The Lord has a much better lifestyle in mind for His people. He wants us to stop existing and start living—in other words, to be bullish. This divine plan is embedded in Ecclesiastes 11:1–6, where we'll learn how to leave timidity behind and grab with gusto the life God offers.

COMMON HUMAN COUNSEL FOR THE AGING

Friends, family, and society in general are good at dictating to us what getting older should look like. We're bombarded with images like the crusty duo in *Grumpy Old Men,* the crabby Archie Bunker, or the near-blind Mr. Magoo. Once we hit retirement, our families may present us lifetime memberships to the golf course, and suddenly our friends can't stop talking about the latest arthritis drug to hit the market.

 What are some of the images and symbols of aging that permeate our culture? Do you think these are accurate or exaggerated? Why?

_____

_____

_____

_____

Let's face it. All too often the advice handed to us as we grow older prods us to adopt a lifeless lifestyle. People tell us to stop exerting ourselves and to take it easy. Others exhort us to avoid risks and live cautiously. Some counselors encourage us to hold on to what we have because the times are going to get worse and people will try to take advantage of us. While life undoubtedly changes as we age, many of the changes are in our attitudes rather than in our bodies.

Most of the stereotypical lifestyles we're expected to adopt as we age are not supported by Scripture. Aging is a fact—it's happening to all of us right now. But this doesn't mean we need to stop pursuing life with the passion of youth.

Consider your current attitude toward new endeavors, active pursuits, or adventurous changes in life. Has your attitude changed from ten or twenty years ago? If so, what is the reason for this change?

_____
_____
_____
_____
_____

If somebody were to accuse you of allowing the world's view of aging to negatively influence your lifestyle, how would you be able to defend yourself?

_____
_____
_____
_____
_____

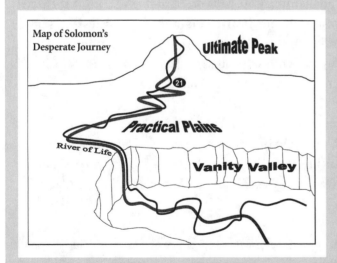

Map of Solomon's Desperate Journey

ROAD MAP FOR THE JOURNEY #21

Commencing his steep ascent up the side of Ultimate Peak, Solomon begins to reflect on life in the most profound and practical terms. He reasons that since God is in control of life's events and we don't know what will come (11:2, 5), we should not fear the uncertainties of life (11:3–4) but should work and plan for the future in light of His sovereignty (11:1–2).

GOD'S UNCOMMON COUNSEL FOR ALL AGES

The last two major sections of Solomon's journal can be summed up in three commands: Be bold! Be joyful! Be godly! When these directives are pursued, they turn a boring life into an exciting and contagious one, regardless of whether we're young, middle-aged, or elderly. In Ecclesiastes 11:1–6,

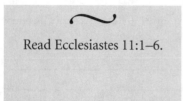

Read Ecclesiastes 11:1–6.

Solomon exhorted us to adopt a bold lifestyle—in other words, to be bullish—having a healthy fear of God, not a fear of uncontrollable circumstances. Solomon communicated this message through four instructions. As we examine each one, take special note of how God's counsel contradicts much of the human advice we receive and challenges our tendencies as we mature in age.

First Instruction: Instead of Protecting, Release Yourself!
(Ecclesiastes 11:1)

Solomon wrote, "Cast your bread on the surface of the waters, for you will find it after many days" (Ecclesiastes 11:1). Regarding the literal meaning of this passage, commentator R. N. Whybray writes, "[The writer] advises his readers to take the risk involved in sea-trade."[1] Walt Kaiser notes:

The figure may come . . . from the realm of foreign commerce, wherein ships finally return with a gain after an indefinite period of time. Likewise, men and women must judiciously and courageously venture forth in benevolent charity without selfish motives, for such help must be given with the confidence that there is a dependable order and plan in the world and a "God who does all."[2]

We can comprehend Solomon's meaning in Ecclesiastes 11:1 this way: "Give of yourself generously, for eventually you will be repaid abundantly." Of course, we may not always receive the kind of return for our generosity that we might expect. But we can look forward to the Lord honoring our service to Him in His way and time.

According to Philippians 4:15–19, what was the blessing received by the Philippian church for their participation in supporting Paul's ministry?

_____

_____

_____

_____

What are some spiritual blessings that result from giving generously, according to 2 Corinthians 9:6–12?

_____

_____

_____

_____

How have you experienced some of these blessings as a result of your giving?

_____

_____

_____

_____

Second Instruction: Rather Than Hoarding, Give and Invest!
(Ecclesiastes 11:2)

We live in a hoarding culture. Under the guise of "good stewardship," we often bury our time, treasure, and talents for a rainy day that never seems to come. How many of us are saving up, gathering interest, increasing shares, and banking on profits in an effort to obtain a comfortable future for ourselves while the work of the kingdom of God is constantly underfunded? This doesn't mean that planning for the future is wrong, but it's easy to let our money-driven culture, rather than the needs of the kingdom, dictate the standards of our stewardship.

Sometimes we congratulate ourselves when we give our weekly offerings to our churches, feeling we've done our part. But Solomon's principle regarding earthly investment—and its application to investment in God's kingdom—can be rather convicting. As a follow-up to his challenge to take certain risks (Ecclesiastes 11:1), Solomon wrote, "Divide your portion to seven, or even to eight, for you do not know what misfortune may occur on the earth" (11:2). Applying this to our New Testament situation, Ray Stedman writes, "Be generous. Do not stop with a few close needs around you. Do not say, 'I gave at the office,' when someone asks for help at your door. You do not know what evil may be averted by your gift; that is the implication of this verse."[3]

Read the following passages and note how they address positive benefits of giving or negative results of hoarding earthly riches.

	Positive	Negative
Proverbs 19:17		
Proverbs 21:13		
Matthew 6:19–20		

We often avoid giving to people or ministries because we don't know for sure how the money will be spent. While good stewardship requires that we invest God's resources wisely, Solomon's instructions concerning risk and diversifying serve to counter many of our excuses as we seek to invest ourselves and our resources in God's kingdom.

Can you think of any person or ministry in need of your assistance right now? How can you contribute your time, treasures, or talents more widely? What is preventing you from helping with this need today?

_____

_____

_____

_____

_____

Third Instruction: In Place of Drifting, Pursue! (Ecclesiastes 11:3–4)

The natural occurrences described by Solomon in these verses are both inevitable and unpredictable. We have no control over the rain—whether it will be a light mist or a violent storm. We have no way of determining when a tree may fall; we can only hope it doesn't fall on us! Because these events are unpredictable and in God's hands alone, we shouldn't base our plans on the "what ifs" of life.

Solomon wisely wrote, "He who watches the wind will not sow and he who looks at the clouds will not reap" (Ecclesiastes 11:4). If we let fear of the unknown future dictate our everyday activities, we'd just stay inside and hide all day and get nothing done at all! Similarly, people spend a lot of time observing the obvious, talking about the inevitable, and worrying about both. What profit is there in living one's life this way? None. The implication of Ecclesiastes 11:3–4 is that we should be pursuing life with faith rather than watching it pass by in fear. We should be working on things God has given us the ability to affect rather than worrying about those things over which we have no control.

Are there activities you've been avoiding due to fear of unknown results? Are there things you would like to try but you're intimidated by the "mights" and "what ifs"? If so, what is the worst that could happen if you stepped out in faith and did that activity with boldness?

_____

_____

_____

_____

Could a worst-case scenario happen to you even if you didn't step out? List some examples.

_____

_____

_____

_____

What are some of the positive benefits that could result from taking a leap of faith?

_____

_____

_____

_____

Fourth Instruction: As an Alternative to Doubting, Trust!
(Ecclesiastes 11:5–6)

There are many things we don't fully understand. As science advances, the number of questions about our universe only increases. It seems like every year we find smaller and smaller particles in the universe, or more and more distant stars, planets, and galaxies. Theory replaces theory, evidence counters evidence, and humans are forced to step back and drop their jaws in awe over the vastness and complexity of God's creation.

Solomon's final piece of counsel in Ecclesiastes 11:5–6 states this fact: there's no way we can know the work of God, who alone controls all things. If we wait for perfect knowledge before we launch a new project or attempt a challenging task, we'll stand frozen by ignorance as the world passes us by. Solomon rightly urged us to throw out the desire for certainty and be content with God's wisdom and a good dose of faith in His sovereignty. We simply don't know which earthly activities or investments will bring an abundant return, or which ones will be set aside by God's better plan. So let's just dig in and leave the results to God!

For Those Who Dare to Be Bullish

As we wrap up our study of this section from Solomon's ancient journal, let's consider three challenges that can help us become more bullish and less timid in our approach to life.

1. *Start living it up today and never quit.* Before we become set in our ways, let's volunteer our services, find somebody to invest our lives in, and refuse to allow our lives to collect dust. The older we get, the harder this will be. Like clay, we need to stay soft and malleable so we will be able to respond to the Potter's hands. If we set too early, He'll need to pull out the chisel to chip away. Ouch!

2. *Remember that wisdom must accompany action.* Although we shouldn't let fear of the unknown or the lure of comfort and security dictate how we live, we must also be careful not to rush out unprepared in our zeal to plunge into life. While unbendable rigidity may be a sign of becoming set in our ways, reckless abandon may be a sign of gross immaturity. Neither of these extremes is appropriate. Ecclesiastes calls us to discernment and balance.

3. *Watch out for enemy attacks during lulls in the action.* When we set out to boldly live for Christ, we ought to expect that times of little excitement and low productivity will come. It's often during these periods that we are prompted by others to entertain doubts regarding the value of living a bold Christian life. Aggressive living is threatening to those who refuse to live that way. Remembering this will help keep us from giving in to mediocrity and will motivate us to press on with enthusiasm.

As we grow older, we're constantly tempted by our families, friends, and society to drop anchor and rest safely and securely in our vessels. Some may even attach such a view of worldly peace and security to anchoring our souls in God. But the fact is, hitching your anchor to God is more like dropping it into the mouth of a whale—get ready for a ride! When you're connected with the Lord, there's no such thing as coincidence, accident, or luck. All things come from His sovereign hand, and they all come for a reason, most often known only to Him. What are you waiting for? Weigh anchor and start sailing!

22 Enjoying Life Now, Not Later

[ECCLESIASTES 11:7–12:1]

Family road trips have long been a staple of American summers. Road tripsters can be divided into two groups: those who drive straight through, and those who take it easy. The "straight-through" folks focus on the destination. The vacation begins when a certain location is reached, and only then do they start to relax and enjoy themselves. In contrast, the "take-it-easy" people appreciate the journey. The vacation starts when they get in the car and includes many stops and even detours along the way. Their final destination could turn out to be a total disappointment, but they find joy in unexpected twists and turns they never could have planned.

People approach life in the same two ways. Some enjoy the journey itself. But many make the mistake of indefinitely putting off the enjoyment of life until they reach a certain destination. They spend their energy and time building toward some distant day when they can sit back, relax, and finally kick off their shoes and enjoy life. This philosophy of life would be just fine if not for one problem: it's unbiblical.

Is there a goal you're seeking to achieve or a circumstance you're awaiting so you can enjoy life more? If so, what is it?

_____

_____

_____

_____

On a scale of 1 to 10, what is the likelihood of your achieving this in the next year?

Impossible   Certain
    1   2   3   4   5   6   7   8   9   10

Is it possible to fully enjoy your life without having achieved this goal or circumstance? If so, what prevents you from doing so now?

_____

_____

_____

_____

Suppose we were to conduct a poll and ask, "What are you waiting for in order to enjoy life?" We would probably get one of three typical answers:

- "I'll be happy when I have all the things I've ever wanted."
- "I'll find fulfillment when I have a certain person (spouse, child, etc.) in my life."
- "When I have achieved certain goals and realized certain dreams, then I'll have really lived."

These may represent common responses, but the Bible has something different to say about enjoying life.

Choose one of the means of finding happiness below and read the corresponding passages.

1. Happiness through possessions (Luke 12:15; John 10:10)

2. Happiness through other people (Matthew 14:31; Mark 14:50)

3. Happiness through the pursuit of personal goals (James 1:11; 1 Timothy 1:5)

How do you think Jesus might respond to somebody who is trying to find happiness through the means you selected to study?

_____

_____

_____

_____

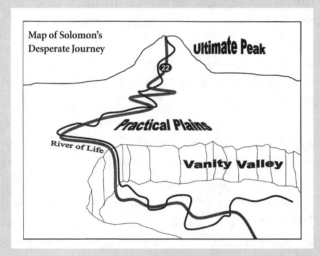

Map of Solomon's Desperate Journey

ROAD MAP FOR THE JOURNEY #22

After contrasting living wisely in the fear of God with living foolishly in ignorance of His sovereignty, Solomon continues his ascent up Ultimate Peak. From its slopes, he sees a bigger picture of life as he surveys where he's been: the darkness of the Valley of Futility and the practical solutions to life from Practical Plain. He then summarizes his exhortation to enjoy life as a gift from God, even from our youth (11:7–9). Warning against wasting our years on grief and anger, he encourages us to live wisely in the fear of our Creator (11:9–12:1).

What Does Solomon Say About Enjoying Life?

As we will quickly discover, Solomon linked joy in life not to our material possessions, personal relationships, or ambitious pursuits, but to our relationship with God and contentment with the simple things He gives us by His grace. Let's take a closer look at what Solomon said.

Read Ecclesiastes 11:7–12:1.

God Gives Us Permission to Enjoy Life (Ecclesiastes 11:7–8)

Solomon began answering the question of how we can enjoy life in the present with these words: "The light is pleasant, and it is good for the eyes to see the sun" (Ecclesiastes 11:7). Solomon could have been referring to life in general, along with its simple pleasures, as gifts from God. The message? It's good to simply be alive.[1]

Another way to understand this passage is in keeping with the imagery of the Old Testament poetic books, in which light and the sun are frequently used to represent the warmth and security of God's loving presence (Psalm 27:1; 84:11).[2] But these two interpretations aren't contradictory. Having an awareness of God's love and grace requires us to acknowledge that He gives us the simple things to enjoy. This is a common theme throughout Ecclesiastes (5:18; 9:9). Solomon reinforced it in Ecclesiastes 11:8: "Indeed, if a man should live many years, let him rejoice in them all." We don't have to wait for that new job, that perfect opportunity, that longed-for relationship—or even until we get our own sinful act together—to enjoy the light that comes from God. We can begin basking in His love and grace now!

List three simple activities or things that have recently brought you joy in life.

1. _____

2. _____

3. _____

Take a moment to thank God for providing these.

_____
_____
_____
_____

All the Traditional Limitations Have Been Removed (Ecclesiastes 11:8–9)

Some people declare that the time to appreciate life is during childhood. Others insist that because young people have many difficult adjustments to make, the best time to find happiness is when we're independent of our parents and "in touch" with our own identities. Then for some there comes a midlife crisis when they try to "find themselves" again and begin enjoying life in a new and exciting way. When this fails, people look forward to retirement, when they will finally be able to relax and enjoy life apart from the demands and dictates of people and responsibilities.

Solomon's words suggest all of these approaches to life are wrong. He exhorted his readers to rejoice in *all* the years we spend on earth (Ecclesiastes 11:8). He even spoke specifically to the young person: "Rejoice, young man, during your childhood, and let your heart be pleasant during the days of young manhood. And follow the impulses of your heart and the desires of your eyes" (11:9). In other words, Solomon broke the traditional limitations we place on people because of their "imperfect" place in life. Enjoy life now, not later!

If you were to put off real enjoyment of life until retirement, what would be two advantages?

1. _____
2. _____

What would be two disadvantages?

1. _____
2. _____

God Inserts Just Enough Warnings to Keep Us Obedient (Ecclesiastes 11:8–10)

That last statement in Ecclesiastes 11:9—to follow the impulses of our hearts and desires of our eyes—could be ripped out of context and used to fuel all sorts of extremes, from leaving our families to going on a credit-card shopping spree. But the Bible student won't need to find other passages to provide the proper balance; Solomon did this himself. He couched this statement with sobering warnings.

First, Solomon said, "Remember the days of darkness, for they will be many" (Ecclesiastes 11:8). Tough times will come—guaranteed. They will be marked by pain, disappointment, struggles, and sorrow. While these trials will certainly set limits on what kinds of activities we engage in, they need not disillusion us or steal our underlying joy that comes from God (Matthew 5:10–12; James 1:2–4, 12; 5:11). If we come to grips with the fact that much of life will be dark at times, the light that comes from God will seem all the more brilliant.

Second, Solomon reminded his readers that God will judge how we have lived, so we must pursue our desires with wisdom and prudence (Ecclesiastes 11:9). In short, if you go hog wild, you might end up roasting on a spit! Believers will be held accountable for their actions in this life; they themselves will be saved, but the loss endured at the judgment seat of Christ will be no laughing matter (Romans 14:10–12; 1 Corinthians 3:12–15; 2 Corinthians 5:10; 1 John 2:28).

A third warning Solomon gave is in Ecclesiastes 11:10: "Remove grief and anger from your heart and put away pain from your body, because childhood and the prime of life are fleeting." The internal responses of anger and resentment toward external events are most often out of our control and rob us of our joy. We may not be able to control circumstances in life, but with God's help we can remove the bitterness, anger, and rebellion that can easily materialize in our souls. In keeping with Solomon's tone throughout Ecclesiastes, one commentator adds a realistic perspective on this verse: "The point is that one should not allow consternation over human ills to consume one, not that one should be stupidly oblivious to human troubles."[3]

But Solomon knew other things that cause us pain that *are* subject to our control. He told his readers to "put away" things that cause pain in our bodies. These might include habits and situations that we willingly participate in, or at least ones we haven't done anything to avoid. Obvious pain producers in our modern world are drugs, alcohol, poor eating habits, and any form of sexual immorality. Whatever they may be, we need to put these destructive activities out of our lives if we really want to experience the joy God wants for us today.

What negative circumstances are you dealing with that are affecting your joy in life?

_____

_____

_____

_____

Are these things you can change or things that are out of your control?

_____

_____

_____

_____

Who does have control of them? Confess this truth to Him in prayer.

_____

_____

_____

_____

The Essential Ingredient for Happiness Is a Vital Relationship with God (Ecclesiastes 12:1)

Finally, after having written several journal entries on dissatisfaction and despair, Solomon rose above the deep fog of life on the ragged edge and revealed what's absolutely necessary for experiencing joy in our lives. While he hinted at it throughout his desperate journey, in Ecclesiastes 12:1 Solomon's voice rang out clearly: "Remember your Creator in the days of your youth, before the evil days come and the years draw near when you will say, 'I have no delight in them.'" In other words, our happiness is directly linked to our relationship with and obedience to God. When we live according to the Word of God through faith in Jesus Christ and in the power of the Holy Spirit, we can begin experiencing the Lord's abundant joy, regardless of our age or life circumstances.

GETTING TO THE ROOT

The Hebrew word translated "grief and anger" or sometimes "vexation" in Ecclesiastes 11:10 is *kha'as* and refers to the anger and resentment that often come from undeserved negative treatment.[4] It's a response to external conditions that are often outside our control. Solomon used it a few times in Ecclesiastes as the internal emotions of frustration mixed with anger that often come from the futility of life (Ecclesiastes 1:18; 2:23). However, the feeling of vexation can be beneficial, because it turns a person's focus from the futility of life under the sun to the profundity of life from God (7:3). Ultimately, feelings of anger and resentment should be exchanged for wisdom and contentment (7:9).

WHAT HINDERS THE PURSUIT OF HAPPINESS?

Now that we know how we can have true joy, we should briefly look at two obstacles to happiness that will likely fall into our paths. Knowing what these are before the days of evil come will help us to more clearly remember God, our true source of joy.

Self-appointed excuses keep us from claiming daily joy. These are the "if onlys" of life. "If only I had more money." "If only I had more time." "If only my kids would obey me." "If only my spouse would love me." The list could go on. We don't have to wait for our circumstances to change. We can find pleasure in our lives right now by removing anger from our hearts, changing what can be changed, and turning to God alone for contentment that rises above the ragged edge of life (Philippians 4:11–13).

What do you think is the most challenging obstacle in our world that prevents us from applying Ecclesiastes 11:8? Why?

_____
_____
_____
_____

Self-styled independence keeps us from remembering our Creator. Often our lives could be described by the toddler's phrase, "Me do it," meaning, "I'll make it on my own." "I don't need God." "I don't need anybody else." "I know where I'm going." "If I can't get there on my own, I won't get there at all!" Many today consider these to be noble words, but the prideful attitude they convey robs a person of true joy. Why? Because it keeps us from relying on the only one who can give us lasting joy—our loving God. In seeking to enjoy life now, not later, we need to turn away from ourselves and turn to God.

What is one thing you could have done today to enjoy the good things in life given by God?

_____

_____

_____

_____

Did you do it? If not, why not?

_____

_____

_____

_____

What will you do tomorrow to enjoy life? You may want to reference one of the three things you thanked God for on pages 224–225.

_____

_____

_____

_____

Throughout Ecclesiastes, Solomon examined life realistically and concluded that life is to be enjoyed *today*, not delayed to an uncertain tomorrow. Ecclesiastes 11:7–10 brings this truth onto center stage. Enjoy life during childhood, adolescence, adulthood, and the twilight years; don't wait for a day that you may never even live to see! Adopting this mentality also means our true happiness doesn't depend on material possessions, external circumstances, emotional maturity, or even financial security. The biblical approach to enjoying life involves remembering God our Creator and finding joy in Him alone. Are you enjoying life *today*?

23 Gray Hairs, Fewer Teeth, Yet a Big Smile
[ECCLESIASTES 12:1–8]

As the years of our lives slip away, we're less dependent on birthdays to remind us that we're getting older. Stiff joints, gray hair, and poor eyesight point out the obvious. Many of us try to fight the effects of time with vitamins, hair growth formulas, and antiaging creams, while others simply ignore it. But none of us can stop the steady march of time.

The question for those of us living in the real world shouldn't be, "How can we stop aging?" but, "What can we do with the time we've got?" Accordingly, Ecclesiastes 12:1–8 presents a realistic picture of the aging process and couples it with some down-to-earth advice: don't put off your relationship with God and the enjoyment of His good gifts; remember Him today.

Have you ever put off something for so long that it was eventually too late? What was it? How did you disappoint yourself and/or others by your procrastination?

_____

_____

_____

_____

COMMON FEELINGS AMONG THE AGING

Before we take a look at Solomon's realistic picture of growing old and its implication for all of us, let's consider some common feelings about aging. A life lived apart from an awareness of God's sovereign hand and our daily response to Him can result in some pessimistic views on aging. Perhaps you struggle with these yourself or know someone who does. Being aware of these common pitfalls can help equip you to counter them with compassion and godly perspective.

First, some struggle with the sense of *uselessness:* "I'm over the hill, in the way, and have nothing to contribute anymore." This sentiment is especially prevalent among people who were once prominent, resourceful, and highly respected. Kenneth Gangel catches this idea well when he writes concerning the feelings of many retirees, "Above all the physical and emotional changes looms the question, 'Who am I now?'"[1]

Are your identity and value as a person inseparably tied to what you do for a living or to your role in your home or community? If you were to lose this position, who would you be?

_____

_____

_____

_____

_____

Read 2 Corinthians 5:17 and Galatians 2:20. What do these verses indicate our true identity is based on?

_____

_____

_____

_____

_____

Another feeling that often grows with age is *guilt.* People think, *I blew it! If only I could go back and give life a second try, but I can't.* A poem by Thomas S. Jones, Jr illustrates these feelings of remorse, regret, and guilt.

SOMETIMES

Across the fields of yesterday
He sometimes comes to me,
A little lad just back from play—
The lad I used to be.

And yet he smiles so wistfully
Once he has crept within,
I wonder if he hopes to see
The man I might have been.[2]

What thoughts or emotions are sparked when you read that poem and think of your own life? Why?

_____

_____

_____

_____

Experiencing an occasional "what if" in life is normal and can actually help us make decisions for the remainder of our lives, but dwelling on the lives we could have lived or imagining the person we could have been is fruitless. We can't change the past, only our attitudes toward it.

A third common feeling among the aging is a combination of *bitterness* and *resentment*. These feelings result in thoughts of self-pity: "I have been so mistreated. My life would have been so much better if it hadn't been for such-and-such. I've had it rough!" There are few people more difficult to be around than those who have lost the battle against bitterness. They are hardened, unpleasant, and brittle. What they lack is a perspective like Joseph's. Though severely mistreated by his own brothers who sold him into slavery, Joseph held fast to his faith in God's enduring presence and sovereignty over the events of his life, concluding, "As for you, you meant evil against me, but God meant it for good in order to bring about this present result, to preserve many people alive" (Genesis 50:20).

Perhaps you're holding on to bitterness. You know it's wrong to refuse to let go, but the feeling seems so justified! The Bible doesn't deny that unjust things happen; they do. But it teaches that God is the One who will avenge, not us. God's Word challenges us to forgive despite what's been done to us.

A final feeling that often heightens with age is *fear*. "I'm so afraid of losing my home! What if I get sick? I'm scared to be alone." As we age we face several realistic fears, but much of the time we imagine the worst-case scenarios and plan our lives around things that may never happen! Irrational fears can rob us of all the potential joy we could experience in life. Christ told us that rather than fear the people and things of our temporal existence, we should fear (revere) God, who has complete control of all things (Matthew 10:28).

There's no doubt that growing older has its difficulties, but must all the negative feelings listed above accompany us as we age? What does God's Word have to say about our prospects for aging?

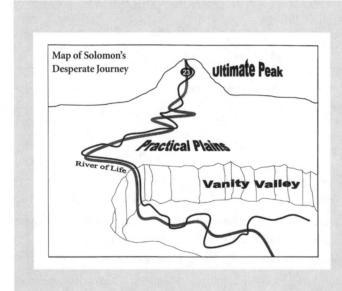

ROAD MAP FOR THE JOURNEY #23

Touching the crest of Ultimate Peak, Solomon begins to share his final conclusions. In this section on aging, he argues that since life apart from God is vanity (12:8), we should remember God all our days, enjoying life as a gift from His hand (12:1–7). Don't wait until it's too late to remember and obey Him—do it now!

SOLOMON'S PORTRAIT OF AGING

Solomon finally lit a beacon of light in a book that thus far illustrated the darkness of life apart from God.

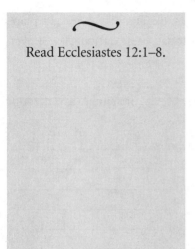

Read Ecclesiastes 12:1–8.

Dark Days (Ecclesiastes 12:1)

Solomon wrote, "Remember also your Creator in the days of your youth, before the evil days come and the years draw near when you will say, 'I have no delight in them'" (12:1). Though we know that God has good things in store for us at every stage of our lives, Solomon painted a bleak picture of aging that drives home his point: why wait to seek the good things of God?

Remembering our Creator means more than just thinking about Him now and then. It means keeping Him at the forefront of our minds so His will affects our attitudes and actions. The important thing to realize from this verse is that we're exhorted to remember God while we are young, not to put it off until we're older. Solomon told his readers that as we age, we will find it more difficult to remember God and to enjoy the good days He's given us as a gift. Sorrow and guilt will rob us of our peace and joy, and our adjustment to the difficulties of aging will be even more challenging.

Solomon described in vivid terms the "dark days" that are coming upon all of us who reach old age. His description serves as a reminder that we ought to remember God and his good gifts *today*.

Mental Dullness and Depression (Ecclesiastes 12:2)

Solomon described the mental and emotional changes that occur as we get older. These can cause changes in our attitudes

GETTING TO THE ROOT

The verb translated "remember" in Ecclesiastes 12:1 is the Hebrew word *zakhar*. While "remember" in English is almost entirely a mental exercise,[3] *zakhar* often emphasizes the action that accompanies a person's reflection.[4] One commentator notes, "To remember our Creator calls for decisive *action* based on recollection and reflection on all that God is and has done for us."[5] Another author says that to remember our Creator is "to revere God, to keep His laws faithfully, to serve Him responsibly, remembering that because He created people, everyone owes Him his life."[6]

and temperament and set a dark tone for all of the physical changes that will inevitably take place. Solomon wisely advised that if we fail to remember our Creator today, these dark days will overcome us like storm clouds.

What "dark clouds" loom over your life today? What challenges, fears, or changes are affecting your frame of mind or outlook on life?

_____

_____

_____

_____

_____

In what ways has getting older contributed to the dark skies of your life?

_____

_____

_____

_____

_____

_____

_____

Physical Ailments and Limitations (Ecclesiastes 12:3–5)

As we age, not only will our minds begin to fail and emotions begin to teeter, but so will our bodies. Solomon brought this fact to light with several symbolic images, painting a picture of a deteriorating home or palace. In his depiction of physical ailments and limitations, Solomon covered everything from cataracts to arthritis, from loss of hearing to the loss of sexual desire.

In the chart on the following page you'll see the ways Solomon creatively illustrated the process of aging. Take a moment to read this section of Ecclesiastes again, referring to the chart for the various possible interpretations of the symbols.

Solomon's Allegory of Aging

Symbol	Probable Meaning[7]
Sun, light, moon, and stars darkened (12:2)	Mental confusion or senility / Alzheimer's disease
Clouds return after the rain (12:2)	Emotional despair or depression
Watchmen of the house tremble (12:3)	Arms and hands shake / Parkinson's disease
Mighty men stoop (12:3)	Legs weaken
Grinding ones stand idle (12:3)	Teeth fall out
Those who look through windows grow dim (12:3)	Eyesight worsens, cataracts, or blindness
Doors on the street are shut (12:4)	Hearing diminishes
One will arise at the sound of the bird (12:4)	Startled or confused by sounds
Daughters of song will sing softly (12:4)	Voice is softened or lost
Afraid of a high place (12:5)	Fear of falling
Afraid of terrors on the road (12:5)	Fear of outside dangers
Almond tree blossoms (12:5)	Hair grays
Grasshopper drags himself along (12:5)	Physical slowing or loss of agility
Caperberry is ineffective (12:5)	Sexual desire or appetite wanes
Silver cord is broken (12:6)	Nervous disorders or paralysis
Golden bowl is crushed (12:6)	Stroke
Pitcher by the well is shattered (12:6)	Heart failure
Wheel at the cistern is crushed (12:6)	Digestive, circulatory, or kidney failure

Read Psalm 19:1–6, which describes how God reveals Himself through His creation. As we experience the symptoms of aging, why might we be less able to enjoy God's creation? How does this relate to a primary theme of Ecclesiastes: to "remember our Creator" and enjoy the gifts of His creation while we are still young?

_____

_____

_____

_____

Life's Final Factor (Ecclesiastes 12:6–8)

At the close of his illustration about the deterioration of life, Solomon returned to his opening command, exhorting us to live for God in light of our approaching death.

> Remember Him before the silver cord is broken and the golden bowl is crushed, the pitcher by the well is shattered and the wheel at the cistern is crushed; then the dust will return to the earth as it was, and the spirit will return to God who gave it. (Ecclesiastes 12:6–7)

The gradual signs of aging point us to the fact that unless the Lord returns, every one of us will die one day. After this, there will be no further opportunity to serve God and enjoy His good gifts on earth. More importantly, after we die, there will be no second chance to get right with God. Hebrews 9:27 contains a serious warning: "It is appointed for men to die once and after this comes judgment."

But this need not be a frightening prospect! The rest of the sentence in Hebrews 9:28 gives hope to those who have trusted in Christ alone for forgiveness and eternal life: "So Christ also, having been offered once to bear the sins of many, will appear a second time for salvation without reference to sin, to those who eagerly await Him."

What do the following passages teach us about the two different destinies people can have after physical death?

Revelation 20:10–15 _____

_____

_____

_____

Revelation 21:1–7 _____

_____

_____

_____

What about you? Are you living in fear of death or in eagerness to be with the Lord forever? If you are neither afraid of physical death nor eager to be with God in heaven, perhaps you're experiencing spiritual apathy, or perhaps something is holding you back from loving God with your whole heart. Pray that God would reignite your passion for intimacy with Him. Also, you may wish to read Matthew 10:37–38; Romans 12:9–13; 1 John 1:5–10, and 2 Timothy 4:2–5.

SOME PRACTICAL ADVICE BETWEEN THE LINES

As we reflect on Solomon's comments about aging and our relationship to God, we can discern at least three thoughts that are communicated between the lines.

1. *We must face the fact that we aren't getting any younger.* Ignoring old age won't make it go away. Aging is inevitable and can propel us toward greater dependence on and a deeper relationship with God. But if we fail to remember our Creator today, our golden years can become "dark days," rather than the joyful times He intends.

2. *God has designed us to be empty without Him.* As we've seen before, Augustine once prayed to God, "You stir man to take pleasure in praising you, because you have made us for yourself, and our heart is restless until it rests in you."[8] Our souls will have no peace in life until we remember our Creator. The process of aging and the inevitable tough times in life will only make it more difficult to turn to God if we continue to delay a complete surrender of our lives to Him.

Now is the time to prepare for eternity. Preparing for retirement is commendable, but it's nothing when compared to the importance of investing in the eternal relationship we have with God. The Lord wants us to entrust our lives to Him so we can enjoy His presence endlessly. If we see the effects of aging as signposts that point to our heavenly home, we'll be all the more ready to endure them with patience and even joy.

If somebody were to observe you today, would they conclude that you're remembering your Creator by obeying Him? What evidence could they point to in order to support their observation?

_____

_____

_____

_____

If this were your last day of life, would you be prepared to meet your Creator? Why or why not?

_____

_____

_____

_____

The scope of Ecclesiastes has taken us from the energetic vitality of youth, through the disillusionment and cynicism of middle age, and finally to the very edge of the grave. We have entered into Solomon's deepest struggles and felt the sting of his frustrations. We've nodded in agreement with many of his cries of exasperation and sighed alongside him as he described the reality of growing older. But let's not miss his point! Since our bodies will one day "return to the earth" and our spirits will "return to God," _now_ is the time to remember Him in all our thoughts and deeds.

24 Wrapping Up a Ragged-Edge Journey
[ECCLESIASTES 12:8–14]

From the depths of despair through the slough of despondency to the ragged edge of disillusionment, Solomon's quest has been quite an adventure. At times it has been wearying to hear his echoing cries of "vanity, vanity" and to trace his steps in circles—always moving but seeming to go nowhere. While Solomon was caught in the jaws of the horizontal perspective on life, his trek exposed the utter futility of life apart from God.

But as Solomon approached the very end of his desperate journey—the peak from which he could gain an eternal perspective—a brilliant light began to shine. Hope pierced the darkness and faith illuminated the landscape, driving out fear, doubt, and despair. Solomon exhorted his readers, "Remember your Creator in the days of your youth" (Ecclesiastes 12:1). From that point on, a entirely new perspective burst forth.

Such a perspective doesn't *replace* the realities of everyday life; it *completes* them. With the divine perspective in our right hand and the horizontal in our left, we're equipped to tackle the challenges of life under the sun and get a firm grip on reality.

So in a very real sense, Solomon's desperate pursuit is our own. We may not have understood this when we began studying his journal, but by now there should be no question regarding the relevance of his words to our lives. As we meditate on the last few verses of Ecclesiastes, let's allow Solomon's conclusions to transform our own perspective on life under the sun.

If you were standing on a mountaintop looking back over the landscape of your own life, what would you see? Would it be a rocky, jagged path? A series of valleys? Rolling hills? Flat, bountiful plains? Swamps? Deserts? You may want to draw a picture of your life using these symbols or simply describe it in such terms.

_____

_____

_____

_____

Explain why you depicted your life this way.

_____

_____

_____

_____

THE PREACHER'S CENTRAL THESIS

Solomon never left us in doubt about the major proposition he expounded and defended. He stated it at the beginning of his journal: "'Vanity of vanities,' says the Preacher, 'Vanity of vanities! All is vanity'" (Ecclesiastes 1:2). As he developed his case by giving numerous examples of the emptiness of life apart from God, he used the Hebrew term for "vanity" more than thirty times.

Why did Solomon think this position needed to be developed so thoroughly? Because he recognized that it raises one of the most significant questions that any human being could pose: If life has no purpose or meaning, then what are we doing here? Why go on living at all? Of course, many people ignore this issue rather than face it. They may continue to search for meaning in life apart from a relationship with God, accept the futility of their existence, or even choose to end their lives.

In chapter 12, Ecclesiastes comes full circle to one of its original questions: how can we find meaning and joy under the sun? This time, instead of answering these questions in the negative by telling us where we *can't* find joy, Solomon boiled it down to a simple answer: we find joy in life by looking to our Creator and obeying Him all the days of our lives (Ecclesiastes 12:1). The cure for despair and futility is a relationship with God, which is achieved only through faith in His Son, Jesus Christ (John 3:16; 14:6).

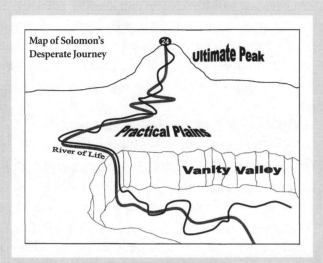

**ROAD MAP FOR THE JOURNEY
#24**

Solomon finally pulls himself to the top of Ultimate Peak and is able to peer down on all of life in one panoramic view. He reasserts his claim that life apart from God is vanity (Ecclesiastes 12:8), but he concludes that amid all human wisdom and learning, the greatest advice is to fear God and keep His commandments (12:13). We are called to do this not because we can gain God's favor or because it will make life on the ragged edge easier, but simply because He is our Creator and Judge (12:14).

The Preacher's Closing Confession (Ecclesiastes 12:8)

As Solomon brought his journal to a close, he recorded the end of his arduous journey. Lest the reader forget his conclusion about life under the sun, he repeated it one last time: "'Vanity of vanities,' says the Preacher, 'all is vanity!'" (Ecclesiastes 12:8). We dare not try to evade this truth. Without God as its center, life really *is* empty. Yet in his position as "the Preacher," Solomon went on to address the role of a teacher of wisdom who combats the futility of the world.

Solomon's Approach to Preaching (Ecclesiastes 12:9–11)

Early in his reign, King Solomon was endowed by God with supernatural wisdom (1 Kings 4:29). God did not give him wisdom, insight, and knowledge so that Solomon could have an inflated ego, increase his own glory, or sit around in an ivory tower thinking big thoughts. Rather, with much understanding came responsibility to others. Solomon took that responsibility seriously and was committed to teaching and instructing people in the ways of righteousness and wisdom (12:9–10).

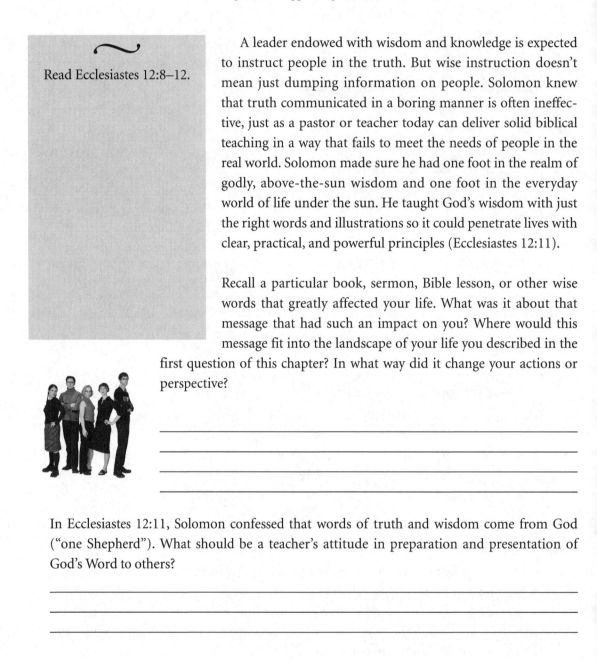

Read Ecclesiastes 12:8–12.

A leader endowed with wisdom and knowledge is expected to instruct people in the truth. But wise instruction doesn't mean just dumping information on people. Solomon knew that truth communicated in a boring manner is often ineffective, just as a pastor or teacher today can deliver solid biblical teaching in a way that fails to meet the needs of people in the real world. Solomon made sure he had one foot in the realm of godly, above-the-sun wisdom and one foot in the everyday world of life under the sun. He taught God's wisdom with just the right words and illustrations so it could penetrate lives with clear, practical, and powerful principles (Ecclesiastes 12:11).

Recall a particular book, sermon, Bible lesson, or other wise words that greatly affected your life. What was it about that message that had such an impact on you? Where would this message fit into the landscape of your life you described in the first question of this chapter? In what way did it change your actions or perspective?

_____

_____

_____

_____

In Ecclesiastes 12:11, Solomon confessed that words of truth and wisdom come from God ("one Shepherd"). What should be a teacher's attitude in preparation and presentation of God's Word to others?

_____

_____

_____

WINDOWS TO THE ANCIENT WORLD

Goads and Nails

Solomon used two items from the ancient world to illustrate the power of a teacher's wise words to a student. First, he compared the words of wise men to "goads" (Ecclesiastes 12:11). Each of these long sticks had a sharp spike on one end that was used to prod oxen along as they plowed a field. On the other end was a small shovel-like tool used to remove built-up dirt from the plow itself.[1] Similarly, words of wisdom serve to prick the conscience of the student, to prod him or her on to righteousness and fear of the Lord (Acts 26:14). Wise words can serve to clean away the sin that often prevents us from being effective or moving in a straight line.

In another simile, Solomon likened to "well-driven nails" those who have mastered the teaching of wisdom (12:11). This is "a picture of that which makes something fixed and immovable, a symbol of the stabilizing and sure character of wise teachings."[2] While the storms of life will overcome a fool, wise God-fearers will be well anchored.

What real-life experiences has God given you that could help you relate His principles of wisdom in your unique way to those who may be struggling through similar things in their lives?

_____

_____

_____

_____

_____

Solomon's Warning to All (Ecclesiastes 12:12)

While the clear and practical teaching of God's wisdom brings guidance and stability (Ecclesiastes 12:11), there are innumerable books advancing worldly wisdom with no basis in divine truth. Solomon wrote, "But beyond this, my son, be warned: the writing of many books is endless, and excessive devotion to books is wearying to the body" (12:12). When we recall that this warning was written during a period without printing presses, word processors, computers, or the Internet, it becomes even more significant. Each year, thousands of new books are published and countless pieces of information are distributed by e-mail or posted on Web sites. No human being on earth would have the time or energy to scratch the surface of this mountain of information, let alone the one Solomon referred to here.

Solomon told us that even if we *could* climb this mountain, it would be a futile task. The Lord has given us the answers we need to the most fundamental questions of life, and He has brought them together in one book—the Bible. While books and information from various sources can be beneficial, only God's Word is our authoritative guide for living. All other sources of "truth" must be weighed against the Bible's clear answers to life's most profound questions.

Discuss a couple of non-Christian "self-help" or "how-to" books on the market these days. What are the questions about life these books are trying to answer? What answers are they giving?

_____

_____

_____

_____

According to 2 Peter 1:2–3, what knowledge is needed for life and godliness?

_____

_____

_____

_____

_____

Read 2 Timothy 3:16–17. How can Scripture be used in the life of the believer?

_____

_____

_____

_____

_____

DIGGING DEEPER

God Is God, and We Are Not

We saw in the first chapter that Solomon's main theological theme through-out Ecclesiastes could be summed up in one simple statement: "God is God, and we are not." The rest of the book details Solomon's unpacking of that dense concept. Under this overarching theme, four related ideas emerge.

GOD IS GOD AND WE ARE NOT

I God does as He pleases according to His perfect plan	II Our exploits apart from God are futile	III God gives all things to us as gifts to enjoy	IV Our response should be to fear God and obey God in wisdom
Ecclesiastes 1:9, 14; 2:14–15, 26; 3:1–11, 14–15; 6:10–12; 7:13–14; 8:6–8, 16–17; 9:1–2, 11–12; 10:14; 11:1–6	Ecclesiastes 1:2–17; 2:1–23; 3:9, 16–21; 4:1–8, 13–16; 5:8–17; 6:1–9; 7:6, 15, 19–29; 8:9–11, 14; 9:3–6; 11:8; 12:8	Ecclesiastes 2:24–25; 3:12–13, 22; 4:6, 9–12 3:12–13, 22; 4:6, 9–12 5:18–20; 7:14; 8:15 9:7–10; 11:7–10	Ecclesiastes 3:14; 5:1–7 7:1–18; 25–29 8:1–5, 12–13; 9:13–18; 10:1–20 11:9; 12:1–14

I. Arguing with God or trying to figure out His exact plan only leads to frustration, because Solomon tells us that God's plans are unknowable apart from His special revelation and unalterable apart from His sovereign will.

Cont'd

247

Digging Deeper (Cont'd)

II. We should place no confidence in our exploits to provide a sense of meaning, security, or happiness. Our own goals pursued in our own strength will always come up short when compared to the purpose and joy God wants to develop in us in His own time and by His own means.

III. God gives us the simple things in life we take for granted—the food we eat, the clothes we wear, the family and friends we enjoy. Because they're gifts, we should enjoy them while they last, because in God's good plan, they may only be ours for a short time.

IV. If we're despairing or feeling frustrated with life, we shouldn't wait to turn to God when things get better—they might not! If we're content, secure, and happy with our lives, we shouldn't put off trusting in God until calamity strikes—by then it might be too late!

Consider the Conclusion (Ecclesiastes 12:13–14)

After seemingly endless cycles of futility and frustration, seasoned with occasional bursts of insight and wisdom, Solomon's desperate journey came to a close as he gazed across the landscape of his life and processed the theological and practical lessons he had learned about living. From this vantage point, he was able to sum up his conclusions in a simple, pointed exhortation:

> The conclusion, when all has been heard is: fear God and keep His commandments, because this applies to every person. For God will bring every act to judgment, everything which is hidden, whether it is good or evil. (Ecclesiastes 12:13–14)

God is the answer to our despair, and a relationship with Him is the cure for our dissatisfaction. We can choose to believe or deny what He says, but all of us will one day have to face Him and give an account of our lives. And nobody will receive everlasting joy apart from personal faith in Christ (John 14:6; Acts 4:10–12).

Read John 3:18–19. According to this passage, who will fall under the judgment of God's condemnation?

_____

_____

_____

_____

Read 1 John 5:11–13. Who does John say has eternal life?

_____

_____

_____

_____

Through each page of the journal of Solomon's desperate journey along the ragged edge of life, we've seen snapshots and episodes of a sometimes harsh reality. Solomon made no attempt to smooth the rough edges, hammer out the dents, patch the holes, or polish the dull facade of life. He incorporated no dreams or fantasies, no "spin" and no "fluff." This was tough stuff. Solomon told the truth about life under the sun and pulled no punches in doing so.

Solomon gradually revealed the truth about those same hard realities from another perspective—God's. He moved us from the darkness of worldly, foolish living into the light of a life filled with faith, wisdom, and purity. He taught us to have a proper attitude toward the world, toward ourselves, and toward God. Ray Stedman once wrote this:

> The record is plain for all to see. Life without God is dull, empty, vain. Life with him is full and satisfying. Even the tears and pain have meaning and value when we see they are chosen by him. The purpose behind it all is the increase of joy.[3]

When we come to the end of our own resources and have consumed what the world offers, we'll be left empty-handed and alone unless we have a relationship with God through His Son, Jesus Christ. After all, it was Jesus who came down from glory and majesty above the heavens to enter our drab world below the sun so we could not only experience _eternal_ life but enjoy _abundant_ life in the present (John 10:10).

How to Begin a Relationship with God

~

Have you ever stroked the velvety petal of a rose? Or listened to the restful cascade of a mountain stream? Or strolled in awe through a redwood grove? In these quiet moments, a thought may well up from your soul: only God could create such beauty.

Most people who have experienced moments like these come away believing that there must be a God. But how do we obey Solomon's concluding exhortation to remember our Creator? How do we come to know God?

The Path to God

The most marvelous book in the world, the Bible, marks the path to God with four vital truths. Let's look at each marker in detail.

1. Our Spiritual Condition: Totally Depraved

The first truth is rather personal. One look in the mirror of Scripture, and our human condition becomes painfully clear:

There is none righteous, not even one;
There is none who understands,
There is none who seeks for God;
All have turned aside, together they have become useless;
There is none who does good,
There is not even one. (Romans 3:10–12)

We are all sinners through and through—totally depraved. Now, that doesn't mean we've committed every atrocity known to humankind. We're not as *bad* as we can be, just as *bad off* as we can be. Sin colors all our thoughts, motives, words, and actions.

You still don't believe it? Look around. Everything around us bears the smudge marks of our sinful nature. Despite our best efforts to create a perfect world, crime abounds, divorce courts are full, and families keep crumbling.

Something has gone terribly wrong in our society and in ourselves, something deadly. Contrary to how the world would repackage it, "me-first" living doesn't equal rugged individuality and freedom; it equals death. As Paul said in his letter the Romans, "The wages of sin is death" (Romans 6:23)—spiritually, emotionally, and physically.

2. God's Character: Infinitely Holy

Solomon observed the condition of the world and the people in it and concluded, "Vanity of vanities, all is vanity" (Ecclesiastes 1:2; 12:8). The fact that we know things are not as they should be points us to a standard of goodness beyond ourselves. Our sense of injustice in life "under the sun" implies a perfect standard of justice "above the sun." That standard and source is God Himself. And God's standard of holiness contrasts starkly to our sinful condition.

Scripture says, "God is light, and in Him there is no darkness at all" (1 John 1:5). God is absolutely holy—which creates a problem for us. If He is so pure, how can we who are so impure relate to Him?

Perhaps we could try being better people, try to tilt the balance in favor of our good deeds, or, like Solomon, seek out wisdom and knowledge for self-improvement. Throughout history, people have attempted to live up to God's standard by keeping the Ten Commandments. Unfortunately, no one can come close to satisfying the demands of God's law. J. B. Phillips's translation of

Romans 3:20 says, "No man can justify himself before God by a perfect performance of the Law's demands—indeed it is the straight-edge of the Law that shows us how crooked we are."

3. Our Need: A Substitute

So here we are, sinners by nature, sinners by choice, trying to pull ourselves up by our own boot-straps and attain a relationship with our holy Creator. But every time we try, we fall flat on our faces. We can't live a life good enough to make up for our sin, because God's standard isn't "good enough"—it's perfection. And we can't make amends for the offense our sin has created without dying for it.

Who can get us out of this mess?

If someone could live perfectly, honor God's law, and bear sin's death penalty for us—in our place—then we would be saved from our predicament. But is there such a person? Thankfully, yes!

Meet your substitute—*Jesus Christ.* He is the One who took death's place for you!

> [God] made [Jesus Christ] who knew no sin to be sin on our behalf, that we might become the righteousness of God in Him. (2 Corinthians 5:21)

4. God's Provision: A Savior

God rescued us by sending His Son, Jesus, to die for our sins on the cross (1 John 4:9–10). Jesus was fully human and fully divine (John 1:1, 18), a truth that ensures His understanding of our weaknesses, His power to forgive, and His ability to bridge the gap between God and us (Romans 5:6–11). In short, we are "justified as a gift by His grace through the redemption which is in Christ Jesus" (Romans 3:24). Two words in this verse bear further explanation: *justified* and *redemption.*

Justification is God's act of mercy, in which He declares believing sinners righteous, while they are still in their sinning state. Because Jesus took our sin upon Himself and suffered our judgment on the cross, God forgives our debt and proclaims us pardoned.

Redemption is God's act of paying the ransom price to release us from our bondage to sin. Held hostage by Satan, we were shackled by the iron chains of sin and death. Like a loving parent whose child has been kidnapped, God willingly paid the ransom for you. And what a price He paid! He gave His only Son to bear our sins—past, present, and future. Jesus's death and resurrection broke our chains and set us free to become children of God (Romans 6:16–18, 22; Galatians 4:4–7).

Placing Your Faith in Christ

These four truths describe how God has provided a way to Himself through Jesus Christ. Since the price has been paid in full by God, we must respond to His free gift of eternal life by trusting in Him and Him alone to save us. We must step forward into the relationship with God that He has prepared for us—not by doing good works or being a good person, but by coming to Him just as we are and accepting His justification and redemption by faith.

> For by grace you have been saved through faith; and that not of yourselves, it is the gift of God; not as a result of works, that no one should boast. (Ephesians 2:8–9)

We accept God's gift of salvation simply by placing our faith in Christ alone for the forgiveness of our sins. Would you like to enter a relationship with your Creator by trusting in Christ as your Savior? If so, here's a simple prayer you can use to express your faith:

> *Dear God, I know that my sin has put a barrier between You and me. Thank You for sending Your Son, Jesus, to die in my place. I trust in Jesus alone to forgive my sins, and I accept His gift of eternal life. I ask Jesus to be my personal Savior and the Lord of my life. Thank You. In Jesus's name. Amen.*

If you've prayed this prayer or one like it and you wish to find out more about knowing God and His plan for you in the Bible, contact us at Insight for Living. You can speak to one of our pastors on staff by calling or writing to us at the address below.

The next time you ponder a rose or admire a sunset, remember the One who created our wonderful world, and remind yourself that you know Him personally. Rejoice in His indescribable gift![1]

~

Insight for Living
P.O. Box 269000
Plano, Texas 75026-9000
(800) 772-8888

Notes

Chapter 1: Journal of a Desperate Journey

Unless otherwise noted below, all material in this chapter is based on or quoted from "Journal of a Desperate Journey," a sermon by Charles R. Swindoll, June 5, 1983, and chapter 1 in the *Living on the Ragged Edge* hardcover book.

1. Richard Winter, *Still Bored in a Culture of Entertainment: Rediscovering Passion and Wonder* (Downers Grove, Ill.: InterVarsity, 2002), 88–100.
2. Francis Brown, S. R. Driver, and Charles A. Briggs, *The Brown-Driver-Briggs Hebrew and English Lexicon* (Boston: Houghton Mifflin, 1906; reprint, Peabody, Mass.: Hendrickson, 1996), 874–75.
3. Walter Bauer and others, eds. *A Greek-English Lexicon of the New Testament and Other Early Christian Literature,* 2d rev. ed. (Chicago: University of Chicago Press, 1979), 240–41.
4. James C. Dobson, *Straight Talk to Men and Their Wives* (Waco, Tex.: Word, 1980), 114. Used by permission of Multnomah Publishers, Inc.
5. Dobson, *Straight Talk to Men and Their Wives,* 114.
6. R. N. Whybray, *Ecclesiastes,* New Century Bible Commentary, ed. Ronald E. Clements and Matthew Black (Grand Rapids, Mich.: William B. Eerdmans, 1989), 37–38.
7. Raymond B. Dillard and Tremper Longman III, *An Introduction to the Old Testament* (Grand Rapids, Mich.: Zondervan, 1994), 247.

Chapter 2: Chasing the Wind

Unless otherwise noted below, all material in this chapter is based on or quoted from "Chasing the Wind," a sermon by Charles R. Swindoll, June 12, 1983, and chapter 2 in the *Living on the Ragged Edge* hardcover book.

1. Richard Winter, *Still Bored in a Culture of Entertainment: Rediscovering Passion and Wonder* (Downers Grove, Ill.: InterVarsity, 2002), 18–19.
2. Francis Brown, S. R. Driver, and Charles A. Briggs, *The Brown-Driver-Briggs Hebrew and English Lexicon* (Boston: Houghton Mifflin, 1906; reprint, Peabody, Mass.: Hendrickson, 1996), 210–11.

3. James L. Crenshaw, *Ecclesiastes: A Commentary,* The Old Testament Library, ed. Peter Ackroyd and others (Philadelphia: Westminster, 1987), 58.

4. George Aaron Barton, *A Critical and Exegetical Commentary on the Book of Ecclesiastes,* The International Critical Commentary, ed. Samuel Rolles Driver, Alfred Plummer, and Charles Augustus Briggs (Edinburgh: T. & T. Clark, 1980), 78.

5. R. C. Sproul, "Vanity of Vanities, All Is Vanity," in *Vanity and Meaning: Discovering Purpose in Life,* ed. R. C. Sproul, Jr. (Grand Rapids, Mich.: Baker, 1995), 12.

6. Norman L. Geisler and William Watkins, *Perspectives: Understanding and Evaluating Today's World Views* (San Bernadino, Calif.: Here's Life Publishers, 1984), 46–47. Used by permission of Norman L. Geisler.

7. Francis A. Schaeffer, *How Should We Then Live? The Rise and Decline of Western Thought and Culture* (Westchester, Ill.: Crossway, 1976), 180.

8. C. S. Lewis, *Mere Christianity,* rev. and enlarged ed. (New York: Macmillan, 1952), 120. © C. S. Lewis Pte. Ltd. 1942, 1943, 1944, 1952. Extract reprinted by permission.

Chapter 3: Eat, Drink . . . and Be What?

Unless otherwise noted below, all material in this chapter is based on or quoted from "Eat, Drink . . . and Be What?" a sermon by Charles R. Swindoll, June 26, 1983, and chapter 3 in the *Living on the Ragged Edge* hardcover book.

1. *Merriam-Webster's Collegiate Dictionary,* 11th ed., s.v. "hedonism."

2. William J. Petersen, *Those Curious New Cults* (New Canaan, Conn.: Pivot Books, 1975), 93, see 91–93.

3. R. Laird Harris, Gleason L. Archer, Jr., and Bruce K. Waltke, eds., *Theological Wordbook of the Old Testament,* vol. 2 (Chicago: Moody, 1980), 879; Francis Brown, S. R. Driver, and Charles A. Briggs, *The Brown-Driver-Briggs Hebrew and English Lexicon* (Boston: Houghton Mifflin, 1906; reprint, Peabody, Mass.: Hendrickson, 1996), 970.

4. Derek Kidner, "The Search for Satisfaction: Ecclesiastes 1:12–2:26," in *Reflecting with Solomon: Selected Studies on the Book of Ecclesiastes,* ed. Roy B. Zuck (Grand Rapids, Mich.: Baker, 1994), 252.

5. Kyle Henderson, "Too Much Pleasure," in *Vanity & Meaning: Discovering Purpose in Life,* ed. R. C. Sproul, Jr. (Grand Rapids, Mich.: Baker, 1995), 21.

6. James L. Crenshaw, *Ecclesiastes: A Commentary,* The Old Testament Library, ed. Peter Ackroyd and others (Philadelphia: Westminster, 1987), 81.

7. Edward M. Blaiklock and R. K. Harrison, eds., *The New International Dictionary of Biblical Archaeology* (Grand Rapids, Mich.: Zondervan, 1983), see "Solomon."

Chapter 4: More Miles of Bad Road

Unless otherwise noted below, all material in this chapter is based on or quoted from "More Miles of Bad Road," a sermon by Charles R. Swindoll, July 3, 1983, and chapter 4 in the *Living on the Ragged Edge* hardcover book.

1. Derek Kidner, *A Time to Mourn and a Time to Dance: The Message of Ecclesiastes* (Downers Grove, Ill.: InterVarsity, 1976), 34.

2. Ray C. Stedman, *Solomon's Secret: Enjoying Life, God's Good Gift* (Portland, Ore.: Multnomah, 1985), 32. Used by permission. Also published as *Is This All There Is to Life? Answers from Ecclesiastes* (Grand Rapids, Mich., Discovery House, 2000.)

3. Walter C. Kaiser, Jr., *Quality Living* (Chicago: Moody, 1979), 70.

Chapter 5: Do You Know What Time It Is?

Unless otherwise noted below, all material in this chapter is based on or quoted from "Do You Know What Time It Is?" a sermon by Charles R. Swindoll, July 10, 1983, and chapter 5 in the *Living on the Ragged Edge* hardcover book.

1. *Merriam-Webster's Collegiate Dictionary,* 11th edition, s.v. "time."

2. For a more in-depth study on God and time, see Gregory E. Ganssle, ed., *God & Time: Four Views* (Downers Grove, Ill.: InterVarsity, 2001).

3. For one secular example of the beginning and end of the universe apart from God, see Stephen W. Hawking, *A Brief History of Time from the Big Bang to Black Holes* (New York: Bantam, 1988).

4. J. A. Loader, *Ecclesiastes: A Practical Commentary,* trans. John Vriend, Text and Interpretation (Grand Rapids, Mich.: William B. Eerdmans, 1986), 33.

5. Francis Brown, S. R. Driver, and Charles A. Briggs, *The Brown-Driver-Briggs Hebrew and English Lexicon* (Boston: Houghton, Mifflin and Company, 1906; reprint, Peabody, Mass.: Hendrickson, 1996), 773.

6. For an analysis of the structure of Ecclesiastes 3:2–8, see J. A. Loader, *Ecclesiastes: A Practical Commentary,* trans. John Vriend, Text and Interpretation (Grand Rapids, Mich.: William B. Eerdmans, 1986), 33–38. Also see R. N. Whybray, *Ecclesiastes,* New Century Bible Commentary, ed. Ronald E. Clements and Matthew Black (Grand Rapids, Mich.: William B. Eerdmans, 1989), 65–74.

7. Donald R. Glenn, "Ecclesiastes," in *The Bible Knowledge Commentary: Old Testament Edition,* ed. John F. Walvoord and Roy B. Zuck (Wheaton, Ill.: Victor, 1985), 983. Used with permission by Cook Communications Ministries. May not be further reproduced. All rights reserved.

8. C. S. Lewis, *The Problem of Pain* (New York: Macmillan, 1962), 93.

9. Augustine, *Confessions,* trans. Henry Chadwick, Oxford World's Classics (New York: Oxford University Press Inc., 1998), 1.1.

Chapter 6: Interlude of Rare Insight

Unless otherwise noted below, all material in this chapter is based on or quoted from "Interlude of Rare Insight," a sermon by Charles R. Swindoll, July 17, 1983, and chapter 6 in the *Living on the Ragged Edge* hardcover book.

1. Richard Winter, *Still Bored in a Culture of Entertainment: Rediscovering Passion and Wonder* (Downers Grove, Ill.: InterVarsity, 2002), 38.

2. Earl D. Radmacher, "Salvation: A Necessary Work of God," in *Understanding Christian Theology*, ed. Charles R. Swindoll and Roy B. Zuck (Nashville, Tenn.: Thomas Nelson, 2003), 846.

3. Radmacher, "Salvation," 847–52.

4. Thomas Dubay, *The Evidential Power of Beauty: Science and Theology Meet* (San Francisco: Ignatius Press, 1999), 38–41.

5. Dubay, *Evidential Power of Beauty*, 34.

6. Thomas O. Chisholm, "Great Is Thy Faithfulness," in *The Hymnal for Worship and Celebration* (Waco, Tex.: Word Music, 1986), no. 43. Used by permission.

7 James L. Crenshaw, *Ecclesiastes: A Commentary*, The Old Testament Library, ed. Peter Ackroyd and others (Philadelphia: Westminster, 1987), 100.

Chapter 7: Confessions of a Cynic

Unless otherwise noted below, all material in this chapter is based on or quoted from "Confessions of a Cynic," a sermon by Charles R. Swindoll, August 14, 1983, and chapter 7 in the *Living on the Ragged Edge* hardcover book.

1. *Merriam-Webster's Collegiate Dictionary*, 11th ed., s. v. "cynical."

2. Some Christian scholars have pointed to the presence of an innate moral sense as evidence for the existence of a divine universal Lawgiver. For more information and discussion on this topic, see C. S. Lewis, *Mere Christianity*, rev. ed. (New York: Macmillan, 1952), 17–39.

3. Robertson McQuilkin, *An Introduction to Biblical Ethics*, rev. and updated ed. (Wheaton, Ill.: Tyndale, 1995), 41–42; see also 43.

4. Norman L. Geisler and Ronald M. Brooks, *When Skeptics Ask* (Wheaton, Ill.: Victor, 1990), 24.

5. Thomas Dubay, *The Evidential Power of Beauty: Science and Theology Meet* (San Francisco: Ignatius Press, 1999), 94–95.

6. Ray C. Stedman, *Solomon's Secret: Enjoying Life, God's Good Gift* (Portland, Ore: Multnomah, 1985), 51. Used by permission. Also published as *Is This All There Is to Life? Answers from Ecclesiastes* (Grand Rapids, Mich.: Discovery House, 2000).

Chapter 8: The Lonely Whine of the Top Dog

Unless otherwise noted below, all material in this chapter is based on or quoted from "The Lonely Whine of the Top Dog," a sermon by Charles R. Swindoll, August 28, 1983, and chapter 8 in the *Living on the Ragged Edge* hardcover book.

1. Frank Minirth and others, *The Workaholic and His Family: An Inside Look* (Grand Rapids, Mich.: Baker, 1981), 28.

2. Based on Minirth and others, *Workaholic and His Family*, 29–30.

3. James C. Dobson, *Straight Talk to Men and Their Wives* (Waco, Tex.: Word, 1980), 174. Used by permission of Multnomah Publishers, Inc.

Notes

Chapter 9: One Plus One Equals Survival

Unless otherwise noted below, all material in this chapter is based on or quoted from "One Plus One Equals Survival," a sermon by Charles R. Swindoll, September 4, 1983, and chapter 9 in the *Living on the Ragged Edge* hardcover book.

1. Gary Inrig, *Quality Friendship* (Chicago: Moody, 1981), 15.
2. R. N. Whybray, *Ecclesiastes,* New Century Bible Commentary, ed. Ronald E. Clements and Matthew Black (Grand Rapids, Mich.: William B. Eerdmans, 1989), 87.
3. Whybray, *Ecclesiastes,* 87.
4. James L. Crenshaw, *Ecclesiastes: A Commentary,* The Old Testament Library, ed. Peter Ackroyd and others (Philadelphia: Westminster Press, 1987), 111.
5. J. R. R. Tolkien, *The Return of the King,* in The Lord of the Rings, (Boston: Houghton Mifflin, 1994), 919. Copyright © 1955, 1965, 1966 by J. R. R. Tolkien. 1955 edition copyright © renewed 1983 by Christopher R. Tolkien, Michael H. R. Tolkien, John F. R. Tolkien and Priscilla M. A. R. Tolkien. 1965/1966 edition copyright © renewed 1993, 1994 by Christopher R. Tokien, John F. R. Tolkien and Priscilla M. A. R. Tolkien, Reprinted by permission of Houghton Mifflin Company. All rights reserved.
6. Crenshaw, *Ecclesiastes,* 111.
7. Elisabeth Elliott, *Loneliness* (Nashville, Tenn.: Oliver-Nelson, 1988), 22.
8. Inrig, *Quality Friendship*, 73.

Chapter 10: What Every Worshiper Should Remember

Unless otherwise noted below, all material in this chapter is based on or quoted from "What Every Worshiper Should Remember," a sermon by Charles R. Swindoll, September 18, 1983, and chapter 10 in the *Living on the Ragged Edge* hardcover book.

1. Zane C. Hodges, "Hebrews," in *The Bible Knowledge Commentary,* New Testament edition, ed. John F. Walvoord and Roy B. Zuck (Wheaton, Ill.: Victor, 1983), 790. Copied with permission by Cook Communications Ministries. May not be further reproduced. All rights reserved.
2. R. N. Whybray, *Ecclesiastes,* New Century Bible Commentary, ed. Ronald E. Clements and Matthew Black (Grand Rapids, Mich.: William B. Eerdmans, 1989), 94.
3. David Allan Hubbard, *Beyond Futility: Messages from the Book of Ecclesiastes* (Grand Rapids, Mich.: William B. Eerdmans, 1976), 70.
4. Louis A. Barbieri, Jr., "Matthew," in *The Bible Knowledge Commentary,* New Testament edition, ed. John F. Walvoord and Roy B. Zuck (Wheaton, Ill.: Victor, 1983), 31.
5. Hubbard, *Beyond Futility,* 71.

Chapter 11: Straight Talk to the Money-Mad

Unless otherwise noted below, all material in this chapter is based on or quoted from "Straight Talk to the Money-Mad," a sermon by Charles R. Swindoll, September 25, 1983, and chapter 11 in the *Living on the Ragged Edge* hardcover book.

1. Alan Loy McGinnis, *The Friendship Factor: How to Get Closer to the People You Care For* (Minneapolis: Augsburg, 1979), 20–21.

2. Walter Bauer and others, eds., *A Greek-English Lexicon of the New Testament and Other Early Christian Literature,* 2nd rev. ed. (Chicago: University of Chicago Press, 1979), 631.

3. A. Duane Litfin, "1 Timothy," in *The Bible Knowledge Commentary: New Testament Edition,* ed. John F. Walvoord and Roy B. Zuck (Wheaton, Ill.; Victor, 1983), 746. Copied with permission by Cook Communications Ministries. May not be further reproduced. All rights reserved.

4. Philip H. Towner, *1–2 Timothy & Titus,* The IVP New Testament Commentary Series, ed. Grant R. Osborne, D. Stuart Briscoe, and Haddon Robinson (Downers Grove, Ill.: InterVarsity, 1994), 139–40.

5. Ray C. Stedman, *Solomon's Secret: Enjoying Life, God's Good Gift* (Portland, Ore.: Multnomah, 1985), 68. Used by permission. Also published as *Is This All There Is to Life? Answers from Ecclesiastes* (Grand Rapids, Mich.: Discovery House, Inc, 2000).

Chapter 12: The Few Years of a Futile Life

Unless otherwise noted below, all material in this chapter is based on or quoted from "The Few Years of a Futile Life," a sermon by Charles R. Swindoll, October 2, 1983, and chapter 12 in the *Living on the Ragged Edge* hardcover book.

1. Francis Brown, S. R. Driver, and Charles A. Briggs, *The Brown-Driver-Briggs Hebrew and English Lexicon* (Boston: Houghton Mifflin, 1906; reprint, Peabody, Mass.: Hendrickson, 2000), 648–49.

2. George Aaron Barton, *A Critical and Exegetical Commentary on the Book of Ecclesiastes,* International Critical Commentary, ed. Samuel Rolles Driver, Alfred Plummer, and Charles Augustus Briggs (Edinburgh: T. & T. Clark, 1980), 134.

3. D. F. Payne, "Solomon," in *The International Standard Bible Encyclopedia, Volume 4: Q-Z,* rev. ed., ed. Geoffrey W. Bromiley and others (Grand Rapids, Mich.: William B. Eerdmans, 1988), 568.

Chapter 13: Wise Words for Busy People

Unless otherwise noted below, all material in this chapter is based on or quoted from "Wise Words for Busy People," a sermon by Charles R. Swindoll, October 23, 1983, and chapter 13 in the *Living on the Ragged Edge* hardcover book.

1. D. A. Hubbard, "Proverb," in *New Bible Dictionary,* 2d ed., ed. J. D. Douglas, and others (Wheaton, Ill.: Tyndale, 1987), 988.

2. See Nicholas H. Ridderbos and Herbert M. Wolf, "Poetry, Hebrew," in *The International Standard Bible Encyclopedia,* vol. 3, K–P, rev. ed., ed. Geoffrey W. Bromiley and others (Grand Rapids: Mich.: William B. Eerdmans, 1986), 892–94.

3. Sid S. Buzzell, "Proverbs," in *The Bible Knowledge Commentary, Old Testament Edition,* ed. John F. Walvoord and Roy B. Zuck (Wheaton, Ill.: Victor, 1985), 904. Copied with permission by Cook Communications Ministries. May not be further reproduced. All rights reserved.

Notes

Chapter 14: Putting Wisdom to Work

Unless otherwise noted below, all material in this chapter is based on or quoted from "Putting Wisdom to Work," a sermon by Charles R. Swindoll, October 30, 1983, and chapter 14 in the *Living on the Ragged Edge* hardcover book.

1. D. A. Hubbard, "Wisdom," in *New Bible Dictionary,* 2d ed., ed. J. D. Douglas and others (Wheaton, Ill.: Tyndale, 1987), 1255–56.
2. Theophilus, *To Autolycus* in *The Ante-Nicene Fathers: Translations of the Writings of the Fathers down to A.D. 325,* ed. Alexander Roberts, James Donaldson, and A. Cleveland Coxe, vol. 2, *Fathers of the Second Century,* American reprint edition (New York: Christian Literature Company, 1893), 101.
3. Irenaeus, *Against Heresies, in The Ante-Nicene Fathers: Translations of the Writings of the Fathers down to A.D. 325,* ed. Alexander Roberts, James Donaldson, and A. Cleveland Coxe, vol. 1, *The Apostolic Fathers,* American reprint edition (New York: Charles Scribner's Sons, 1899), 406.

Chapter 15: The Qualities of a Good Boss

Unless otherwise noted below, all material in this chapter is based on or quoted from "The Qualities of a Good Boss," a sermon by Charles R. Swindoll, November 6, 1983, and chapter 15 in the *Living on the Ragged Edge* hardcover book.

1. R. N. Whybray, *Ecclesiastes,* New Century Bible Commentary, ed. Ronald E. Clements and Matthew Black (Grand Rapids, Mich.: William B. Eerdmans, 1989), 128.
2. Ray C. Stedman, *Solomon's Secret: Enjoying Life, God's Good Gift* (Portland, Ore: Multnomah, 1985), 108. Used by permission. Also published as *Is This All There Is to Life? Answers from Ecclesiastes* (Grand Rapids, Mich.: Discovery House, 2000).
3. Robertson McQuilkin, *An Introduction to Biblical Ethics,* rev. and updated ed. (Wheaton, Ill.: Tyndale, 1995), 483-86.
4. Bob Ricker and Ron Pitkin, *A Time for Every Purpose* (Nashville, Tenn.: Thomas Nelson, 1983), 122.

Chapter 16: Mysteries That Defy Explanation

Unless otherwise noted below, all material in this chapter is based on or quoted from "Mysteries That Defy Explanation," a sermon by Charles R. Swindoll, November 13, 1983, and chapter 16 in the *Living on the Ragged Edge* hardcover book.

1. *Merriam-Webster's Collegiate Dictionary,* 11th ed., see "mystery."
2. Walter Bauer and others, eds., *A Greek-English Lexicon of the New Testament and Other Early Christian Literature,* 2d rev. ed. (Chicago: University of Chicago Press, 1979), 530.
3. Francis Brown, S. R. Driver, and Charles A. Briggs, *The Brown-Driver-Briggs Hebrew and English Lexicon* (Boston: Houghton Mifflin, 1906; reprint, Peabody, Mass.: Hendrickson, 2000), 1112.

Notes

4. Philip Yancey, *Disappointment with God,* paperback ed. (Grand Rapids, Mich.: Zondervan, 1992), 177. Used by permission of Zondervan Corporation.

5. Jerry Bridges, *Trusting God* (Colorado Springs: NavPress, 1989), 125–26.

6. Deborah Tannen, *You Just Don't Understand: Men and Women in Conversation* (New York: Ballantine, 1991), 51–53.

Chapter 17: Have a Blast While You Last!

Unless otherwise noted below, all material in this chapter is based on or quoted from "Have a Blast While You Last!" a sermon by Charles R. Swindoll, December 4, 1983, and chapter 17 in the *Living on the Ragged Edge* hardcover book.

1. See Kenneth O. Gangel, *Thus Spake Qoheleth: A Study Guide Based on an Exposition of Ecclesiastes* (Camp Hill, Penn.: Christian Publications, 1983), 116–17.

2. Jerry Bridges, *Trusting God* (Colorado Springs: NavPress, 1989), 37 (emphasis in original).

3. Tremper Longman III, *The Book of Ecclesiastes,* The New International Commentary on the Old Testament, ed. R.K Harrison and Robert L. Hubbard, Jr. (Grand Rapids, Mich.: William B. Eerdmans, 1998), 228 and Roland Murphy, *Ecclesiastes,* Word Biblical Commentary, vol. 23A, ed. David A. Hubbard, Glenn W. Barker, and John D. W. Watts (Dallas: Word, 1992), 92.

4. R. N. Whybray, *Ecclesiastes,* New Century Bible Commentary, ed. Ronald E. Clements and Matthew Black (Grand Rapids, Mich.: William B. Eerdmans, 1989), 142.

Chapter 18: An Objective View of the Rat Race

Unless otherwise noted below, all material in this chapter is based on or quoted from "An Objective View of the Rat Race," a sermon by Charles R. Swindoll, December 11, 1983, and chapter 18 in the *Living on the Ragged Edge* hardcover book.

1. *Merriam-Webster's Collegiate Dictionary,* 11th ed., s.v. "rat race."

2. Roland E. Murphy, *Ecclesiastes,* Word Biblical Commentary, vol. 23A, ed. David A. Hubbard and others (Dallas: Word, 1992), 100; R. N. Whybray, *Ecclesiastes,* New Century Bible Commentary, ed. Ronald E. Clements and Matthew Black (Grand Rapids, Mich.: William B. Eerdmans, 1989), 147.

Chapter 19: Be Sensible!

Unless otherwise noted below, all material in this chapter is based on or quoted from "Be Sensible!" a sermon by Charles R. Swindoll, January 8, 1984, and chapter 19 in the *Living on the Ragged Edge* hardcover book.

1. Walter Bauer and others, eds., *A Greek-English Lexicon of the New Testament and Other Early Christian Literature,* 2d rev. ed. (Chicago: The University of Chicago Press, 1979), 802, 866.

2. Donald R. Glenn, "Ecclesiastes," in *The Bible Knowledge Commentary: Old Testament Edition,* ed. John F. Walvoord and Roy B. Zuck (Wheaton, Ill.: Victor, 1985), 1001. Copied with permission by Cook Communications Ministries. May not be further reproduced. All rights reserved.

3. For one perspective to help you move toward your own answer on the issue of our responsibility for spiritual growth under God's sovereign grace, see Jerry Bridges, *The Discipline of Grace: God's Role and Our Role in the Pursuit of Holiness* (Colorado Springs: NavPress, 1994).

Chapter 20: A Fool's Portrait

Unless otherwise noted below, all material in this chapter is based on or quoted from "A Fool's Portrait," a sermon by Charles R. Swindoll, January 15, 1984, and chapter 20 in the *Living on the Ragged Edge* hardcover book.

1. Francis Brown, S. R. Driver, and Charles A. Briggs, *The Brown-Driver-Briggs Hebrew and English Lexicon* (Boston, Mass.: Houghton, Mifflin and Company, 1906; reprint, Peabody, Mass.: Hendrickson, 2000), 698.

2. Brown, Driver, and Briggs, *Brown-Driver-Briggs Hebrew and English Lexicon,* 614.

3. J. D. Douglas and Merrill C. Tenney, eds., *The New International Dictionary of the Bible,* pictorial ed., (Grand Rapids, Mich.: Zondervan, 1987), 358.

4. James Dobson, *Love Must Be Tough* (Waco, Tex.: Word, 1983), 206.

Chapter 21: Be Bullish!

Unless otherwise noted below, all material in this chapter is based on or quoted from "Be Bullish!" a sermon by Charles R. Swindoll, February 19, 1984, and chapter 21 in the *Living on the Ragged Edge* hardcover book.

1. R. N. Whybray, *Ecclesiastes,* New Century Bible Commentary, ed. Ronald E. Clements and Matthew Black (Grand Rapids, Mich.: William B. Eerdmans, 1989), 159.

2. Walter C. Kaiser, Jr., *Quality Living* (Chicago: Moody, 1986), 143.

3. Ray C. Stedman, *Solomon's Secret: Enjoying Life, God's Good Gift* (Portland, Ore.: Multnomah, 1985), 147. Used by permission. Also published as *Is This All There Is to Life? Answers from Ecclesiastes* (Grand Rapids, Mich.: Discovery House, 2000).

Chapter 22: Enjoying Life Now, Not Later

Unless otherwise noted below, all material in this chapter is based on or quoted from "Enjoying Life Now, Not Later," a sermon by Charles R. Swindoll, February 26, 1984, and chapter 22 in the *Living on the Ragged Edge* hardcover book.

1. Donald R. Glenn, "Ecclesiastes," in *The Bible Knowledge Commentary: Old Testament Edition,* ed. John F. Walvoord and Roy B. Zuck (Wheaton, Ill.; Victor, 1985), 1003.

2. Ray C. Stedman, *Solomon's Secret: Enjoying Life, God's Good Gift* (Portland, Ore.: Multnomah, 1985), 151–52. Used by permission. Also published as *Is This All There Is to Life? Answers from Ecclesiastes* (Grand Rapids, Mich.: Discovery House, 2000).

3. Duane A. Garrett, *Proverbs, Ecclesiastes, Song of Solomon,* The New American Commentary, vol. 14, ed. E. Ray Clendenen, Kenneth A. Mathews, and David S. Dockery (Nashville, Tenn.: Broadman, 1993), 340.

4. Francis Brown, S. R. Driver, and Charles A. Briggs, *The Brown-Driver-Briggs Hebrew and English Lexicon* (Boston: Houghton Mifflin, 1906; reprint, Peabody, Mass.: Hendrickson, 1996), 495.

Chapter 23: Gray Hairs, Fewer Teeth, Yet a Big Smile

Unless otherwise noted below, all material in this chapter is based on or quoted from "Gray Hairs, Fewer Teeth, Yet a Big Smile," a sermon by Charles R. Swindoll, March 11, 1984, and chapter 23 in the *Living on the Ragged Edge* hardcover book.

1. Kenneth Gangel, *Ministering to Today's Adults* (Nashville, Tenn.: Word Publishing, 1999), 126.

2. Thomas S. Jones, Jr., "Sometimes," *Shadow of the Perfect Rose: Collected Poems of Thomas S. Jones, Jr.,* ed. John L. Foley (New York: Farrar & Rinehart, 1937), 17.

3. Merriam-Webster's Collegiate Dictionary, 11th ed., s.v. "remember."

4. Francis Brown, S. R. Driver, and Charles A. Briggs, *The Brown-Driver-Briggs Hebrew and English Lexicon* (Boston: Houghton Mifflin, 1906; reprint, Peabody, Mass.: Hendrickson, 2000), 269–70.

5. Walter C. Kaiser, Jr., *Quality Living* (Chicago: Moody, 1979), 149.

6. Donald R. Glenn, "Ecclesiastes," in *The Bible Knowledge Commentary: Old Testament Edition,* ed. John F. Walvoord and Roy B. Zuck (Wheaton, Ill.: Victor, 1985), 1004. Copied with permission by Cook Communications Ministries. May not be further reproduced. All rights reserved.

7. For a larger variety of interpretations on these metaphors, some of which differ from those suggested here, see George Aaron Barton, *A Critical and Exegetical Commentary on The Book of Ecclesiastes,* The International Critical Commentary, ed. Samuel Rolles Driver, Alfred Plummer, and Charles Augustus Briggs (Edinburgh: T. & T. Clark, 1980), 186–91.

8. Augustine, *Confessions,* trans. Henry Chadwick, Oxford World's Classics series (Oxford: Oxford University Press, 1998), 1.1.

Chapter 24: Wrapping Up a Ragged-Edge Journey

Unless otherwise noted below, all material in this chapter is based on or quoted from "Wrapping Up a Ragged-Edge Journey," a sermon by Charles R. Swindoll, March 18, 1984, and chapter 24 in the *Living on the Ragged Edge* hardcover book.

1. J. A. Patch, "Goad," in *The International Standard Bible Encyclopedia, Volume 2: E-J,* rev. ed., ed. Geoffrey W. Bromiley and others (Grand Rapids, Mich.: William B. Eerdmans, 1987), 491.

2. Duane A. Garrett, *Proverbs, Ecclesiastes, Song of Songs,* The New American Commentary, vol. 14, ed. E. Ray Clendenen, Kenneth A. Mathews, and David S. Dockery (Nashville, Tenn.: Broadman, 1993), 344.

Notes

3. Ray C. Stedman, *Solomon's Secret: Enjoying Life, God's Good Gift* (Portland, Ore.: Multnomah, 1985), 171. Used by permission. Also published as *Is This All There Is to Life? Answers from Ecclesiastes* (Grand Rapids, Mich.: Discovery House, 2000).

How to Begin a Relationship with God

1. Adapted from *God's Word, God's World, and You* (Anaheim, Calif.: Insight for Living, 1997), 41–48.

Books for Probing Further

In the following list, you'll find selected books that can increase your knowledge and application of several of the major themes of Ecclesiastes. These resources offer a variety of perspectives and insights that can be helpful for in-depth study. We hope that you will use them wisely, testing everything they say in light of the clear teaching of Scripture (Acts 17:11; 2 Timothy 3:16–17) and never forgetting that "the writing of many books is endless and excessive devotion to books is wearying to the body" (Ecclesiastes 12:12).

Popular and Devotional Books on Ecclesiastes

Glenn, Donald R. "Ecclesiastes." In *The Bible Knowledge Commentary: Old Testament Edition,* ed. John F. Walvoord and Roy B. Zuck. Wheaton, Ill.; Victor, 1985.

Kaiser, Walter C., Jr. *Quality Living.* Chicago: Moody Press, 1979.

Sproul, R. C., Jr., ed. *Vanity and Meaning: Discovering Purpose in Life.* Grand Rapids, Mich.: Baker, 1995.

Stedman, Ray C. *Solomon's Secret: Enjoying Life, God's Good Gift.* Portland, Ore.: Multnomah, 1985.

Wiersbe, Warren. *Be Satisfied.* Wheaton, Ill.: Victor, 1990.

Scholarly Studies on Ecclesiastes

Barton, George Aaron. *A Critical and Exegetical Commentary on the Book of Ecclesiastes.* The International Critical Commentary, ed. Samuel Rolles Driver, Alfred Plummer, and Charles Augustus Briggs. Edinburgh: T. & T. Clark, 1912.

Kidner, Derek. *A Time to Mourn and a Time to Dance: The Message of Ecclesiastes.* Downers Grove, Ill.: InterVarsity, 1976.

Longman, Tremper, III. *The Book of Ecclesiastes.* New International Commentary on the Old Testament. Grand Rapids, Mich.: William B. Eerdmans, 1998.

Murphy, Roland. *Ecclesiastes.* Word Biblical Commentary, vol. 23A, ed. David A. Hubbard, Glenn W. Barker, John D. W. Watts, and Ralph P. Martin. Dallas: Word, 1992.

Whybray, R. N. *Ecclesiastes.* New Century Bible Commentary, ed. Ronald E. Clements and Matthew Black. Grand Rapids, Mich.: William B. Eerdmans, 1989.

Zuck, Roy B., ed. *Reflecting with Solomon: Selected Studies on the Book of Ecclesiastes.* Paperback edition. Wipf & Stock, 2003.

Coming to Terms with the World

Bridges, Jerry. *Trusting God.* Colorado Springs: NavPress, 1989.

Colson, Charles and Nancy Pearcey. *How Now Shall We Live?* Wheaton, Ill.: Tyndale, 1999.

McQuilkin, Robertson. *An Introduction to Biblical Ethics.* Revised and updated ed. Wheaton, Ill.: Tyndale, 1995.

Nash, Ronald H. *Worldviews in Conflict: Choosing Christianity in a World of Ideas.* Grand Rapids, Mich.: Zondervan, 1992.

Schaeffer, Francis A. *How Should We Then Live? The Rise and Decline of Western Thought and Culture.* Westchester, Ill.: Crossway, 1976.

Winter, Richard. *Still Bored in a Culture of Entertainment: Rediscovering Passion and Wonder.* Downers Grove, Ill.: InterVarsity, 2002.

Yancey, Philip. *Disappointment with God.* Paperback ed. Grand Rapids, Mich.: Zondervan, 1992.

ISBN: 0-8499-1813-8

The pace of life, and the demands of life, just keep getting more intense. And for many, that combination may lead to a life crisis.

GETTING THROUGH THE TOUGH STUFF is a book of *encouragement*, *hope* and *freedom*. It's an invitation to meet Christ at the crossroads of our lives and move beyond the tough times.